The Last Cowboys
at the End of the World

The Last Cowboys at

The Story of the Gauchos of Patagonia

the End of the World

N I C K   R E D I N G

Crown Publishers • New York

Grateful acknowledgment is made to Zagier & Urruty Publications
for permission to reprint partial images from the map *Patagonia Ecomapa.*
Adapted from *Patagonia Ecomap,* Zagier & Urruty Publications.

Published by Crown Publishers, New York, New York.
Member of the Crown Publishing Group.

Random House, Inc. New York, Toronto, London, Sydney, Auckland
www.randomhouse.com

CROWN is a trademark and the Crown colophon
is a registered trademark of Random House, Inc.

Printed in the United States of America

DESIGN BY LEONARD HENDERSON

Library of Congress Cataloging-in-Publication Data
Reding, Nick.
The last cowboys at the end of the world : the story of the gauchos of Patagonia / by
Nick Reding.
1. Patagonia (Argentina and Chile)—Description and travel.   2. Aisén (Chile : Province)—
Description and travel.   3. Gauchos—Chile—Cisnes Medio—Social conditions.
4. Gauchos—Chile—Coihaique—Social conditions.   5. Frontier and pioneer life—
Patagonia (Argentina and Chile).   6. Reding, Nick.   7. Cisnes Medio (Chile).   I. Title.
F3134.R43   2001
983'.622—dc21   2001028063

ISBN 0-609-60596-8

10 9 8 7 6 5 4 3 2 1

First Edition

For Giselle

Acknowledgments

First on the list of people to thank are the gauchos of Middle Cisnes, most of all Duck and Edith; without their willingness to take me in—and have their lives disrupted as part of the deal—this book would never have been possible. I was constantly amazed by the matter-of-fact kindness of the gauchos, who always concerned themselves first with feeding a visitor, second with giving him a place to sleep, and third with making sure he would stay long enough to enjoy the unending hospitality endemic to that part of the world.

Second, I could never express sufficient gratitude to my parents, who supported me emotionally and financially when I left New York to pursue an obsession with Patagonia that must have seemed at best misguided, and at the very worst complete folly. The same is true of my sister, who, through her marriage to my brother-in-law and the birth of their first child, always found time to speak patiently and intelligently with me. She is the most evenhanded advice-giver anyone could want.

Many writers claim to have the best agent in the world. What separates Elizabeth Kaplan from the rest is that she really is the best. She saw potential as far back as 1997 where even I, as determinedly as I might have been looking, could not see it. Since then she's proven herself to be not only my greatest ally, but a friend as well.

It's only partially true that writing is not a collaborative effort. At the top of the list of people who helped me shape this story is Tom Harpole, who, aside from being an unequaled inspiration as a human being and a journalist, took countless hours out of his own busy schedule to read and comment not just on one draft of this book, but on all of them. Tom once said to me that if you can't tell a story without maintaining the dignity of the people involved, you should not be telling the story in the first place. I hope I've achieved something like that in this book.

Thanks to Will Bourne—as a dear friend, as an astute reader, and, along with Beau Woodring, as a part of all the long nights in bars that kept me from going nuts throughout the past three years. Also to Judy Budnitz and Phil Monahan, whose criticisms were invariably warranted, perceptive, and totally integral. And to John Michel and Marysue Rucci for helping me to find an agent, see the story more clearly than I might have, and to begin to understand the realities of publishing. Thanks also to Doug Pepper at Crown for bringing the book through to completion.

This book is based almost entirely on firsthand reporting and interviews. Much of the history that appears here was related to me patiently and in great detail by Dr. Mario González Kappes, Peter Hartmann, and Oscar Aleuy Rójas, three Coihaique historians who have devoted part of their lives to anonymously compiling the unrecorded facts of Aisén's settlement and recent development. I hope I've done justice to their work.

Finally, living away from home for long periods would not have been possible were it not for the generous help of a few essential people, and I'm indebted most of all to Rex Bryngelson and Tania Figueroa Mesa, both of whom gave me places to stay, food to eat, and companionship.

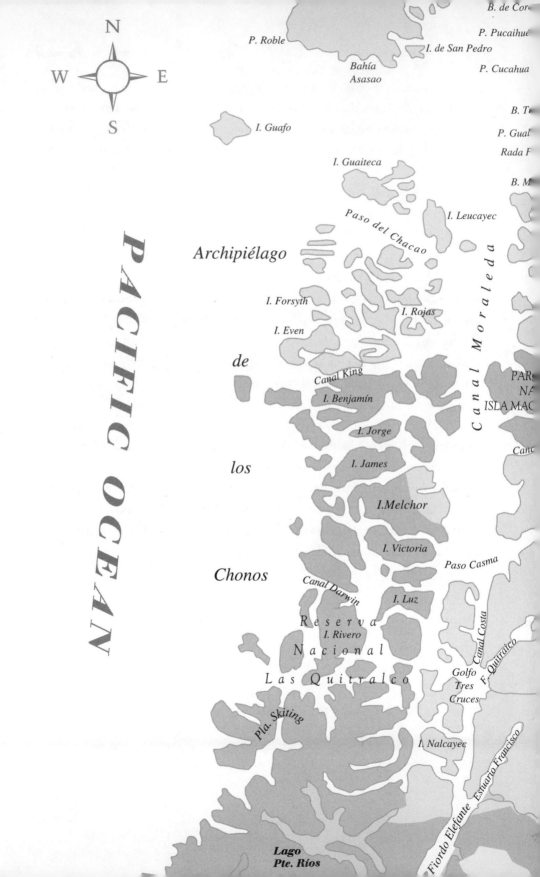

N
W E
S

P. Roble

B. de Cor

P. Pucaihué

I. de San Pedro

P. Cucahua

Bahía
Asasao

B. T

P. Gual

Rada F

I. Guafo

I. Guaiteca

B. M

I. Leucayec

Paso del Chacao

Archipiélago

Canal Moraleda

I. Forsyth

I. Rojas

I. Even

PAR
NA
ISLA MAC

de

Canal King

I. Benjamín

I. Jorge

Canc

los

I. James

I.Melchor

I. Victoria

Paso Casma

Chonos

Canal Darwin

I. Luz

Reserva

I. Rivero

Canal Costa

Nacional

F. Quitralco

Las Quitralco

Golfo
Tres
Cruces

Pta. Skiting

I. Nalcayec

Fiordo Elefante

Estuario Francisco

Lago
Pte. Ríos

PACIFIC OCEAN

"Do not try to save the blood of the gauchos. . . . Blood is the only thing they have in common with human beings."

— BARTOLOMÉ MITRE,

as quoted in 1861 by

Leroy R. Sheldon in

The Gaucho Works of Sarmiento

The rest of that country is notable primarily for its weather, which is violent and prolonged; its emptiness, which is almost frighteningly total; and its wind, which blows all the time in a way to stiffen your hair and rattle the eyes in your head. . . . If you owned it, you might be able to sell certain parts of it at a few dollars an acre; many parts you couldn't give away. Not many cars raise dust along its lonely roads—it is country people do not much want to cross, much less visit. But that block of country . . . is what this book is about.

—WALLACE STEGNER

Wolf Willow

PART ONE

The End of the Road

❀

CHAPTER ONE

Middle Cisnes

Duck and Edith lived with their three small children in a tiny two-room cabin in Middle Cisnes, Chilean Patagonia. They were twenty minutes on horseback from the nearest neighbors, who were rumored to be cattle thieves, and an hour from the next-nearest neighbor. Inside of the main room of the cabin, there was a cabinet, a wood-burning stove, a table, five chairs, and a couch. There was no bathroom and no electricity; seven candles stuck together in their own drippings on the table provided the light. Duck was behind me with a wad of my long hair in one hand, the same hand in which he also held a knife, and he was using my hair like a handle with which to force my neck into the crook of his elbow; I could see his shadow on the bedroom door, against which I'd braced my arms. An hour before, Edith had barricaded herself and the children in the bedroom with a fifty-pound barrel of flour. I could not hear them in there.

Duck, who was a gaucho, a Patagonian cowboy, had been drinking nonstop for five hours. I had been drinking with him, first to keep from offending him and then, as he got more and more violent, so that he would pass out. I was hopelessly drunk; Duck was not. I had tried once already to walk out of the cabin. Duck had been sharpening his knife; he had sharpened it so many thousands of times before slaughtering a ewe that he did it by feel, watching me instead of the knife as he went. If I looked left—at the stove, for instance, wondering if I could get to it and open the door to retrieve a burning log before

Duck stabbed me or sliced my hamstring—or right—at the guitar on the wall or the sharp-lipped frying pan he'd thrown on the floor—Duck looked, too. There was no way to get outside.

"Sit down," he said. When I didn't move, he nodded at the chair behind me. "Sit down," he'd said again, and I did. Behind Duck was a chair we called the throne, which Duck had fashioned with a hatchet from the trunk of a *coigue* tree and covered in sheep skins. He'd sat on the throne and said, "Why are you here?" Then he had dropped the whetstone and thrown the newly sharpened knife so that it stuck in the floor between us. He had reached for the liter bottle of beer next to the throne and drunk from it, watching me watch the knife. "Why are you here?" he had repeated. The knife had been closer to me than to him.

For two months, I'd been living in a tent in the pasture outside of Duck's cabin. He'd taken me with him on a long cattle drive and shown me how to make chaps from the skin of a butchered ewe—things gauchos have done for three centuries. Now a road had been built that connected Duck to central Patagonia's only town and, by virtue of this fact, connected the eighteenth century to the twenty-first. I'd come to Patagonia to see what would happen to men like Duck. I told him, "I came because of the road, *che*."

Duck had passed me the bottle of beer at the same time that he had seesawed the point of the knife out of the floor. It was hard to believe I'd let him have it that easily. He said, "That's correct, Skinny. Because of the road."

Then Duck had picked up two of the plates that had spilled out of the cabinet when he'd pulled it down onto the floor. He'd held one plate in each hand, like cymbals, then put one plate over the other and thrown the bottle of beer into the air. "There I am," he said, and watched the bottle fall to the floor. "Duck!" he had yelled. "Hold on," he'd said, "I forgot a part of the trick."

Starting over, Duck had tossed the bottle in the air and, when it passed in front of him, had crushed it between the plates. The plates had shattered, though the bottle had not. Duck had looked at the floor "There I am," he'd said. He'd looked at me. That's when I got up from the chair and tried to make it to the door, but Duck had caught me by the back of the hair.

He pushed my neck harder against the crook of his arm and said, "I want you to come outside with me, *che*."

My eyes were watering, and I thought I could feel the walls of my windpipe rubbing against one another under the pressure of Duck's grip. He loosened it to permit me a response. I retched and said, "One more drink, *che*."

"Nico," he said, "if you don't come outside with me, I'm going to gut you and hang you from the fucking ceiling."

"One more drink," I said.

Duck moved his head close to mine. He raked his whiskers against my ear. Then he said, in a voice I didn't recognize, "Duck has waited so long for you, *che*."

*   *   *

Sometime very early on my first morning in Middle Cisnes, a fog bank had settled into the valley. I crawled out of the two-man tent I'd pitched the night before in the pasture in front of Duck and Edith's cabin. I could see the green, knee-high grass and the midriffs of the cottonwood trees behind the corrals; and, though I couldn't see the mountains, they were there, pressing and close in every direction.

Duck had already ridden across the river to the neighbors' to see about getting me a horse, and I could see her, too, tied and unsaddled at the hitching post next to Duck's two horses, Happy Fat and Happy Slim. Duck and I were leaving in a couple of hours for a cattle drive, and he was walking along the river to get a sheep to butcher. I got to my feet.

Duck passed low huts of handhewn wood with corrugated roofs and roofs of hatchet-cut wood shingles—the slaughterhouse, the smokehouse, a hay barn. Duck's two dogs, Sheep Shearings and Country Dog, slunk behind him, their brown eyes partially hidden behind tufts of tawny fur. I followed, watching. Each time the dogs tried to creep ahead, Duck raised his hand and mumbled, "Go behind," and they dropped back into his slipstream, crossing and recrossing one another's track. Two hundred meters ahead of Duck, one white head after another raised from the tall grass. By the end of the day, the unluckiest among the sheep would be skinned and gutted, and a quarter of her would be with Duck and me, fifteen kilometers deeper into the Andes.

Duck whistled carelessly as he walked, as though he would not have the sheep know what was coming. At the age of thirty-four, Duck, though he was by no means old, was curiously unmarred. All gauchos are preternaturally misformed in some way, their bodies warped about the shoulders or hips or sternum like tectonic plates forced under one another by one too many falls from a horse. Duck, though, was not, with one exception: one of his brown eyes played higher on his face than the other. And the youthful effect of their missetting was heightened by their close proximity to his long, drop-point nose. It was as though his face were still forming.

Duck was a large man by any standards; but at five feet nine and two hundred fifty pounds, he was huge among gauchos. That morning, he was dressed in gray warm-up pants and an untucked white dress shirt with maroon pinstripes. On his feet he wore black, steel-toed construction boots. He had gained sixty pounds in the last two years, though in the vestigial sinew of his forearms there still existed the skeletal blueprint of a mesomorph, a tall, thin, and muscular Mapuche Indian, the tribe of which his mother is a full-blooded member. Duck had the full, indigenous lips, the wide forehead, and straw-straight hair. He wore it cut army-short, and when he smiled, his hairline shot up. When he frowned, it fell with the near-audible certainty of a closing window. When he laughed, Duck raised his hands as though waving to two people at once.

As he approached the sheep, his whistling stopped. He let the grass blade that he'd been chewing fall from his mouth as he and the dogs moved well past the flock and into the woods; there the dogs paced anxiously in the shadows until Duck said, very quietly, "Go." Then they slithered into a dried creek and came out into the pasture at full speed. The sheep went for the riverbank, where uneven, fist-sized rocks slowed the dogs' sensitive paws. Country Dog rolled end over end, yelping, and Sheep Shearings slowed briefly to watch. When the dogs recovered their momentum, Sheep Shearings, the younger and faster of the two, attacked, as Country Dog stayed back, using the river as a natural barrier to control the frightened, confused movements of the flock. In a few minutes, the dogs had cornered the sheep into a holding corral, a labyrinth whose only exit was the slaughterhouse.

"Get out of here, fuckers," warned Duck, and kicked at Country Dog, who limped now on three legs. Duck waded into the flock, looking closely at the sheep. He bent his knees to get a better view of the hams on one old ewe and kneed another against the wall, as though gauging her tenderness. Satisfied, he reached down and grabbed the ewe by a hind leg and dragged her in through the darkened door. The dogs whined outside the fence.

The slaughterhouse smelled of lanolin and damp wood. On the windowsill was an aluminum baking pan, and in the center of the room was a thing like a sawhorse with two slanted boards running across the top like a gutter. A hole had been cut into the raised floor, and the sawhorse was positioned over the hole. The ewe's front hooves scratched against the floorboards, and Duck looked coolly around the place before flipping the ewe on her back. Then he grabbed her by a hind and a front leg and hefted her onto the horse so that her head hung over the hole.

Duck put three fingers in the ewe's mouth the way you would with a six-pack, middle and ring fingers across the tongue. To look at Duck's face, he might have been selecting a fresh piece of grass to chew on. He asked me to put the aluminum pan over the hole in the floor; then he turned the ewe's head down, drew his knife, and poked against the thick wool. When he found the jugular, he smoothly ran the knife through to the handle and withdrew it, careful not to sever the windpipe so that the ewe could bleed herself to death. Then Duck threw the knife so it stuck in the floor.

Each time the ewe exhaled, blood poured thick and rhythmic from the wound, filling the room with the elemental reek of an open body cavity. Duck turned the ewe's head further, like a trainer stretching an athlete, then centered the wound over the pan on the floor. Blood fell into it audibly and in clumps, like brilliant red dollops of heavy metal. With his free hand, Duck pressed on the ewe's stomach slowly and with great assurance. Each new place that Duck touched on her body trembled, and the trembling sent a convulsion forward through the ewe's torso and ended with a quickened suck of air. Duck grunted softly, and so did she, though her hind legs no longer moved and her stomach was still. The ewe, it seemed, was already dead below the chest. Then she coughed and coughed again and was empty.

Duck's wife Edith stood watching silently from the doorway. I'd not heard her, and then I turned and she was there. Mariana, their youngest daughter, was at Edith's side. Duck looked at his wife. His face was pale and sweating, and his close-set eyes were moist along the lids. Edith had two handfuls of mint and cilantro that she'd picked from where the plants grew wild along the river, and she came forward and stood above the pan, tearing the leaves with her hands and dropping the bits to float on the warm blood. When Edith was done, Mariana came and took the pan and set it to steam and congeal on the windowsill.

Now Edith took the ewe by the hind legs, and together she and Duck dumped the animal to the floor. Edith squatted and held the ewe's back legs open luridly while Duck slid his knife under the hide, just above the sex organs. He cut away the mammary glands, the teats, and the urinary tract, and threw each, in turn, to the pacing dogs. The whole time, Mariana stood braiding Edith's hair; Mariana's tongue was in her cheek as she concentrated on the task, looking quickly at the ewe and then not looking again.

Duck skinned the ewe. When he was done, he hung the hide over a rafter like clothing on a line. He aligned the blade of the knife across her spine and used a wooden mallet to crack the spine vertically from anus to collarbone with three exacting shots. He pulled a deposit of gelatinous fat from around the ewe's diaphragm and slopped it on the floor. He and Edith gleamed with sweat as they struggled to hang the flayed ewe by her hind legs from hooks in the ceiling. When Duck wiped his brow, smearing blood across his eyes, Edith walked out the door and across the pasture, followed by Mariana.

As Duck and I threw the guts into the pasture and filled buckets of water from the pump in front of the slaughterhouse, the dogs set their legs on either side of the pile of offal, pulling and slipping in the gore until the single unit of innards was a mess of many parts. Duck and I sloshed the floor of the slaughterhouse and refilled the buckets over and over till it was clean. "There it is," said Duck, though when I looked back, all evidence of what had just happened there had been erased.

*   *   *

We went to see about my horse. Duck smiled and said, "She's crazy, *che*. She won't like you because you're a gringo." The mare was a stubborn fifteen-year-old, he said, and ought to have been eaten instead of ridden. Pork Rind, the neighbor across the river, had warned Duck about her temperament. But it was the only horse Duck could get: the next-nearest neighbor lived an hour away, and we had to leave soon.

The mare sidled away as Duck approached; when the rope holding her came tight, she nodded her head with such force that the hitching post creaked back and forth. She was long and wiry, a horse for the flat Argentine *pampas*. There seemed to be nothing Chilean about her, nothing that had been systematically engineered for the mountains, and alongside Happy Fat and Happy Slim, with their deep chests and thick legs, Pork Rind's horse seemed completely out of place. Duck looked under her belly, ran his eyes along her long neck, and frowned. "Built for speed," he said. "Good thing my fat ass isn't riding this thing. All I can say is, when the time comes, get your feet in the stirrups fast, *che*."

The night before, when Duck said he was going on a cattle drive that would last at least a week, depending upon the weather, I'd asked if I could go with him. He'd said he planned to take Pork Rind with him but that he would take me instead, assuming that I could ride well enough to be trusted. If I couldn't, he'd said plainly, it would not only be my life that I was risking, but also his, for it was not uncommon during the short Patagonian fall for sudden blizzards to overtake the riders. Nor was it uncommon for those blizzards to obscure the steep trails so thoroughly that horses at times slid off cliffs to their deaths, and that, should the rider not be killed outright—should he, for instance, grab onto something and be left hanging over the side—it would take another expert and decisive horseman to come to his aid. When Duck had asked me if I was an experienced rider, I said the first thing that came to mind: "I've been around horses all my life."

The truth was that not only had I never ridden a horse before, but my fear of them made me almost physically ill. I'd been to Patagonia once, three years before, long enough to know that, in order to have any hope of getting the story of the gauchos, I would have to adapt myself to the central characterizing factor of their lives: riding horses. But thinking about this in an apartment on Tenth Street and thinking about this while standing before a gaucho with whom you're about to go on a cattle drive are two very different things. Duck looked at Pork Rind's horse and then at me, expecting that I would draw whatever obvious conclusions there were to draw from looking at an animal. And I decided that I would try to hide my secret from Duck, at least until we got far enough into the cattle drive that we couldn't turn back.

The mare had a bald spot the size of a quarter on her ribs where Pork Rind's spurs had exposed her gray hide, and the hide showed through against the deep chestnut of her coat. As I looked at the horse's legs and at the tight skin stretched about the awesome muscles of her hams, I could feel the muscles around my stomach contracting and warm saliva filling my mouth. She smelled of hay, and mixed with this was the faintly pungent odor of urine. I turned away from Duck and swallowed the bile in my throat.

For some reason, Duck didn't force me to admit the truth. He didn't say anything about it then and he didn't say anything about it for the next year that we knew one another. Instead, he simply smiled, looked from the horse to me, and said, "I guess we ought to get ready, Skinny."

* * *

When we went inside the cabin, Duck washed the blood from his face and put fried bread called *sopapillas* into an old plastic detergent bottle with the top cut off. We ate ewe ribs and threw the bones out the window to the dogs, their muzzles still wet with offal. Duck put a kilo of *mate* and an old dirty rag and a container of salt in a little bag that looked like a dop kit. We rolled sleeping bags and shoved them deep into burlap sacks; in another sack we put four rolled sheep skins with which to make our beds and tied everything shut inside woven horsehide *chiguas,* or packsaddle bags. The name *chiguas* is derived from the Brazilian word for chigger, a nasty insect whose bites, like overfilled packsaddle bags, cause pain and inflammation of the joints. Then Duck handed me a pair of goatskin chaps, the white fur curly and thick on the outside, to slide over my legs.

Edith nervously watched us do all of this. She kept coming over to help and then sitting back down again. When she went to the window, Duck looked up. The only road in all of Chilean Patagonia was behind the cabin, completely out of sight, a quarter mile away. "What?" said Duck.

"Felt hooves," said Edith, by which she meant she thought she'd heard a noise. Perhaps a truck, which was not likely, since traffic was limited to four or five vehicles a week.

Duck shook his head. "Wasn't anything," he said.

"I felt it," insisted Edith.

"Well," said Duck. In his hand he had a liter-sized box of red wine that the gauchos call a "battery," as much for its size, which is roughly as long and wide as a car battery, though only half as deep, as for its energizing effects. "Time to eat the blood, Nico," said Duck.

We went to the slaughterhouse again. The blood in the pan was congealed, with a leathery skin across the top in which the clumps of cilantro and mint had been cooked by the ewe's residual body heat. Duck drew his knife and carved a hole in the top of the battery and pulled the aluminum bladder inside the box through the hole so that it protruded like a nipple. He sliced the tip of the nipple off and set the box in the windowsill. Then he cut lines across the blood so that it was divided into squares, like brownies.

The skin of the blood was chilled and slightly chewy, though the body of each square was warm and wobbled in your mouth like Jell-O. I could taste the raw iron, and it remained dry along my tongue, like spinach. The mint was cool and the cilantro, too, and after each square we would pass the battery of wine and drink in long, arching streams. The rush of the protein and the alcohol was so strong that it made my head swim and the backs of my eyeballs tingle. After I'd had five squares, I felt as though I'd eaten a long, multicourse dinner. We wouldn't be eating again until nightfall.

When half the blood and all the wine was gone, Duck took the pan and slopped the remaining squares down into the grass for the dogs to fight over, though it was a fool's reward, for each time they licked at a square it dissolved so that, after a few moments, the dogs began eating clumps of stained grass. Duck washed the pan at the water pump and set it once again on the windowsill. I said, "And Edith?"

"She doesn't want anything to do with the blood," said Duck.

*   *   *

We unhooked the ewe from where she hung from the slaughterhouse ceiling and carried her—with some difficulty, and followed by the loping dogs—a hundred meters across the pasture to the tack room. The tack room was built as an addition to the barn, and it, like the slaughterhouse, was dark and cool. In one corner was a long, vertical cabinet frame walled with small-gauge screen. There were two hooks in the ceiling of the cabinet, and we hung the ewe on them by the hocks. Duck cut away most of the ribs from one side of her and then he cut the meat away from one of her forelegs. Satisfied that it was enough to last us until we got back from the drive, he placed the meat in a burlap sack. One sheep lasted the family four weeks, and each day that Duck and I were gone, Edith would come to the tack room and take from the carcass what she needed for the day's cooking.

Duck carried the sack over to the horses and affixed the packsaddle to Happy Slim. When he asked me to saddle the other two horses, I told him that because I was used to a western saddle—and because that was so different from a Chilean—I'd have to see how it was done first. Emboldened by the wine early in the morning, I figured it was an excuse I could use for at least two days: long enough, I hoped, for me to figure out how to saddle a horse by myself.

Duck seemed to buy this line of reasoning, and when he was done saddling Happy Fat and my horse, he put on his poncho and tossed a second poncho to me and mounted up. He said, "What's your horse's name?" I told him Marión— it was the first thing that came to mind. "Well, *che,*" he said, "lead her a few minutes so she gets used to you, then see if she'll let you get on her back. When you do it, though, *che,* do it fast, and get your feet right in the stirrups. When she tries to rub you off against the barn, don't jump off; just fight her away, *che.*"

Edith stood near Duck, holding their son Oscar in her arms, her eyes narrowed with anticipation. Mariana hid between Edith's legs, giggling. "It's been nice knowing you, Skinny!" called Edith. It was the first time in the eighteen hours that I'd been in Middle Cisnes that Edith had spoken to me.

Marión led smoothly around the pasture for several minutes, but each time I tried to slip the reins over her head, she nodded and backed down till it was all I could do to keep my feet. We did this three more times before the crowd grew impatient.

"Quit inflating your nuts!" piped Mariana—quit wasting time.

Marión accepted the reins calmly on the fourth attempt. But before I could get in the saddle, she was pirouetting wildly. I had one foot in a stirrup and the other leg over her back and I was falling off to the side. I held on to the reins for balance as she bolted at the barn and tried to rub me off against the wall. I pulled harder at the reins, nearly bringing her down on top of me. Finally, I fell off.

Edith clapped. She said, "Okay, now do that again, *che.*"

I'd not let go of the reins, and I got Marión settled long enough to hold the stirrup in one hand and get my boot in. She moved forward and I moved with her, hopping on one leg, and then I swung up and nearly got in the saddle. But before I could do so, she galloped at the hitching post and stopped just short so that my groin slammed into the metal pommel.

"Ooooohhh," said Edith. "No more inflated nuts."

Duck tried not to laugh, but it was hopeless, and he turned his horse, embarrassed. I got my other foot in the stirrup while Marión backed away from the hitching post and looked around for something else to charge. Before she could make up her mind, I got her head anchored against her chest by pulling down on the reins. I was leaning forward in the saddle, trying to catch my breath from the pain. Then I sat up and looked at Duck. He rode over and we were at eye level, each of us atop his horse. I started to laugh. I put Marión forward and reined her, so amazed by the feeling of control over such a large animal that I did it again. Only this time Marión took off at a gallop across the pasture toward the cabin. I thought she would run right through the window, but instead she stopped and swiveled around and charged back toward the river, two hundred meters away. My feet were out of the stirrups again, and Duck was yelling, "Fight her head down, *che!* Fight it down."

I did, and Marión stopped near the riverbank. She wanted to cross back to Pork Rind's, and each time I swung her head toward Duck and the other horses, she would turn in quick circles on her hind legs. Finally, she relented and galloped back at the barn and stopped. Edith was bent double. She had to put Oscar down, she was laughing so hard.

Duck shook his head reproachfully at her, and I watched as he swung Mariana briefly into the saddle for a kiss and did the same with tiny Oscar. Patricia, the oldest child, was still at school in Amengual, the nearest village, though she was coming home that afternoon. By the time we'd gotten back from the mountains, she'd have gone back to school for another week and come home again. Duck said, "Tell Pati goodbye for me." Then he rode past me, his body rocking easily to and fro, Happy Fat farting under his weight. "Sucks to be a gringo on my mother's cunt of a crazy fucking horse," he offered.

We rode through the first gate and gained the trail uphill, following it for several hundred meters to where it ended at a second gate. Duck leaned down and undid the latch and swung the heavy gate open. After we were through, he latched it again and looked at me. "Don't worry, *che,*" he said. "I won't let anything happen to you. I'll teach you how to ride. I'll teach you everything you need to know." Then we turned the horses onto the road.

*   *   *

The ranch where Duck and Edith lived was called Santa Elvira. Like most medium-sized cattle ranches in Chilean Patagonia, it was split into three pieces of land of varying size, from thirty-five hundred acres to over ten thousand. (Collectively, Santa Elvira was twenty thousand acres—large ranches in Patagonia are ten to twenty times this size—though only one piece was actually ever referred to as Santa Elvira: the one where Duck and Edith lived.) Duck, who was the head cowboy at the ranch, worked for a *patrón,* or landholder, called Carlos Asi. Duck had in his employment two other gauchos: the Eagles brothers, Tito and Alfredo. Duck and I were going to the *veranada,* the summer grazing grounds, an outranch of twelve thousand acres seventy-five kilometers farther into the Andes. There, Alfredo Eagles lived in utter isolation from December till May—the austral spring, summer, and fall—with the *patrón's* five hundred head of cattle as they grazed along the Argentine border.

Duck and I were going to get the fifteen bulls in the herd, who, done breeding for the year, needed to be separated from the cows and younger bulls, which they might kill. We were to drive the bulls down to the *invernada,* the winter grazing grounds, where Duck lived with Edith along the Río Cisnes.

Much of Middle Cisnes—in fact, much of the state of Aisén, of which Middle Cisnes is but a small sector—had at one time been covered in thick, coniferous rain forest. But the gauchos, so that their herds could graze, had burned much of the land, and between 1925 and the end of World War Two, Aisén lost an estimated fifteen million acres of forest, or nearly half its virgin growth.

Burning coniferous rain forest to make pastureland, because of the high annual rainfall, which was, before the fires, measured in the hundreds of centimeters, is at best an imprecise and labor-intensive process, and the result was a quiltwork of old forest and burned pastures littered with dead trees—dead trees that took up critical surface area, so that the sheep and cattle could not remain for the entire year in one area. The *invernadas* were located along the river, a couple hundred feet above sea level, where the yearly mean temperatures were relatively high, and where the rainfall, though markedly less than it had been before the fires, rarely turned to snow. Because the winters at the *invernadas* were so mild compared to the high mountains, they were referred to in a play on words that translates as "nothingwinters."

In order for the grass at the *invernadas* to rejuvenate after a long winter of grazing pressure, the herds were shuttled each spring, usually in mid-December, to the *veranadas*, the nothingsummers, two or three thousand meters higher into the Andes. There, the stock could graze until it started snowing in earnest, which was, depending on the year, any time between March and May.

Santa Elvira was one of two nothingwinters owned by Carlos Asi. Tito Eagles lived much of the year at the south end of Santa Elvira, an hour away on horseback from Duck and Edith's cabin. In another month, Duck would once again make the trip to the nothingsummer where Alfredo lived, this time accompanied by Tito. The trio would then drive the remainder of the herd down from the mountains. Half would be kept through the winter with Duck and Tito at Santa Elvira; the other half would go with Alfredo to the second nothingwinter, also of thirty-five hundred acres, where Alfredo would once again pass the months completely without human contact. All of which would have been easier to understand, perhaps, were Alfredo not deep into his sixties.

"Fucking Alfredo," said Duck. "I guess we get to see fucking Alfredo tomorrow or the next day, depending on how fast we go."

To say that Alfredo was deep into his sixties is partly incorrect. No one, most of all he, was sure of his age. What was sure was that, since he was a teenager, Alfredo had preferred to spend, between the nothingsummer and the second nothingwinter, the twelve months of every year in one of two *puestos*—shacks of handhewn logs that have neither plumbing nor electricity—solely in the company of horses and cows and cats and dogs.

Duck said, "We took Alfredo a woman one time, and he wouldn't speak to her. We left her up there when we went for the bulls, and he just went inside his *puesto* and closed the door. We came back three weeks later to get the rest of the herd, and she was standing right in that same spot, and fucking Alfredo's door was still closed. I bet he never even invited her in. Then he comes out and saddles his horse and rides off to start gathering the herd. I said to the woman, 'Well?' She says, 'Well what? He hasn't said a single word in three weeks.'" Duck shook his head. "She had a horse, and we drove the cattle down the mountain and she went to Tapera. She was from Tapera. I looked to Alfredo after she left off, and I said, 'Well?' He just looked at me. I don't even know if he knew what I was talking about."

I said, "Is that all true?"

"As injustice," said Duck.

I said, "Maybe he's gay."

"I don't know if Alfredo's got his umbrella turned inside-out or not," said Duck, using a common euphemism for homosexuality. "There's plenty of that around. I think it's just that he doesn't like to be around anyone. All the *viejos* are like that, I guess. I mean, Tito is probably ten years older than Alfredo; he must be eighty by now. And he doesn't live much different. I mean, at least Tito's got a woman and fourteen children."

None of this, given the country through which Duck and I rode, sounded out of place. We were headed due east on a one-and-a-half-lane dirt road deeper into the mountains from a place that was already as magnificently and anonymously interred as any place I could imagine. According to a decade-old census, the river valley that the road followed was home, in its sixty-kilometer course, to one hundred nineteen people. But because these same people were so often coming and going for months and even years at a time, and because the river was flanked on the north by thousands of square miles of *cordillera* that no one had ever settled, the number had hardly any significance. No one knew how many people really lived in Middle Cisnes.

Happy Fat stretched at the bit, and Duck unconsciously pulled back on the reins. In the western sky, several shades of gray—the light, unretractable tint of a snowstorm moving across the mountains and, over the valley, the church-pants hue of a rainstorm—flowed past one another like bruises in differing stages of ripeness. Duck said, "Alfredo won't talk to you when we get there, *che*. I don't know what he'll do, but I guarantee he won't answer questions. When Alfredo has the other half of the herd in the winter, he's like four or five hours up above Tito on horse, depending on the snow. But as a witch flies, it's like two kilometers. They can practically see one another's cabin." Duck leaned forward, confidentially. "They communicate," he said, "by smoke signal. How's that for crazy?"

*   *   *

Counting south from the Peruvian border, Aisén del Carlos Ibáñez del Campo is the eleventh of Chile's twelve governmental states. At 107,153 square kilometers, or 42,000 square miles, it is roughly the size of the state of Mississippi, though only 85,000 people live there. Between 45,000 and 55,000 of them, depending on whom you talk to, live in one place, Coihaique, the state capital, and another 10,000 live in a port town to the west of Coihaique, making Aisén, the middle state of three in Chilean Patagonia, one of the least populated tracts of land remaining in South America. Outside of those two towns, the population density of Aisén is reportedly lower than that of the Sahara Desert.

Aisén is bordered on the west by the Pacific and on the east by the Andean *cordillera,* which forms the border running north-south between Chile and Argentina. A hundred kilometers north of Coihaique, the border veers deeply east for several dozen kilometers toward Argentina, then careens back out again to form an island of land surrounded on three sides by the mountains and that seems to be cut off from both countries. This is the sector called Cisnes, for the river, the Swan, that runs through it from the Argentine border in the northeast all the way to the Canal Puyuhuapi in the southwest.

Cisnes sector is divided into three parts: Upper, Middle and Lower Cisnes. They are, despite their proximity, three immensely different areas. The Upper Río Cisnes is a quiet, elegant spring creek that winds its way across a virtual desert of *pampa,* or prairie, that has bled through a crease in the Andes from Argentina and into Chile. Two hundred kilometers away, the lower river is a wide glacial torrent that empties into a maze of fjords. But it is Middle Cisnes, or simply Cisnes, that is the most mountainous and secluded. There is a crushing immediacy to the isolation in Cisnes that the openness of the Upper *pampa* and the Lower coast do not share, as though you are literally caught in the middle of nowhere.

As Duck and I rode, a queer paradox settled into place, for I was at once aware of the infinite possibility of so much space and of the pressing, claustrophobic impossibility of infinity. Five or six kilometers from the point where the clopping of our three horses kept time with one another was Argentina. To get there, though, we'd have had to go up and over mountains whose peaks were six thousand feet high and whose sides fell more or less straight down into the road, which was built only a few hundred feet above sea level. It was, even for the gauchos who had passed six or seven decades there, very difficult to get out of Cisnes. For the younger gauchos like Duck, who wanted more than anything in the world to leave the valley for good, it was nearly unthinkable.

We urged the horses up a steep rise in the road walled on the south by an exposed shale cliff ten stories tall. Below us, the river sliced the Andes into shards of black igneous rock the size of pickup trucks. In between rapids, the water rolled as smooth as glass at a deceptively dangerous clip. Along the banks, boulders lay on top of one another in layers six and seven deep and protruded at sharp angles. We rode down the rise, all the while shielded on one side by the bluff, until we got to its base, at river level. Here, a fence came down out of the forest, nearly met the road, and ran to the east as far as you could see. It breasted the uneven swells of rocky soil and veered around thorn-encrusted *calafate* plants as big as horses. Yet the wire was somehow stretched so tight that the wind parted and moaned. I tried to remember if I'd ever seen a fence that looked as though it had been as difficult to build as this one.

But as difficult as it was to imagine how the posts had been given purchase on the rocky slope with only a digging bar, it was more difficult to believe how obsessively uniform the fence was. And how beautiful. Each post was perfectly shaved to the exact same diameter and smoothed by hand. It seemed only fitting that people living within the confines of such an awesome cage—people relegated to communication via smoke signal—would honor their captivity with such mathematical precision.

CHAPTER TWO

El Eggo and El Che

It was through a series of coincidences that I ever went to Chilean Patagonia in the first place. In October 1994, the year I graduated from college, I was living in Dillon, Colorado, and working as a fly-fishing guide, which is the same job I'd had during the university summers. I didn't have any idea that Chile even had a Patagonia, nor that one of the crowning projects of General Augusto Pinochet, Chile's dictator from 1974 to 1990, had been to begin building a road from one end of Patagonia nearly to the other, a distance of fifteen hundred kilometers. Nor that the road had succeeded in opening, for the first time in history, places that few people had ever known existed.

What I did know was that I wanted to continue to go to rivers and figure out how to catch the trout in them, and to show people I'd never met how to do it. The deeper I could get into an unknown place, the better. So that October, I called a friend who has a fly-fishing travel agency in California and asked him to help me get a job guiding. He gave me the name of a man from Edina, Minnesota: Rex Bryngelson. Rex, he said, had been guiding for years in Alaska on a river called the Goodnews, which, though I'd never met Rex, also happened to be a river I'd fished for several weeks in the mid-1980s. Now that Alaska, like Argentine Patagonia and New Zealand, had gotten too popular, said my friend, Rex was starting a lodge in Chile.

I called Rex that night. He said he'd leased some land and fishing rights on a ranch called Santa Elvira in exchange for fixing up the dilapidated main house, which was where the four guests a week that the agent in California had promised to send him would stay. Rex said there was a chickenhouse across the pasture that he thought I might, with a little creativity, make habitable. There was no mention of anyone living at Santa Elvira. Rex said only that a couple years before a road had made the ranch accessible by truck, and that, until then, the valley had been reachable from the nearest town only after a three-week trip on horseback. At the end of a fifteen-minute conversation, Rex said to meet him on December 19 at the bus stop in that same town, which was called Coihaique. He said he'd be the only guy there at the hour the bus pulled in. I didn't even ask him what he looked like.

Rex and I and his girlfriend, Rhonda, who was from South Africa, left for the mountains the morning after I arrived in Patagonia. Rex gave me a 1973 Land Rover Santana to drive which had one temperamental headlight and battery wires that were held on with duct tape and this organic caulking the gauchos use to seal their windows. For three weeks, Rex and Rhonda and I worked on fixing up the main house during the mornings; in the afternoons and on days off, we'd get in the Land Rover to explore any parts of the Río Cisnes that were accessible by road—or, in many cases, by horse trails that we could, with enough disregard for the theoretical consequences, get the Land Rover to negotiate.

The main house of the ranch was in a complete shambles. Carlos Asi was an absentee landowner who had little interest in the workings of his holdings, so long as the cattle were brought to market on time, and under the ruined floors of the main house were the skeletons of rats with skulls the size of baseballs, and the skeletons of the newborn sheep and kittens and puppies that the rats had dragged there to eat. By the time the first clients arrived in mid-January, though, the house had a working kitchen, three bedrooms, two hot-running showers, and a living room with new, varnished floors. A generator provided the lodge with the only electricity for thousands of square kilometers. New windows looked out from the house onto the pasture and, at the other end of the pasture, a hundred and fifty meters away, onto a little shack.

How the people who lived in the shack had gotten there or what they did was a mystery to me, and would remain so, for the time I spent off the river was limited to eight or nine hours a week, during which time there were flat tires to change and wood to be cut for the stoves. Once a week, Rex and I would make the eight-hour round trip to Coihaique, where we would spend a day and a half buying supplies and picking up clients at the airport. The three people I did see with regularity were the lodge cook, Luísa, her son Jimmy, and her father, Don Luis. They lived in the cabin that fronted the barn, and the four of us would sit around the stove at night after dinner and play dominoes.

And the more time I spent with them, the more I began to understand what was happening at Santa Elvira, and, I suspected, all over Aisén, in Río Baker and Chile Chico and a dozen other places like Cisnes. And when I drove down the Southern Road nearly to its end during my last week in Patagonia in 1995, my suspicions were confirmed: I saw people just like those living in the shack across the pasture at Santa Elvira—people who, despite living without electricity and hot running water, were suddenly witness to Land Rovers and tourists. And all of it had come out of nowhere, with the building of the road.

In the end, though, I was as fascinated by what I saw at Santa Elvira as I was unsure what to do with the information. And so, at the end of four months in Patagonia, I left for New York, where I'd been given a fiction-writing fellowship at NYU. Classes were in the evening, and I worked the late-night shift at an ad agency, proofreading copy. A year later, I got a job as a magazine editor, and, not long after that, a job teaching fiction writing at NYU. Everything, it seemed, was fine.

Except that I couldn't get Patagonia, and particularly Aisén, out of my mind. I'd go to the New York Public Library on days off looking for anything that might shed some light on the history of the state. I tried computer searches in Spanish and English and French and German and Italian and Portuguese. Aside from a few tangential entries, there was next to nothing about anyone who had gone to Aisén or when or why they'd gone or what they'd found. Above all, there was nothing about what, to me, as a fiction writer, was the central question: what was it like for a man and woman suddenly to wake up one day and have an entirely different idea about the size of the world and their changing place within it?

In 1997, I began writing a novel about what I imagined Duck's and Edith's lives to be like. At the same time, I was researching my grandmother's life, about which I had planned to write a nonfiction book. My grandmother, sometime around 1925, had headed for St. Louis, leaving her brothers Winfred and Chris and Lawrence to care for their widowed mother. My grandmother's name was

Mildred Viola Wehmueller, and she was sixteen years old when she moved to St. Louis. She was from a family farming commune called Ebo, after the creek that separated the homestead from one of the smallest towns in Missouri. At the time, St. Louis was, for anyone from Missouri or southern Illinois or northern Arkansas or Kentucky, the center of the world. And because, compared to places like Ebo, life in St. Louis happened in a different century, it was the place to which thousands and thousands of people migrated like salmon, fueled by the desire to spawn new lives; and where, also like salmon, they would let their old lives die as part of the agreement. It's safe to say my grandmother spent the rest of her life trying to get there. Or, rather, that she spent the rest of her life trying to shed an old skin, a skin that was as obvious—because of her thick accent and because she said things like "ain't" instead of "isn't," which marked her as uneducated and, therefore, "backward"—as it was impossible to shed. She'd had, when she left Ebo, no idea what she was up against.

I'd always wanted to know what, exactly, that trip had been like and, more to the point, what it had been like to decide to make the trip in the first place. In my grandmother's case, though, I was never going to find out, because she'd lost her memory to Alzheimer's and her speech to Parkinson's. Now, in Cisnes, there was another chance. A better one, for the change there—one that was many times more severe—had not occurred ten months or ten years or ten decades before. It was occurring at that very moment. And fictionalizing Duck and Edith's story seemed to me a waste when the cabin across the pasture at Santa Elvira held most everything that there was to know. All I had to do was get inside.

*　　*　　*

Once I'd decided in late summer of 1997 to go back to Patagonia, I began spending more and more time at the public library. What I wanted to know, quite simply, was who—and what—were Duck and Edith?

It's not as ridiculous a question as it sounds. What I'd found as I'd widened my computer searches and read more and more books about Patagonia was that, for every little bit of information there was on Chile, there were several volumes about Argentina, and that, in each of these volumes, the focus was invariably on the gaucho. Nearly all of the research cited in these books came from the journals of people who had traveled through Argentina between 1700 and 1890, and the breadth of their observations was the only thing as stunning as the specificity with which they recorded them. There were descriptions of everything from the breast-feeding habits of the gauchos (they often, according to one historian, extended the practice to eighteen or even twenty-four months after birth, thereby elongating the birth interval significantly when compared to that of Europe) to the gauchos' particularity with reference to the colors of their horses, "the most esteemed being roan and pyeballed." What stuck out the most, though, was that every book either began or ended by saying that the gaucho no longer existed. And, moreover, had not existed for at least a century. As Richard W. Slatta put it in *The Gauchos and the Vanishing Frontier:* "Gauchos disappeared as a recognizable social group in the last third of the nineteenth century. . . . Vanquished in reality . . . only the name remained."

So who were Duck and Edith and all the dozens of people I'd seen in Cisnes in 1995 if not gauchos, when so much about their lives mirrored exactly the descriptions in the journals? How could the gaucho be dead? And how might the fact that Duck supposedly did not exist be affected by the other central fact: that he was now connected by the road to a place that was two centuries further into the future than he was?

To understand how a culture universally associated with Argentina—and with a particular period in that country's history—could be at once alive and dead in neighboring Chile, it's first necessary to understand what a Coihaique high school student once told me with great conviction: Santiago *is* Chile, in the same way that Coihaique *is* Aisén. Both places hold over half the population of their respective areas (eight of Chile's fourteen million people live in Santiago) and account for a massive portion of the economy. Each is the government seat, and each is the place that large numbers of people consider the starting point of a new and better life, and, for this reason, each is absorbing people at an astounding rate.

But as apt as the student's observation is, Chile is a far more complicated place. Like many Latin American countries, its immensely distorted population distribution makes for a kind of split personality. There is at once in great supply the mind-bogglingly urban and the epically rural. Perhaps the best illustration of this is Chile's bifurcated obsession with soccer, a team sport whose powers (France, Germany, England, Brazil) are some of the world's industrial megaliths; and rodeo, an individual, grassroots spectacle built upon solidarity fostered in isolation. In many ways, Santiago has nothing to do with Chile.

Nor do most Santiaguinos seem to care about what happens outside the city limits. When I approached the LanChile desk (Lan, as it's known, is one of three Chilean airlines) in the Santiago airport in 1995 and asked an attendant what time my flight was leaving for Coihaique, she replied without the slightest bit of irony, "Where's Coihaique?" Which is precisely the kind of thing that Coihaiquinos despise. It's funny, then, that they apply the same aloof disinterest to the outlands of their own state.

Downtown Coihaique is decidedly not Patagonia. It is, rather, the only place in an area the size of Mississippi—more to the point, it's one of a handful of places in something like six Mississippis—where the twentieth century is in full swing. Downtown Coihaique is glass-fronted computer shops, well-stocked hardware stores filled with chain saws and drills, showrooms with Toyota four-door trucks, and inflationary cafés with expensive lighting and big-screen TVs: a sort of southern Santiago made to much smaller scale.

But walk along Calle Cruz out from the town square, turn left onto Calle Ramón Freire, and, with each uphill block, time begins steadily to regress. It's slow at first—the initial change is from business district to residential neighborhoods. Then, somewhere along the way, Calle Freire, like all Coihaique's streets, gives way to dirt and stone. Sidewalks begin to crumble. White picket fences turn to flimsy chicken-wire parodies of fences against which cur dogs hurl themselves, bulging and stretching the alloyed latticework. The *pampa* begins to creep into town, wild and overgrown; horses stand hobbled at the sides of rusted trucks.

Calle Freire then re-forms its identity altogether, breaking into a chaotic grid of tiny streets with the blind corners of a labyrinth. The walls are the tiny shacks of the gauchos who have filtered into town. Another few blocks uphill, and what was long ago Calle Freire becomes a winding, northbound crease in the *pampa*. There's no fence; there are no street signs. This is where Patagonia begins, and with it, the story of the gauchos.

*　　*　　*

Alfonzo Mansilla lives on Calle Freire one block above the point where the pavement stops. In front of Alfonzo's house, two medium-sized Marco Polo buses sag into a patch of grassless dirt two hundred square yards. The front axle of one bus rests awkwardly on two cinder blocks; the hood is propped open with a lead pipe. The other bus, possessed of all four wheels, leans at an appreciable angle toward the deserted street. It is this one that will take Alfonzo tomorrow, at 10:00 A.M., as it does every Sunday, the one hundred twenty kilometers to Cisnes, and, forty kilometers beyond that, to the village of La Tapera. Along the way, he'll make brief stops in the villages of Mañihuales (pop. 275), for a cup of coffee and a chat with the owner of the bar there, and Amengual (pop. 150), this time for a cheese sandwich and *mate* at a friend's house.

It's only 4:00 A.M., though I expect, looking in the window of Alfonzo's clean, white house, to see him already awake and drinking his *mate*. Alfonzo has remained incredibly youthful into his sixties. He is tall and fit, and he carries himself with the unmistakable, easy confidence of a military man pleased with his own handsome virility. He wears handspun wool sweaters over his dress shirts and jeans. He does not drink, and his skin is tanned.

But Alfonzo is also kind in a way that suggests guilt. He is disciplined in a way that recognizes the dangerous potential of any hairline fracture. In another life, he was Sergeant Alfonzo Mansilla, one of the elite, a Carabinero, or state policeman, under Pinochet. What part he played in the "disappearances" that plagued Coihaique and all of Chile in the '70s and '80s is unclear; and, to the gauchos of Cisnes, largely considered moot, for since retiring, Alfonzo Mansilla has become, aside from the occasional truck driver or *patrón,* the only Coihaiquino who will even come to Cisnes. For a modest price—500 *pesos,* or about a dollar—he will forward letters, bring people to the hospital, and deliver odds and ends (solid wooden oxcart wheels the size of those on tractors; kilos of *mate;* saddles and stirrups and cigarettes) to the gauchos who ride down out of the mountains to the road.

It's March 12, 1998, and in a month of wandering Coihaique at all hours, I've come to find out that it's less a good time now than it was three years ago to be sitting against a fence at the farthest reach of the slums an hour before dawn on a Sunday morning. Thanks in part to Señor Mansilla, Coihaique is increasingly occupied by the poor, who have come to understand how little they have, and how little chance of advancement. In the mountains, you might listen to radio ads telling you what you don't own. But if you can't see it and cannot imagine what it looks like, there is a certain lack of immediacy in your desire to possess it. Not so in town, where men with good shoes hurry from shop to shop jangling car keys in their pockets, and neatly uniformed schoolchildren sit on benches in the square leafing through textbooks.

So it is that kids who months before wore goatskin chaps now rove in groups, clad in baggy jeans and black Alice in Chains T-shirts. They carry the homemade knives with which they once slaughtered sheep. To make a living, they sell marijuana and cocaine; to differentiate their territories, they paint antique fences with the Spanglish names of their gangs, like Los MegaRapers and Los Reyes del Hood. All of this is a means of quelling the frustration of a place more impenetrable than even the valleys that surround sectors like Cisnes and the Northern Ice Country.

For my part in all of this, I have nowhere to go and nothing to do but sit here and wait for Alfonzo to wake up and take me out to the mountains. I'm afraid to leave his house because, if I do, I don't think I'll ever regain the nerve it's taken me a month to muster. The fly-fishing lodge at Santa Elvira has been shut down now for two weeks. Rex, whom I saw a few days ago, told me that it had been a slow season, and that, although there may still be a couple of clients later in April, even that's iffy at best. He also told me that Duck and Edith were still at Santa Elvira. Which is no guarantee that they will be tomorrow. If they are, then I'll ask to pitch a tent in the pasture; if not, I'll hike one of the trails along the river that I remember from three years ago and ask to live with whomever I find at the trail's end. Either way, I've got the tent and a water filter and a fly rod with which to catch trout, and I figure the worst that can happen is I'll have to flag down Señor Mansilla on his way back to Coihaique in a week.

All night I was at a bar called the Red Skin, where middle- and upper-class kids on break from faraway universities came to watch Mariah Carey and Ricky Martin videos on the big-screen TV over the gothic fireplace. Every now and again above the noise I could pick out the bass line of the latest Argentine or Colombian *rok-en-rol* as it filtered through the high, heavy wood floor of the upstairs dance room.

I was sitting with a young woman from Santiago who'd come south a year earlier to start a nightclub. She had fair skin and green eyes. Her name was Verónica Schenke. "My people," she said, "came to Santiago from Spain two hundred years ago," then added with a pride only vaguely masked by a self-deprecating smile: "We would only mix with the Prussians, catch it?"

She said her father, who lived in La Junta, a village in the north of Aisén, "had animals," which was to say he was a *patrón* and may very well have owned two or three hundred thousand acres, which is not an uncommon size for a ranch in Patagonia. "He's a brute," she said, "like, practically barbarian, catch it? He won't leave the country." Before her parents separated, her father had tried to live in Santiago with her mother, who kept a nice apartment there and had a woman to cook and clean, but he'd been unable to stay away from the mountains. Unlike Carlos Asi, I suspected, Verónica's father was one of the traditional *patrones* who worked alongside his gauchos. In any event, Verónica's nightclub wasn't doing well, and now she sat in the Red Skin (the newest and most successful of her several competitors), drinking *pisco* and Coke.

"It's so boring," she said, looking at the table next to us, where a mixed lot of Coihaiquino fly-fishing guides, Chileans and Americans and Australians and an Uruguayan, were talking about the wealthy American, English, and Brazilian clients they'd been guiding that season. Outside of the two massive windows, groups of seventeen-year-olds on vacation from Munich and Buenos Aires and London gathered in the street, waiting their turn to come in or protesting the $2 entrance fee, the girls in platform leather shoes and tight black pants, the boys wearing baseball caps and suede jackets.

Verónica watched them. "It's tourists," she said, "then it's winter. That's the progression. And a woman with a business isn't going to *get* the business, catch it? Especially not in Patagonia. The opportunity for expansion here is absolutely unlimited. But a place like Coihaique, it's developing *too* fast, like, so fast there isn't any control. I don't know," she said. "At least the fumes from the exhaust keep the snow from sticking in the winter." She lit a cigarette and blew out the match. "What are you doing here?"

I said I was leaving in the morning for Cisnes.

"Never heard of it," she said, smiling politely. "You must have the name wrong."

I told her I was sure of the name. "It's on the way to La Junta from here."

"Well," she sighed, "let me tell you something: you'd better be careful. The peasants out there, they're like another race."

*   *   *

Race was the word most commonly used in Coihaique to differentiate between the people who lived either in the mountains or in the slums of town and those who lived in residential neighborhoods, and because living in either of the two former places was synonymous with extreme poverty, race actually described socioeconomic differences. No one, however, had been able to tell me what race that was, though it did not stop them from reacting incredulously when I suggested that the people of the mountains and the slums were gauchos. For starters, I was told, Argentina had the rights to the very concept of the gaucho.

As it turns out, the first written record of the word "gaucho," in 1743 in a journal called *The Secret American News,* was not in Argentina, but across the Andes in Chile. If language serves as an imitator of social fact, then it's no surprise, given the vacuum of knowledge surrounding Aisén, that the word "gaucho" has several meanings, none of which has anything to do with the others. Depending upon the tone of voice you choose and the context into which you fit "gaucho," you might be using it as an adjective or a noun to mean "cowboy" or "Indian" or "noble" or "untrustworthy" or "thief" or "reliable." All of this despite the fact that no one knows from where, exactly, the word comes.

The leading theory is that "gaucho" was derived from *huachó* or *guache,* which means "orphan" in several Indian languages indigenous to Argentina, and that this word was used in the mid-eighteenth century to describe a mixed lot of horsebound men who hunted wild cattle on the *pampa* of Buenos Aires province. How they got there and who they were is as much a mystery as when and how the gauchos eventually got to Chile—or, for that matter, why the word was first recorded in Chile.

All that is sure is that Buenos Aires was founded in 1536 by the Spanish nobleman Don Pedro de Mendoza, who came to the twenty-eight-mile-wide River Plate delta with twelve hundred men and one hundred horses and mares.

By 1541, Mendoza was dead of syphilis; and the colonists, unable to feed themselves on the harsh, dry *pampa,* had abandoned Buenos Aires to the Indians.

What they left behind, though, were their horses, which had not existed anywhere in South America (or North America) until the Spanish came. After two more failed attempts to restart the colony (one of the unsuccessful governors was Cabeza de Vaca, or Cow Head), Juan de Garay founded, in 1580, and once and for all, the city of Buenos Aires, not with Spaniards, but with *mestizos* from what is today Paraguay and northern Argentina.

What de Garay found when he came was that the *pampas* were now rich with wild horses and cattle and that groups of men were hunting the cattle from horseback. Had some of Cabeza de Vaca's men, like their stock, gone feral, and from them the word "gaucho" come into being? Was the first gaucho a newly horsebound Guarani Indian, or was the first gaucho one of de Garay's *mestizos?*

The only thing that makes the question interesting, as far as I'm concerned, is not what the answer is, but how obsessively people pursued—and continue to pursue—the answer. In all the dozens of books written about the Argentine gaucho, race is perhaps the most common topic. And there in Coihaique, nearly three hundred years after de Garay's death, people didn't even know who was living in the mountains, though they still felt comfortable boiling the conversation down to what was deemed the essential element. I was reminded that night at the Red Skin of a quote attributed to an English entrepeneur traveling through Buenos Aires province in 1826: "The gauchos . . . are, in appearance, a fine race, but, in comparison with the peasantry of England or France, little better than a species of carnivorous baboon."

In both Argentine and European literature, the race question often gives way to a list of legendary personality traits attributed to the gauchos, which include, not surprisingly, a number of other paradoxical terms best summed up in Frederick Mann Page's 1893 article in *Modern Language Notes 8,* entitled "Remarks on the Gaucho and His Dialect": "The average gaucho is generous, crafty, liberal, irreligious, ignorant, immoral, ferocious, hospitable, brave, 'moderately' honest, fond of display, eager for novelty, a natural gambler, libertine and dandy." Gauchos are also often portrayed as having no sense of linear time, a trait that is at once romanticized (as in Borges's famous short story "Funes, the Memorious") and thought to demonstrate a complete lack of work ethic. Even Darwin took note. He is quoted as asking two gauchos near Mendoza, Argentina, in 1833, why they didn't work. When one remarked that the days were too long, and the other that he was too poor, Darwin concluded that: "The number of horses and profusion of food is the destruction of all industry."

Whoever the gaucho was and whatever he was like, it was industry—billable hours—that, according to historical consensus, spelled the gaucho's demise at the end of the nineteenth century, when *latifundismo,* a movement in Argentina to fence the *pampa* into immense *fundos,* or ranches, effectively ended his semi-nomadic way of life. Which only begged the question: How long had the gauchos been living in Cisnes? A hundred years? Two hundred years? How had they gotten there? And what, now that they'd been connected by road to the most industrialized century in history, would happen to them?

* * *

With this in mind, I'd gone while I was in Coihaique to the hospital to speak with Dr. Mario González Kappes. I'd been told by a dozen people that Mario knew more about Aisén than anyone in Chile. He'd even written two of the few books on the place, though I discovered they largely contained the same episodic information that everyone does know—of Darwin's brief time there, for instance, and of the partial mapping of Aisén by the German Hans Steffan. Mario seemed the perfect man to ask how it was that no one knew any more than this.

"To say there are no more gauchos," said Mario, who is also an amateur paleontologist, "would be like me telling you there's only one place in all of Patagonia to find mylodon skeletons. We know very little about how and where that animal lived. But we do know there's a cave in Argentina where you can find their skeletons. Does that mean that's the only place in all of Patagonia that they lived or that it's time to stop looking? Of course not."

We were in his office. Mario had brown hair that he wore slicked back off his wide forehead, and a thin, scraggly beard; under his white doctor's coat he had on a nice suit. His eyes were blue and he was seated behind a gunship-gray metal desk. Above us, a single, unrelenting tubelight basted the room in the white glow of an autopsy lab. He pulled a burlap sack out from under the desk, and said: "The gaucho lives right here."

I said, "In the sack?"

"No, eggo," he said. "In the sack live apples, eggo." Eggo, or *huevón,* is the most famous of all the words indigenous to Chile; it comes from *huevo,* or egg, and it's a euphemism for testicle that can be familiar or aggressively skeptical or, as Mario chose to use it, both. "Didn't you see the men waiting in the hall to be seen by a doctor? And they want to say the gaucho is extinct? It's madness, eggo."

I had, indeed, seen the men in the hall while waiting for Mario to be done with a series of phone calls. I had listened carefully to the things they said. More to the point, I had listened for the one thing they did not say: eggo. They used the word *che* instead. There is, syntactically, no difference between the two, and either of them can serve, within the same sentence, as a proper or interrogative noun, an imperative, and a verb. But the cultural difference between *el* eggo and *el che* is immense.

"*Che*" is to Argentina what "eggo" is to Chile. Walking around downtown Coihaique saying "*che*" made people smirk. Walking around Santiago saying it made them ignore you altogether, because maintaining poor relations between Chile and Argentina seems in both countries to be a matter of national pride. In Coihaique, which had been settled initially by Argentines and then, later, predominantly by Chileans, the physical lines drawn between the two words were remarkably clear: if the sidewalk beneath your feet was new, you used "eggo"; if it was in severe disrepair, you switched to "*che.*"

"*El che,*" Mario told me, comes from the Mapuche language. "*Mapu*" means "earth," and "*che*" means "man." The Mapuche were the only tribe of Indians in South America never to be defeated by the conquistadors, due in part to the singularly prideful view of the world they espoused. According to them, the place of the Mapuche, the EarthMan, was absolute in its centrality, and from it was derived the location of all others. A man or tribe that occupied a place to the west was "West*che.*" A man or tribe to the east was "East*che,*" and so on. The world, because the Mapuche were largely nomadic, was a constantly shifting plane upon which they occupied center stage. I said to Mario, "But the Mapuche were a tribe that largely inhabited Chile. So how is it that a word that's supposedly Argentine, like *che,* was developed from a 'Chilean' referent?"

"It wasn't," said Mario. "It was developed from an indigenous referent that colonialists from Spain referred to as 'Chilean.' The Mapuche are neither Chilean nor Argentine, eggo. They're Mapuche. But as the Chilean government fought them at the end of the last century, they were pushed farther south. And east, into what the Spanish called Argentina and the Mapuche called East. That's probably about the time the Argentines decided to usurp the word. There's nothing like war, eggo, to make people take characterizing features of the vanquished as their own—it's just one of those brilliant ironies that allows people's heritage to live on, albeit sort of like an elephant's head in a trophy room."

Mario was very easy to understand. He spoke beautiful, textbook Spanish, although with a heavy Chilean accent, and, of course, liberally salted with *el* eggo. The slum*che,* on the other hand, were much more difficult to understand. They spoke with mixed Argentine and Chilean accents that often sounded more like Italian than Spanish. More than adding *el che* to the end of sentences, they fused it to words within sentences: Argentina*che,* Coihaique*che.* Downtown Coihaique was, to them, a place that was Other, just as the slum*che*—the gauchos—were Other when you looked outward from the center of town. Coihaique was a place that was located in Chile, albeit a specialized geographic and historical part of Chile: Patagonia. Eggos lived in Chile, but I felt sure that Duck and Edith's world—all of Aisén outside of downtown Coihaique, in fact—would be a place where *el che* dominated.

I said, "So that's why the gaucho uses the word *che,* because he's seminomadic and because, like the Mapuche, he's neither Argentine nor Chilean. He's gaucho."

"An orphan," said Mario, "because neither country knows where he is. The Argentines think they own the word. They think the history began and ended there. The word is their trophy. And the Chileans, on whose land the gaucho now lives in his purest and most historical form, couldn't give a shit. To us, he's lesser. Another race."

I said, "Because he came from Argentina."

"Precisely," said Mario.

"And that's how come gauchos, long before the road and even still, could bring cattle to market and no one considered them gauchos: it'd be some kind of blight on their national pride. And no one follows them back to the mountains or goes to the slums to hang around with them because in a place that's modernizing as fast as Coihaique, no one has any interest in what's backward and poor. "

"Right again, eggo," Mario smiled. "Apple?"

According to the principal theory, *latifundismo* forced the gaucho to domesticate and care for the very cattle he'd been hunting. He became a cowboy, and the moniker gaucho stuck. Eventually, the fences were stopped cold in what is today Argentine Patagonia by the violent resistance of the very Indians who may have originally given the gauchos their name and much of their blood. The government gave the gauchos a choice: fight or be shot. It was not, according to the theory, a simple case of whites versus Indians, as it was in the United States. It was gauchos—mixed bloods—against people who were probably at least half their own kind. The gauchos were the only horsemen skilled enough to ride against the Indians, perhaps because the gauchos were, effectively, Indians.

The apple Mario gave me was at once sour and sweet. It was delicious. I said, "So the gauchos came to Chile to be left alone."

"They may have been in Chile for centuries," said Mario. "All I know for sure is that while all this genocide is happening in Argentina, Chile is fighting the War of the Pacific against Peru. This is the 1870s. And at the end of the War of the Pacific, the Chilean army sacks Lima, and everyone's happy. Except for one little thing: during the war, Argentina had taken advantage of Chile's north-turned eyes to declare sovereignty over what is today Argentine Patagonia, leaving Chile with the comparatively small area we have now. But Chile didn't argue, because the War of the Pacific had depleted us, and we just couldn't go fight with Argentina right away.

"So, what happens?" said Mario. "The triumphant Chilean army returns from Lima, and because the Chilean personality is one that becomes more . . . barbaric when it has booze, the bingeing victors start treating Santiago as though it were Lima.

"So the government sends its army of reprobates south to fight the Indians, and Chilean settlers follow. But between the army and the Indians, who were very clever, the settlers don't know who's worse. So the settlers say fuck this and move over into Argentine Patagonia. And there the Chileans mix with the men whose forebears survived the ruined colonies at Buenos Aires. And the children of those Chileans who go to Argentina get raised as gauchos."

I said, "With the exception that instead of hunting cattle with spears and *bolas,* they're raising them. Cowboying them."

"Right," said Mario. "There's just not that much difference between the people in Buenos Aires province in the seventeeth and eighteenth centuries and the people in Argentine Patagonia in the late nineteenth. They dress the same, they hunt the same, they move around. It's just that they have some domestic cattle that keep them more or less in the same area. But even the original gauchos, from what the journals say, weren't completely nomadic. They hunted the cattle on the *pampa,* yes, but the *pampa* is a harsh place, eggo. You can't, if you're a cow or a gaucho, just get water wherever you want it. The gaucho had a cabin or a tent or whatever that he came back to, and it was near water. But the thing that made him gaucho was that he did something akin to the Aboriginals—he went on a kind of walkabout. Nothing religious in the gaucho's case. He'd just disappear when he wanted. I'm sure you'll see this in Cisnes, that the men just . . . go away.

"So as the Argentines got more and more roads in their Patagonia, the government realized they had a bunch of Chilean expatriates running around, and they started getting nationalistic and pushing the foreigners out. Then the sons and grandsons and great-grandsons of the original Chileans in Argentine Patagonia come through the passes into Chile, at Cisnes and Lago Verde and La Junta and all down around Cochrane, looking for new land."

I said, "And because at this point they aren't really Chilean and they aren't really Argentine, they're kind of orphans themselves. They're gaucho. They're settling land that technically belongs to Chile but that the Chilean government hasn't even mapped. And they brought with them *el che* and the *bolas* and the dialect and all of it."

"And," Mario smiled, "the blood. Out in Cisnes, eggo, it's like a time warp."

I said, "But what are the gauchos like?"

Mario wiped his mouth on his sleeve and put the sack of apples back in his desk. "That," he said, "is something I've always wanted to know."

*   *   *

When the sun finally rose above Señor Mansilla's, the gauchos began coming in twos and threes. By nine o'clock, there were a dozen of them standing around Señor Mansilla's front yard and in the dirt street, waiting for the bus to leave. Through their number moved only one man who stood out, a large-boned Coihaiquino with a mess of curly strawberry blond hair, half-muttonchop sideburns, pale blue eyes, and a red Wyatt Earp mustache. He spoke loudly as he walked, and smoked one cigarette after another. Occasionally, he would lean sympathetically into the ear of an old gaucho and say something just between them. When we all filed onto the bus, he sat in the jump seat alongside Señor Mansilla. His name was Red Duck.

Señor Mansilla pulled off the yard and shifted smoothly down the hill. We passed the square and the silent churches and turned onto Avenida General Baquedano. A hundred meters later, the road became gravel and then pavement again. We wound up into the mountains, and Coihaique glistened below us, flanked by yellow fields of hay and green fields of grass, and all around the mountains ranged off into the half-circular distance.

We passed hills split open by the shadowy depths of great crags. The very landscape seemed to breathe and move and undulate. Streams flowed out of sight under canopies of rock and waterfalls spilled over cliffs. Under one of them an altar sat in a shallow cave where dozens of candles twinkled. In the distance was a sign that pointed north but said nothing, and here the road turned to stone and dirt for good. A gaucho man and woman and their young child sat beneath the sign with their hair going sideways in the wind. Señor Mansilla stopped for them. As they stumbled to navigate the thin and crowded aisle and find their seats, Red Duck watched them intently in the large rearview mirror.

When the bus started again, the steering wheel spun back and forth like a Frisbee in Señor Mansilla's hands, and everyone watched the fight in the mirror's reflection. Near Mañihuales, the road turned into a narrower valley and followed the Río Mañihuales. Several hundred meters outside the village, the road doubled in width, and the bus slowed as gauchos rode at a gallop through the dust ahead of us like messengers racing the very news they would announce. Across from a gas station with no attendant, Señor Mansilla brought the bus to a stop so that one wheel rested awkwardly on a bit of cracked sidewalk.

A woman waited behind the bar inside the cafe. Down a hallway was a door that opened onto a courtyard and then another door across the yard; Señor Mansilla went through them both with Red Duck trailing like a shadow. Two men came down the stairs and followed, leaving me alone in the courtyard with a blind calf that stood with its legs buckling and a perplexed look on its face like it was misunderstanding a conversation.

When I went inside the bar again, Red Duck was sitting there with two men drinking *pisco* with a splash of warm Fanta orange drink and no ice because there was no electricity in the place. The two men with Red Duck were heavily stubbled and leaves clung to the wool of their clothes. One had had his right eye scrambled in his head and the uni-colored mess that had been made of the iris and the pupil looked like a runny egg yolk and stared out at an angle.

I ordered a beer and sat down several seats from them. They stopped talking and watched me in the mirror behind the bar. When the ex-policeman walked through, Red Duck hopped up and clapped him on the back. Then he followed Señor Mansilla to the bus as though the two vagrants were no friends of his.

When we pulled into the village of Amengual an hour later, the village idiot had taken his place in the window of the first house on Calle Opazo, his hair combed and his mustache trimmed and his hand raised. The owner of the Little Huaso, the general store, came running across the street from his house to open for business as Señor Mansilla shut off the bus's engine. When we left, he closed the shop once again. It was anyone's guess when he would have reason to reopen.

Fifteen kilometers out of Amengual, an Indian woman called Julia waited by the side of the road with her horse tied by the reins to a fence. Señor Mansilla slowed to a stop and slid open the window and leaned out on his elbow. Julia wore fur-lined boots, despite the heat, and blue plastic beads in her thick hair. She was waiting for a letter, and Señor Mansilla gave her one; then she asked after her husband, who had ridden off two months before and never come back. "Anything?" said Julia. But Señor Mansilla shook his head and said he was sorry. He said he'd asked around Coihaique and Mañihuales and again in Amengual and no one had seen her husband.

We drove on. After a while, a man was visible through the windshield, sitting on a rock. Behind him the land built itself, terrace after terrace, into squared buttes, and in front of him was a fence and a gate. He wore a beige cap and gray sweats and a maroon wool sweater and a thin black beard. It was Duck. When the bus pulled away we were standing across from one another on opposite sides of the road. It had been three years since we'd seen one another.

Duck looked closer as I started to explain what I was doing there. "Let's worry about all that later." He smiled. "Right now, your lunch is getting cold, Nico*che*."

❈

CHAPTER THREE

The Nothingsummer

Duck and I stopped the first night of the cattle drive at a place called Casa Piedra, or Rock House. Rock House is a gash at the bottom of a cliff; the gash starts chest-high and angles sharply to the ground so that it looks like an initial logger's cut into a tree trunk of rock twenty stories tall. It was deep enough that half a dozen men could lie side by side under it without getting rained on. Across the road was a thin plateau of grass where horses could pasture. Two hundred meters below the plateau, the Cisnes boiled through a canyon, the far wall of which was six hundred meters high. Hiding under Casa Piedra from the rain and looking at the vicious, sheer walls all around, I began to appreciate the conquistador's apathy toward Aisén. Not even their ruthless desire to find the Lost City of Caesars, a sort of Southern Hemisphere version of El Dorado that many were convinced was hidden in deepest Aisén, could persuade them to come back after two aborted expeditions in the sixteenth and seventeenth centuries.

To one side of Casa Piedra, a spring welled out of the grass and moss. Water dripped audibly from somewhere beneath the lush plants that overhung the pool and grew out of the rock walls, some with leaves the size of a horse's hindquarters. With his knife, Duck shaved a length of bark from a tree and sharpened one end into a wedge. He parted the leaves above the pool, exposing a sopping wall of moss, and drove the wedge in so that water ran along the bark like an aqueduct. We filled a bota bag and a teapot, then washed our hands beneath the frigid trickle.

It was part of the etiquette among the gauchos to leave dry wood in the few places that all of them stopped on cattle drives, so that the next party would never be without fire. And although there was an ample supply hidden under Rock House, Duck was unimpressed. "Duck," he said, "is a master of fire. In fact, Duck is crazy when it comes to fire, *che*." Then he crossed the road with his axe and disappeared down the steep bank opposite our camp. When he came back half an hour later, he had the stripped trunk of a small tree over one shoulder.

I'd unsaddled the horses (working backward through the puzzle was much easier than the other way) and gotten a fire going, and Duck set the trunk next to the fire to dry. He reached into the burlap sack and pulled out the side of the ewe he'd killed that morning; the outside of the meat was already maroon and sticky to the touch. Duck carved away half the ribs and took a metal stake three feet long called an *asador* and pushed the ribs onto it, through the ragged meat of one side and out the bottom, then slid the whole thing toward the blunt end of the stake. He wove a thin green stick through the ribs horizontally, to complete the crucifixion of the meat. The stick, which couldn't burn, would keep the cooking meat from wrinkling in on itself. After Duck worked the stake into the rocky ground next to the fire, we made our beds—two sheepskins each with a sleeping bag on top, a saddle for the pillow—and lounged around, watching the meat spit and drool into the flames.

Duck said, "What's the favorite sport in your country?"

"Baseball."

"You Americans do anything for sport. I heard there's some that'll go down whitewater in a boat for fun, *che*. Or climb up the face of a canyon. Is that true?" I said it was. "You people are out of your minds," he said. "Everything I hear about you people on the radio makes me think you're all *loco* for *mate*. Speaking of which . . ." he said. It was getting dark, and he unwrapped a battered AM/FM from within a double swaddling of goatskins; laid next to the radio was a series of wire hangers, one twisted into the next and stored in circles. Duck unwound them with effort. He ran the hanger-antenna along the rock ceiling above us and out the side of Rock House, then wrapped the end around the thick shoot of a *calafate* plant that grew from a crevice. The radio had retained a broken nub of antenna, and Duck twisted the other end of the hanger around the nub. He switched the radio on. A Los Fabulosos Cadillacs song played sporadically through the static on Radio Santa María, then gave way a few moments later to the nine o'clock Messages.

Messages, which airs four times daily, is how the gauchos communicate with one another all over Chilean Patagonia's quarter-million square kilometers. If a gaucho wanted to let relatives in Lago Verde know that he was coming to see them from Cisnes (a distance of two hundred kilometers), he would first have to find someone who, like Duck, had a two-way radio in their cabin. Then he would relay his message to the radio station in Coihaique, where it would be read on the specified day or days.

Duck reached over to turn up the volume; we could barely hear the announcer for the static. "María Ochoa, of Valle Simpson," he said, "writes to Carlos: 'I arrive at Cochrane tenth of April, morning. Usual place. With love, María Esperanza Ochoa Valdez.'"

But Messages also served a much more important, if less practical, function, soap opera, for the majority of the notes read were stunningly personal. Meals were planned around the airing of the program, so that the maximum number of family members were near the radio to translate, by committee, from the crackle, and to share in the mish-mosh of crushed hopes and diverted intentions that poured forth for thirty minutes four times daily.

"The most common message," whispered Duck, "is from women to their men, who've disappeared. It's like with the guy down the river, Tea Kettle Without a Spout, who left Julia. A lot of times a woman will send a message that says, 'Send money—don't come home.'" He giggled. "Julia sent that message a few weeks ago, though it hasn't resulted in him doing either of the two, as far as I know." I asked what the nickname Tea Kettle Without a Spout meant. Duck said, "It means he's useless, Nico." When I laughed, Duck said, "Shhhh."

"Diego in Murta: Coming home. Might be afternoon 28 or 29 March. Much changed. Your loving sister, Fernanda Ordoñez de la Mesa, Coihaique."

Duck nodded. Murta was three hundred kilometers south. He said, "Shit."

"What?" I said.

"Shhhh."

The announcer enunciated every word so clearly that it almost made it harder to understand him. You could tell he spoke very good Spanish, and his accent was urban. Still, he never tried to edit the messages he got. He understood, I think, that many gauchos lived so far from their nearest neighbors that they'd developed a sort of cabin-specific way of speaking, one that identified families to one another in a way that simple names could not. He said, "Village of Cochrane. 17 March. Juan Pablo: Having trouble. Drive to begin week that comes, depend weather. Herd shelled-out—who can tell which way the rabbit'll jump? Ramón Vega."

Duck nodded his head. Cochrane was four hundred kilometers south. He said, "That guy, he's had a hard time of it. The drive was supposed to begin *two* weeks ago. Now the herd's too skinny to make it. God knows what'll happen next."

The tree that Duck had cut was drier now and he pulled it into the flames, roots and all. I moved back. The announcer said, "15 March. Message to Brother Pancho: Coming to El Gato for María Victoria's party. Arrive P.M. three weeks tomorrow. Signed, your loving sister Isabel Rodríguez Fierro."

"That family, too," said Duck, chewing. "I guess they're over it, though."

I said, "What?"

"María Victoria has tuberculosis. They're coming for her birthday party. She's seven this year. There for a while it looked like Isabel wasn't going to make it because her husband's a misfit. Six weeks ago, she was looking for her husband. She must have found him because of Messages."

When the program was over, a disc jockey came on and played "Oh Susannah," in English. Duck and I sliced pieces from the mutton with our knives and ate squatting. The meat was charred on the outside and nearly raw on the bone. Duck pulled an old plastic ketchup bottle of *chimichurri*—salt and garlic and onions that had been left to stew for weeks in vegetable oil and wine—from a saddlebag at his side and cut another piece and doused the meat.

He said, "Me, I like boxing. My favorite is this guy who's making a comeback now. All he was famous for during this decade is beating his wife and wrecking cars. He was the greatest fighter in Chile, Nico. But he was too young, and he didn't understand what to do with it all. Now he's fighting again. He's forty years old—way past his time; but," said Duck, taking another bite, "that doesn't matter. He's fighting again."

When we'd finished eating, we slid inside our sleeping bags and pulled our ponchos over ourselves and laid our heads against the saddles. The disc jockey put on "Camptown Drag." It was close and warm in the cave and the breeze came downcountry from the north and swirled in the cave to feed the fire. Next to it, our empty boots steamed. I said, "Does that boxer have a chance?"

"Not really," said Duck. "He'll get squashed. But, see, that's not really the point." He turned the radio off. His sleeping bag had a detachable hood at the top, and the zipper was broken. Duck put the hood on like a hat. He said, "Do you believe in the Devil?" His face was half hidden in the hood so that he looked at me with one eye. I don't know why, but I felt suddenly very sorry for him. When I didn't say anything, he said, "You think I'm crazy."

"I don't know if you're crazy," I said. "I don't know anything about you."

"And the Devil, Nico?"

I said, "I believe for whatever reason that God created man. But I also believe that man creates God in his image. So I think the same about the Devil. There has to be some name for evil. For me it's the Devil, but it's not the only thing."

"Nicolás," he said, "I don't read books. But I know what I've seen. I do things I can't explain."

"Like what?"

He reached over for the detergent bottle of fried breads and held one out to me. "Like right now," he smiled. "I'm about to eat something I don't need. I have to ride the fattest horse in the world. Happy Fat would be truly happy if she didn't have a pig on her back. When I was eighteen, twenty, I was skinnier than you, *che*. Now I'm fat, no?"

I took a fried bread without saying anything.

"Duck does things he can't explain," he said. He flipped one of the logs, exposing its gutted and charred innards. The heat was painful, and I moved farther into the cave.

I said, "You told me earlier today you hate to leave Edith alone. How come?"

"She's afraid of what'll happen. She thinks the Devil knows when a woman is alone."

I said, "Are you afraid of what'll happen?"

"Doesn't matter," said Duck, chewing. "It's like with that boxer and with the people on Messages—it's just something that's out there, *che*." He looked across the flames at the road, but it was invisible in the night. He said, "I don't know how many people have much of a chance, *che*."

* * *

Duck and I left Rock House at dawn the next morning, the horses steaming and wet with dew, and followed the road northeast. Alfredo's *puesto* lay some seven kilometers directly to the south of us. But to get there, we would first have to ride another fifteen kilometers east, then leave the road to follow the canyon above the Río Moro as it angled into the Cisnes from the southeast. Had you followed our progress from an airplane, you would have seen that, in order to get from Duck's cabin to Alfredo's *puesto,* the route that we described was that of an obtuse triangle of which the road was one leg and the impending and difficult journey above the Moro was another.

The reason for this was that the second-growth and remaining virgin forests, coupled with the sheer drape of the Andes, made much of Middle Cisnes completely impenetrable in all but a few places. The creeks and streams provided the only viable routes upon which even small herds of cattle and sheep and horses could be driven. They were the same routes that the Tehuelche Indians had used for hundreds of years before that, as had, arguably, the first gauchos themselves, though there is no record beyond a few rutted, thin trails and the occasional wickiup made of branches and stones.

Duck and I were moving from a place, the nothingwinter at Santa Elvira, which remained for much of the year in a perpetual state of rainy, autumnal grayness, to the nothingsummer, which might at any time get three feet of snow dumped onto it. The gauchos, as they did for many things, had invented a word to describe not only the two places between which they moved the stock, but the actual process of that movement: *el infiertodo,* the allhell.

We pushed east. Fifteen kilometers ahead of us was the canyon downstream of the Moro confluence; from our high vantage point, we could see where it cut through the flat-topped *cordillera* like a crack between two slabs of concrete. Seventy-five years before, the Chilean government had sold the canyon and the surrounding two million acres to an Anglo-Chileno called Juan Dun. Dun's company, the Anglo-Chilean Pastoral, was one of five heavily subsidized conglomerate livestock *industrias* created in the early 1900s by the Chilean government, which, desperate to populate Aisén, gave the *industrias* free rein to oversee the colonization of the state. Along with several dozen gauchos, Dun had driven eighty thousand sheep in from Argentina and spread them through the valley.

Now, seven decades later, Duck and I followed one of the trails along which Dun had moved his herd, though the trail was now a road.

Each "industrial" ranch had set up an administrative village as its headquarters. The hope was that the villages would become centers of commerce that could compete with the border towns of Argentina. Only one ever achieved its goal, the Industrial Society of Aisén, from which Coihaique was founded and which, ninety years later, had become so influential that the only road in Aisén entered town on the north and left it on the south. The rest of the villages had either remained tiny and inconsequential or had disappeared altogether.

The wreckage wrought by the fires that Dun had started—fires for which the Chilean government rewarded Dun and the other *industrialistas* with additional land allotments based on the amount of forest they could clear—was beautiful in an austere way. Above the canyon, thousands upon thousands of dead trees stood up out of the dry grass like grave markers in a tremendous cemetery. The mountains all around looked eczematic, burned in places and lush and green where the fires had been thwarted by the protective embrace of a series of cliffs or a stream that the flames could not ford. Whole areas of land that had once looked like the Oregon coast now looked like two parts Nebraska and one part New Mexico.

Ironically, it was the sheer organic richness of the soil that had aided in the demise of the land, because the fires would bake through the winter and spring rains by hiding between the nutrient topsoil and an underlayer of clay, simmering for months as though in an oven and popping up again in the summer. The soil, degraded and exposed by the loss of trees, grew grass so sparse that what was meant to be a man-made *pampa* looked more like a man-made desert.

By the 1930s, the Chilean government was under the control of General Carlos "Boots" Ibáñez, the "Chilean Mussolini." Ibáñez was still obsessed with Chile's loss of much of Patagonia to the Argentines during the 1879 War of the Pacific, and he was doubly perturbed that, at this point, the attempts of the *industrias* to lure settlers to places like Cisnes had all but failed.

Ibáñez was a clever man, and he stirred the pot by talking about foreign—meaning Argentine—domination of southern Chile, which resulted in the Argentines once again persecuting the expatriated Chileans who had been ranching there for several generations. Ibáñez then had ads placed in Argentine newspapers proclaiming generous land allotments for every "Chilean" who returned home. No matter that, in order to keep the Argentines out of his country, Ibáñez colonized Chilean Patagonia with the defining symbol of Argentine nationalism.

At the same time, Ibáñez encouraged "gentlemen adventurers" from Europe, particularly France, Germany, and England, to come to Patagonia and help him tame it. The Chilean government, ever since its independence from Spain in 1818, had not only become indebted to these countries for military assistance, it had openly imitated many of their customs, including afternoon English tea, Prussian military uniforms, and French as a required second language in schools. The more notable effect was that as Ibáñez proudly marketed the idea of "continentals" in Patagonia, he succeeded in essentially covering the tracks of the gauchos who had done most of the work.

What could not be ignored was the cultural, racial, and linguistic mix that, bolstered further still by an influx of Chilotes from the Big Island of Chiloé, made for an Aisenino identity as rich as the eroded topsoil had once been. One that, once Ibáñez was out of office and Patagonia was again forgotten, flourished in absolute anonymity.

Duck and I rode the canyon east and watched the river settle into pools and shallow runs with the softening grade of the land. Then the mountains parted into two fingers and the Cisnes, its allegiance decided millennia before, set off to keep step with the western finger of *cordillera*. The eastern vein, meanwhile, swung deep toward Argentina and then broke north again, and, at its farthest reach another hundred kilometers in the distance, regrouped to swing northwest to meet the western finger near Lago Verde.

Duck and I were on the cusp of the *pampa* now, which flowed tawny and rugged between the two fingers of *cordillera* as far as the eye could see. In that seemingly endless and lonely continuance of drab scrub warded over by mare's-tail clouds, buttes rose out of the advancing curvature of the earth like broken black coral, then sank just as readily into the backtrail beneath a reeling sky. The wind blew like a gale, though the grasses were so dry, and the trees so low to the ground, that there was nothing to bend to its will.

There was, in all of this emptiness, only one anomaly, and that was a village aptly named La Tapera, the Ruin. When Edith was born there in 1974, only a hundred twenty people lived in Tapera. Edith's first memories are of a winter storm when she was four or five that dropped two meters of snow on Tapera. After the storm, she and her half-brothers could climb to the top of their mother's house and, in every direction, be just above eye level with the white *pampa.* The shoveled streets seemed to have been cut from the ground like scale canyons; smoke from hidden chimneys seeped into the frigid air and dogs dug holes alongside their masters' houses and tried to extend them through the windows. In the morning, you could watch them sleep, piled on one another for warmth like gerbils in a plastic tunnel.

"Oh, *che,*" Edith recalled to me one day, laughing, "we slept in our shoes. We ate ice because we'd carefully put the wood under the shed to avoid it getting wet, and now we couldn't get to it for the snow, catch it? Everybody would have starved if the army hadn't come, *che.*"

Tapera's only connection to the outside world at the time was an airstrip maintained by the Estancia Río Cisnes, the three-hundred-sixty-thousand-acre remnant of Juan Dun's Anglo-Chilean Pastoral. Early one morning, word went around that the villagers had to dig out the airstrip. The army was coming with food and firewood, and the only thing between that and starvation was getting the airstrip free.

The turnout, considering the task, was far from encouraging, mostly prepubescent boys and girls and middle-aged and old women. Tapera existed to provide infrastructural ballast to the Estancia; it was a central place where gauchos could be kept until needed for work, where their families could live and their children could be rudimentarily educated, and where they could purchase the *mate,* wine, and cigarettes that kept them reasonably happy. At the time of the storm, every male from the ages of fourteen to eighty was stuck somewhere out in the snow and ice with the cattle and sheep, riding out a disaster that, when all was said and done, would kill seventy-five percent of the Estancia's stock. When Edith heard the military plane coming several days later, she hid under the kitchen table.

Duck sat his horse and looked up. The canyon above us was bare and dry and sagebrush grew. The face of it was striated with the ancient cuts of waterlines, for the *pampa* to the north had once been a sea, and the river that had flowed out of it was twenty or thirty times as deep as the Cisnes. I tried to imagine the shock of looking down from the lip of the forested mountains and onto a blue ocean as far as the eye could see. But even now, thousands of years after the waters had receded, the starkness of the confluence of the *pampa* and the mountains was just as striking, and it was heightened by the sudden and brilliant emergence of the sun from behind the storm front that had stalked Duck and me all morning.

We dismounted. Duck took the horses by the fetlocks, and the horses showed their hooves so he could check the shoes. Duck sighed. "Do you have to pee?" he said. I shook my head; Duck pulled down his warm-up pants and urinated on Happy Fat's hooves. He held the stream, walked to Happy Slim, and urinated again. "We need some luck," he said. "With what we have ahead of us, *che*, we need about four hundred pounds of luck."

Having the army come to Tapera was one of the few strokes of good luck that the village ever enjoyed. It was one of the few things the government had ever done for the people of Cisnes or, to a slightly lesser extent, any of the people of Aisén. Until 1976, that is, when General Pinochet saw a way to get a little good press with the people of Chilean Patagonia and, at the same time, shore the country against the omnipresent specter of military ruin at the hands of the Argentines: Pinochet would build a road.

At the time, the half-dozen or so dead-end one-laners in Aisén were extensions of roads that originated in Argentina. To get from Coihaique to Tapera, the Chilean army would have had to cross the border into Argentina near Balmaceda, head north on the Río Mayo road, then recross the border into Chile. So Pinochet ordered his engineers to design the Carretera Austral, the Southern Highway, which would run eleven hundred fifty kilometers, from Puerto Montt, on the northern edge of Chilean Patagonia, almost to the southern tip of South America.

But the Carretera was to be something much larger—a leg of the Pan American Highway, which runs through the United States, Central America, and South America. The Carretera would be an artery that connects isolated Patagonia to the rest of the world—connects it all the way to Deadhorse, Alaska, on the Beaufort Sea, where the Pan American Highway begins. Like the long, thin country it opened, the Southern Highway was built as a straight line designed to run through as many remote villages as possible along its path. One of these was Amengual, the village of a hundred fifty people at the southern extreme of

Middle Cisnes, fifteen kilometers downriver from Santa Elvira. The road reached Amengual in 1983. Other villages that were just out of reach of the Carretera were "favored," or added to it, by secondary roads. One of these, the Argentine Road, wound its way east from Amengual through the Andes, past Santa Elvira, and ground its way in low gear through the mountains toward the *pampa*.

By 1986 the Argentine Road had made it to where Duck and I now sat the horses. By the following year, when Edith was twelve, the Argentine Road had made it another forty kilometers east to "favor" Tapera. And though from there the Camino Argentino finally crossed the border another hundred kilometers beyond the village, it was, for Duck and me, indeed the end of the road.

A trail came down from the southeast, and Duck and I put the horses forward onto it. It was very steep, and the saddles slid back, pulling at the skin behind the horses' forelegs. Dust blew behind us downslope and out over the road, where it swirled up and was gone. When we made the ridgeline and could look down the other side, Duck turned to me and smiled.

The ridge we were on crumbled at the horses' feet and fell at a murderous angle all the way to the Moro in the valley. What might have been a trail fell with it and crossed a bowl of scrub veined with springs from the river. A mountain built its way out of the bowl, and the thing that might have been a trail wove its way along the side of the mountain and up a dirt face, where it disappeared into a talus field three kilometers distant. Duck looked at me. He said, "Are you sure you don't have to pee?"

"Why?"

He pointed at the far ridgeline. "Because between here and there," he said, "there's no way off the horse unless you fall."

* * *

The horses knew the way onto the steep trail. I imitated Duck's posture and leaned back above Marión's haunches, and kept the reins loose to let her look back and forth before each step, like a dog watching the veering flights of bugs in front of its nose. This side of the ridge was scarred by a glacier's retreat, and the trail followed the contours of earth in a series of switchbacks, as though descending into an archaeological site. We rode east for a hundred meters and put the horses down to the next lip and rode back west at head level with the place we'd just been. At the end of an hour, we'd made it into the gorge.

Duck and I moved fast across the bowl to where the trail was knitted into a new fabric of sheer rock from which there grew a dozen kinds of plants, all of them with some manner of thorn or sticker that caught in our chaps and scratched at our hands and faces or grabbed at our hats. At the far end of the bowl, we looked up. Another kilometer above us was the tree-covered ridgeline. In the middle of it were two black rocks that had been dragged ahead of a glacier and set on the ridge like gateposts. To get to them, the trail simply went up and across a dirt face at a forty-five-degree angle. Any misstep by the horses would result in a straight fall onto the rocks where we sat resting.

Behind us, grass grew in a rectangle of three hundred square feet. Duck said, "Put Marión on that grass and turn her hard toward the wall, then give her the spurs. Don't get your boots wedged into the stirrups too far. If you fall, you want to fall clean and not have her on top. You might be able to grab hold of something till I get to you. Go on," he said, and I did.

Marión struggled to keep her footing, and I leaned forward to keep from sliding off her back. She stopped often, and each time she started forward again, she would fall onto her knees and gingerly regain them by pushing with her back legs. I looked back and saw Happy Fat come onto the face slowly under Duck's weight. It was hard to imagine how we'd get a herd of cattle through the same place in two days.

When I made the ridgeline, I turned to see Duck beat Happy Fat across the haunches with his crop, and when he did this, Happy Slim jerked her head back and nearly went off the side. Duck fought ridiculously against the lead rope—had Happy Slim begun to fall, there would have been nothing he could do. It occurred to me that, were Duck to lapse in concentration too many times as he had just done, it would eventually kill him. He let Happy Fat rest for several minutes. Then he slapped her with the crop, and she and Happy Slim chugged up the slope and came over the top like sea animals making their way for the first time onto land.

For the rest of the morning, we skirted the base of the same bald, snow-and-talus-covered mountain. We passed above a river that ran green and white three hundred meters below us, and we descended so that the air became first warmer and then colder, and after an hour we turned and left the river behind. We crossed a charred plateau where wild horses watched us from behind the ruined trunks of trees and moved along our flank, disappearing and reappearing. At the far side of the plateau, we entered the piebald shade of the forest and dismounted to drink on all fours at the side of a brook.

"The trail goes that way," said Duck, standing up. To our right, the foot-deep rut we'd been following continued along the spine of the ridge. To our left there was the faintest line, perhaps a trail or perhaps a shadow highlighting the contour of the land. "Which way?" said Duck.

I shrugged; it was raining again.

Duck said, "That's Alfredo's trail," and indicated the one we'd been following. Alfredo had spent forty years making it. Duck said, "Duck makes his own road. Have you heard of Rambo?" I looked to the left and said I had. "I took an American tourist hiking one time up a mountain. He told me I was the Rambo of Cisnes, whatever that means."

Five minutes after following the trail to the right, we came to a cliff that dropped two hundred meters into an overgrown ravine; a diagonal ledge of rock ran down the cliff's face at a suicidal angle where the ridgeline had been sheared in two. Taking the horses along the ledge was the only way to the other side of the ravine. I said, "You're crazy."

Duck looked at me angrily. He was frustrated, I think, with the difficulty of a job he did not want to be doing. Now he would do something rash to make it more difficult still and, in that way, justify his anger. It was the first of several times when it seemed as though Duck wanted to script his own death. He handed me his whip and put Happy Fat onto the ledge. Happy Slim lifted one leg, then leaned backward against the rope and grunted.

"Beat her," said Duck.

* * *

It was early evening when we sat the horses on the crest of a small rise and looked down onto the nothingsummer. At the edge of the shadows through which we'd ridden for much of the day, the scale of the land was dizzying against the rising cobalt sky. Forty or fifty kilometers deeper into Chile, the Andes ranged off toward the Pacific like sharks' teeth, one peak waiting to take the place of another in the shifting line of vision. Below us lay a backwater eddy of scrub grass fed from the east by a rising sea of mottled Argentine steppe. Duck pointed with his lips toward a cabin. "Alfredo," he said.

Three hundred meters away, Alfredo's *puesto* stood in the middle of the bowl, or, rather, sank into the middle distance, at once camouflaged and queerly out of place. Alfredo stood in the dark slot of the open door, watching us. His white goatskin chaps shone against the hard shadow. He raised his hand and lowered it and blew cigarette smoke. Then he disappeared inside. Four cattle dogs jerked up and down like marionettes against the chains holding them fast to the corners of the cabin, their baying muted by the clear distance.

Marión galloped a hundred feet in the direction from which we'd come before turning quickly and galloping at Happy Fat and Happy Slim, flushing them like quail. Duck lost the pack rope and all three horses spun circles around one another, as though caught within the confines of a shrinking corral.

When we got them calmed, Duck shook his head. "Alfredo, Alfredo, Alfredo," he said.

Then we put the horses forward and rode down into the basin.

CHAPTER FOUR

❊

El Puesto

Cattle do not require populations—they are the population. They are contrary to society and displace and dis-
solve it.

—*Ezequiel Martínez Estrada,* X-Ray of the Pampa, *1933*

At the age of twenty-four, Edith has the look of someone alternately mend-
ing and reopening great, seeping internal cracks. She shuffles slowly,
kneads dough violently, and sits gingerly in her chair. Edith's upper incisors have
decayed to form tainted fangs, and the ridges of her toothless gums, not yet
blunted and smoothed over by disease, stick down like little red pikes. When she
laughs, it is often explosively, and she opens her mouth wide, only to close it
immediately out of embarrassment for her teeth. She is small, five feet two, and
her markedly indigenous features—round face, broad forehead, black eyes and
hair—are at odds with her white, creamy skin. She uses a knife the size of a
machete for a gross of chores, from splitting bones to peeling carrots, and she
often yells at or laughs with her daughters, aged five and eight, as though they
were her little sisters. None of which is at all out of place in Cisnes. What differ-
entiates Edith is the way she talks. That and the fact that she lived, for the first
year she was with Duck, in Coihaique.

"Oh, Wednesday!" she says, slapping herself to stop from saying "shit," which
in Spanish is *mierda*—Wednesday is *miércoles.* She's telling me about the first
night that she and Duck spent in the cabin at Santa Elvira, five years before, and

though Edith is, like her children, given to speaking vulgarly, she tries not to curse in any sentence containing the word God. "God on a Wednesday, *che,* this *puesto* was one room, and in the middle was a stove and a bed. No sink, no running water, not one whoring thing, *che.* And the rain was falling through the holes in the roof onto the bed. There were rats living in the attic where the chickens roosted. And rain, rain, rain, rain—more rain than Sunday in the jungle. Duck went out in that mess and found us some wood. I cooked steaks from a ewe we'd brought with us, and then we slept on the floor on sheepskins, and if that wasn't about the least romantic arrangement imaginable, *che,* I don't know what is, with Patricia between us, wrapped in a poncho like an orphan."

Duck and Edith's possessions were few: a tea kettle, a pot, a frying pan, some clothes, Duck's cowboying accoutrements. He and Edith and Patricia shared everything, right down to the family's lone toothbrush. Everything, that is, except for their *mates* and *bombillas,* the gourds and silver straws with which the gauchos drink a strong herbal tea called by the same name as the gourd: *mate.*

Five years later, things are much changed. Mariana was born during the second summer at Santa Elvira, and Duck added a bedroom to the cabin, with a window and a dresser and a bunk for Mariana and Patricia. Duck and Edith now sleep with their third child, Oscar, in the bed that had been in the cabin when they arrived. Duck covered the raw floor and walls of the *puesto* with particleboard. He built a table, and a sink with cold running water; for decoration, he added several Stihl posters in which buxom blonde women wearing cowboy boots and short skirts strike suggestive poses in the vicinity of chain saws, and, above the stove, a poster of the Mexican rock star Gloria Trevi. In it, she is probably seventeen or eighteen and has long, frizzy hair the color of dried apricots. She wears a tie-dyed Lycra jumpsuit and sits leaning forward with her hands between her legs; her breasts are right in the lens. Above her, in the same large, bubbly letters that evangelical mission-flyers often employ, it reads: "GLORIA."

"So it's true what they say," says Edith, "that the Devil knows more for being old than he does for being the Devil. Then again, the more you know out here, the more you realize how much has stayed the same. Life hasn't changed at all, really. Nor has the fact if I don't drink some *mate* soon, I'm going to be unhappy, Skinny."

Aside from being the fulcrum of social life and a ritual repeated ad infinitum among the gauchos, taking *mate* is an indicator of politics, culture, and finances. Drinking too much *mate*—seven or eight times a day—is a sign that you're backward or even trashy. Drinking it five times a day is a sign of a certain progressiveness. None of which is lost on Edith; she uses the word *mate* in as many ways as possible—about as often as she uses the phrase "catch it" and the word *che*—to say that one is (in addition to drinking a kind of tea from a gourd) relaxing or getting drunk or being lazy.

No matter how often you drink *mate,* its effects are very addictive, because it makes you at once highly alert and very calm. *Mate* is grown predominantly in Paraguay, and it is extremely bitter, leading many people to add mint, sage, warm milk, and even *pisco* to cut the taste. If you're lucky enough to have an orange or an apple, you might bore out the meat and use the husk as a gourd. The most common addition, however, is lots of sugar—a teaspoon or so for every three-ounce serving—which, along with the fact that few people have ever seen a dentist, accounts for so many toothless grins.

Despite its popularity, there's little known about *mate*'s chemical makeup, aside from the fact that it possesses a high level of caffeine. Why this doesn't result in the jumpiness associated with coffee is unclear, as are the reasons behind the searing headaches you get for the first week after you stop drinking it. What's more clear is that one's etiquette while taking *mate* can be used to say any number of things, from welcome to my house to "let's raise knives," the idiom of choice to invite a brawl.

It's two weeks since I began living with Duck and Edith, and, as far as *mate* goes, it appears as though I've finally arrived: Edith has given me the coveted position of pourer. (Though because it's an unseasonably warm day and the pourer sits right next to the stove, I'm more than a little suspicious of Edith's motivations.) "Mariana!" she says, smiling, "bring more wood—Skinny's nose is getting cold!"

The *mate* process is theoretically quite simple, though there's ample room for confusion, beginning with the fact that the dried leaves used for brewing, as well as the gourd in which they steep and the ritual in general, are all referred to as *mate*. It all begins when water is placed in a tea kettle to warm without boiling.

Boiling water is the most egregious *mate* foul, first because it burns the leaves (also called *yerba*), dulling the taste, and then burns the drinker's mouth. To avoid water that's too hot, tradition demands that the pourer use his pinkie as a thermometer.

While the water heats, you get the *yerba* bag, sold by the quarter-kilo, and pour just enough but not too many leaves into the gourd, which is about four times the size of a shot glass, taking into account the *yerba*'s expansion when water is added over and over during the actual drinking. Should you want to take your *mate* sweet, then you must also leave room for sugar and *yuyos*—whatever other herbs that can be gathered by the river and hung over the stove on a nail to dry—which further crowd the tiny cup.

Meanwhile, the *bombilla,* a ten-inch silver or aluminum straw with a teardrop tea-strainer at one end, must be checked for earwigs—which like nothing better than to crawl inside a wet *bombilla* and wait to be sucked in, pincers and all—by removing the strainer and blowing through the hollow shaft. That done, the *bombilla* goes strainer end down under the *yerba* until it leans against the lip of the *mate* at just the right angle. Too close to ninety degrees and it won't draw, too close to sixty degrees and it draws too much.

By then, the water should be ready, and you pour it over your pinkie, splattering it onto the floor for luck. The first two pours into the *mate* are taken by the host, or pourer, to clean the *yerba*. So, with the kettle in hand and a mouth full of dusty, earthy water, I open the back door of Duck and Edith's cabin, select a mangy chicken, and fire a stream at her. After a second shot, we're ready to drink.

Or so I think. When I sit back down, Edith takes the *mate* from my hand. "Too much *yerba,* Flaco!" she yells with mock derision. "You'll spill the water when the *mate* expands so that your mother, all the way over there in the Together States, will cry." She opens the ash drawer on the stove, flicks two small piles of *yerba* into the fire from the gourd, and slaps the drawer shut. Then she hands the gourd back to me before Oscar can knock it out of her hand.

Among the superstitions surrounding *mate*—and everything else among the gauchos, from how to interpret the trajectory of your love life from the flight of certain birds to how to turn yourself into a witch (answer: by kneeling at the side of a river with your head under water for twenty-four hours to reverse your baptism)—is that to spill water while pouring is to have made whomever you were thinking about at the time suddenly, immeasurably, and inexplicably sad.

Mariana drops more wood by the stove. "It was a joke," says Edith. "Uncle Chickenhead doesn't need any more wood for the fire. It's already hot as church in here. Take your brother," says Edith, and when she hands Oscar down, he breaks from Mariana's hug, slips to the floor, and starts to howl. "Fool!" says Edith to Mariana, and picks up Oscar, who belts her in the face. "Come here, my little prince," she gurgles. "Go outside," she says to Mariana. "Maybe you can find something to do other than fuck with me, *india*."

Not inviting a guest to take *mate* is as good as asking the person to get out of your cabin. Passing it with the left hand is dicier still, and requires clarification on other levels. If, for instance, you did this and then failed to refill the kettle after the first round, you'd be telling the other person you'd never really wanted to share *mate* with them in the first place. If, on the other hand, you go through several rounds this way, it might mean you're cursing the person or, more likely, exposing him to the humiliation of having to end the session prematurely and leave.

It's not the first time that Edith has scolded Mariana severely for failing to control an angry brother who is already stronger than she, and I think briefly about passing the *mate* to Edith with my left hand. Instead, I relent and pass the gourd with my right and ask Edith the meaning of a word I've heard her use many times, particularly in reference to Mariana: *huasa,* or, in the masculine, *huaso.*

"It's like," says Edith, casually inserting the *bombilla* into a hole in her upper gum where a tooth used to be, "when someone won't talk to you unless they know you. Maybe not even then."

"Shy is *huaso?*" I say.

"It's more than shy," says Edith. "It's like not having the custom to be around people outside the family. Remember when you first got here and Mariana hid in the corner when you came in the cabin?"

"I remember," I say, "how you wouldn't talk to me."

"That's right," Edith smiles, "and that was *huasa,* too. Only you couldn't have said that I was being *huasa.* It's a word that we can use with ourselves, *che,* but you, for example, would have to be here a long time before you could say it because you're, you know, so obviously foreign. What it really means is kind of like an animal."

According to one linguistic theory, the word *"huaso"* comes from the same Guarani and Quechua origins—*huachó* and *guache,* both of which mean "orphan"—as the word "gaucho." "So," I say, "they must mean kind of the same thing."

"False!" says Edith, and reaches to take the lid off the pot of ewe ribs on the stove. She pours two fingers of boiling water from a milk canister into the pot before shaking lunch like a misbehaved child. "Because here we're all gaucho, but we're not all *huaso, che*. If you lived in town, Nico, you'd probably think we're all *huaso*. Townies see a gaucho come to Coihaique in his poncho and he goes to the bank, catch it, and he doesn't know how to deposit his money and he doesn't speak the same Spanish and he's illiterate—that's *huaso, che*. The people laugh at him like he came out of . . . ," she searched for the word, ". . . the jungle, catch it? It's like calling someone an Indian."

The illiteracy rate in Cisnes, as it is in nearly all of rural Chilean Patagonia, is above ninety-five percent, so that, without written words to learn the "right" way to speak (or the "write" way to speak), the gaucho dialect is itself all but a separate language, a kind of linguistic free-for-all. Or an unending collection of dialects, because each *puesto* (literally, "place"; or as it is translated indirectly, "dwelling") was differentiated by its own particular slang. Never mind the difficulty of a banker understanding a gaucho: neighbors who lived four hours on horseback from one another were often hard-pressed to keep track of the nuances of conversations.

"So that's what I mean, *che,* is that a guy who doesn't know what a bank is, to *me,* that's as *huaso* as it is to a person in Coihaique. In Coihaique, though, they'd call me *huasa,* too, because I look like I'm from the country—whether or not I know what a bank is. In Argentina and down here, to us, a gaucho is a cowboy. *Huaso* is also what they call cowboys in the Central Valley, up around Santiago. You ask someone up there what a Chilean cowboy is, they'll say a *huaso;* ask them what an Argentine cowboy is, they say gaucho.

"Difference is that a *huaso* up there is more a landowning gentleman than what a cowboy is here, which is basically a peasant with horses. Land up there is much richer, *che,* and people live well enough to run expensive horses in rodeos, and drive trucks. And they dress differently, too—riding boots instead of chaps, wide hats instead of berets: finer things. So *huaso* is a mean thing to say here because it, like, reminds you of what you don't have. It reminds you of your place. Catch it or don't catch it?"

Edith was the only person in Cisnes I knew who used this last expression; the verb from which it comes, *cachar*, is a slang invention, one that was associated strictly with urban Chile. She'd gotten it from listening to the radio. Edith did not, though, use "catch it" all the time. It all depended on who was in the room with her—and if they could be counted upon, as it were, to catch it.

The neighbor who visited Edith and Duck most often was Don Tito Eagles. Duck, as the head cowboy of Santa Elvira, was in charge of maintaining the *patrón's* flock, from which he and Don Tito were allowed one sheep every three to four weeks as part of their wage. Once a month, he would ride over to butcher a ewe and, on his way back home, Don Tito would stop in to take *mate*, though he almost never spoke while he did this. Neither Don Tito nor his brother Alfredo ever spoke much unless they were together—at the beginning of a cattle drive, for instance, as they sat in Alfredo's *puesto* at the *veranada*. When the drive started, they were mostly silent again, as though the presence of the other riders impeded their ability to communicate. When either of the brothers did say something to one another or to anyone else, they kept their bodies turned ninety degrees away from their interlocutor. During pauses in the conversation, they would peek around the shoulder closest to their interlocutor, only to look sharply away as soon as they began speaking anew or were spoken to.

"I was born in Tapera," says Edith, "same as where Don Tito thinks he was born. Do you think I understand a word that comes out of his mouth? Negative!" she says, raising her finger and pointing backhand at the ceiling for emphasis. "They speak Turk or something—all kinds of words. Grunts more than words, really."

"Turk" was the word Edith used in reference to anything unfamiliar—words, customs, dress—a fact that dovetailed nicely with one historical school of thought that traced the original gauchos of Buenos Aires province to Spaniards from Andalusia, which had spent seven centuries under Moorish rule. Whether or not Tito and Alfredo actually spoke any Arabic (they did mix in Tehuelche and, on occasion, Italian) was not nearly as interesting as the word the brothers used for anything they didn't like: "Christian."

Whatever linguistic quirks the brothers employed, Duck always understood them perfectly, though he refused, out of what seemed to be pride, to emulate their speech patterns, except when communication on a cattle drive demanded it. Which is to say that the only time Duck spoke like Alfredo and Tito was going to and from one of Alfredo's *puestos*.

"Those *viejos*," says Edith, "are more *huaso* than a tent full of Indians, *che*."

"Can a young person be a *viejo*, or does it only mean someone old?"

"It's more like anyone who won't change," says Edith. "Basically, a *viejo* is anyone who's *huaso*."

"Oopa!" says Oscar, sitting bolt upright on Edith's lap. "Oopa!" he insists. "Oopa! Oopa!"

Edith rolls her eyes as the smell begins to permeate the room. "It's his little word for shit," she says. I watch her face, but there's nothing to indicate that she sees the irony in what she has just said. In one motion, Edith has Oscar on his back on the floor and is untying his diaper. She looks at the contents before folding it and setting it aside, then reaches for a roll of toilet paper.

When I walk to the window to give Edith and Oscar a little privacy and to look for Mariana, I don't initially see her. My eye is drawn immediately to the barn and, beyond that, to the hills a thousand meters across the river that ward over part of an immense area called the Inside, a system of river valleys not unlike several Cisneses where no one lives and few people have ever explored. Looking back at the barn, it seems absurdly small, despite being five or six times the size of the cabin. It's then that I see Mariana sitting in the shadow of one of the barn's corners, her place there nearly obscured by the high, wild grass.

"I bet Don Tito doesn't even use toilet paper," continues Edith. "I bet he hasn't cleaned his behind since he dipped it in the rising waters of the Flood. Waved to Noah with the other hand, then said something even Noah didn't understand," she says. Then she walks over and closes the cabin door.

*   *   *

Duck's real name is Patricio, for which Pato, or Duck, is short. He was born the son of a Mapuche Indian woman from the Big Island of Chiloé and an Argentine gaucho father he hardly knew. Everything about Duck seems *bien* gaucho, and to listen to or look at him, you'd swear he was born in a cabin on the Río

Moro or in Tapera. He was not. He was born in Coihaique, eight or nine years before Pinochet's coup initiated the changes that would make Coihaique and Tapera two radically different places. By the time the Argentine Road made it as far as Tapera, Duck was old enough to remember what life was once like, and to have been imbued with many of the old sensibilities, and young enough that his ideas were shaped almost wholly by the confused and spasmodic making of an amalgamated New World.

On the afternoon of September 11, 1973, Duck and his brother were standing in line to buy bread in a villagelike slum on the outskirts of Coihaique when a detachment of Carabineros (led, perhaps, by then-sergeant Mansilla) told everyone to go home. Anyone left in the street, they said, would be shot. The next day, several of Duck's neighbors were gone. For weeks after that, when Duck walked outside in the morning to go to school, he noticed a decrease in the number of familiar faces. Coihaique gauchos had forever gone—and still go—back and forth to Argentina, and many of them in the fifties and sixties had been enamored of the socialist gospel of Perón, making the Coihaique slums of the seventies and eighties prime targets of Pinochet's police. And in the rising tide of "disappearances," hundreds of gauchos rode to Argentina to pass the Pinochet years there. Their absence created a vacuum that young boys like Duck were all too willing to fill.

When he was thirteen, Duck hired himself out for his first cattle drive. He and three older gauchos from Coihaique—two herders and a man to handle the packhorses—rode the horse trail to the village of Mañihuales, seventy kilometers north of town. By the time they'd turned toward Cisnes, they'd picked up a twelve-year-old boy, with whom they rode the ninety remaining kilometers to Tapera, where fifteen hundred head of the Estancia Río Cisnes's cattle waited. The gauchos also took a half-dozen sheep to slaughter as they went. They loaded the cargo horses with potatoes, salt, flour, sugar, *mate,* and three whole goatskins filled with wine before turning back toward Mañihuales.

For two weeks they rode above the Río Cisnes, urging the animals along creeks that would be redirected by explosives when the Argentine Road went in twelve years later. Each morning, the stringman rode ahead to leave lunch in the same places that Duck would camp and eat his lunch on cattle drives into his thirties; at night, the stringman would build fires and cook the herders' supper in burned clearings left by Juan Dun's gauchos decades before.

At the end of two weeks, the riders reached a valley that split toward the coast above a little creek. Ten years later, the tiny village of Amengual would preside over this place, and the Southern Road would follow the same creek toward the coast, before turning north and running all the way to Alaska. Two of the gauchos turned with the creek, and they rode with half the herd until they reached Puyuhuapi three weeks later. There they sold the cattle for slaughter.

Duck stayed with the men bound for Coihaique. He watched for days as the stock grew thin; when an animal broke his leg or was too exhausted to move on, they roped him, severed his heart, and ate the steaks they cut from his legs. They were not cruel; rather, hooved animals had little business passing through coniferous rain forest and struggling up sheer buttes better suited to mountain goats or red stag. When they were ready to ride on, the old men would have Duck run the herd past them to see that all of the animals were accounted for, though it wasn't in the way of people who apply numerological values to things, for the old men couldn't count. Instead, they had memorized every animal based on subtle differentiating characteristics that to any untrained eye would be impossible to perceive: an asymmetrical pairing of ears or horns, perhaps, or an individuating pattern of scuffs on a hide. In Mañihuales, the riders took on another bunch of sheep and rode out of the village due south. Duck walked into his mother's house in Coihaique just as the weather turned cold, five months after he'd left.

Duck told me once that those months were the most formative in his memory, because they introduced him to the unsatisfying life for which he was destined. Nor did he know what to do about it. Even the political turmoil that defined the country in the seventies and eighties couldn't provide Duck with a word to describe his place in the world, because he was neither a socialist nor a Peronista nor a Pinochetista. He was simply unhappy.

When he arrived in Coihaique after those five months, he saw the town with new eyes. The population had nearly doubled since he was a child, as people came from Santiago and northern Patagonia. Many had arrived to begin a kind of self-imposed exile, a means by which to put as much distance as possible between themselves and the capital, where Pinochet's grip was the tightest. Others had come because they'd made money under the dictator's new economic programs, and they wanted never again to live in a city. A middle class was forming. Everywhere, from what Duck could see, people had things: trucks driven by regular men and women, and the first televisions, and houses with indoor plumbing.

And none of the old men, the kind Duck had just ridden with, seemed to care. The young kid who'd headed west to Puyuhuapi didn't know the difference, either. How could he, living out there in the mountains? Suddenly, Duck's was not a vague distaste; all around him were markers, rocks on the shore by which he judged his progress. Would he end up like the men he'd just been with, or would he end up accumulating things that, suddenly, he wanted? For the time being, Duck was in the middle of the current, a salmon swimming upstream, and it seemed he'd never get there.

For the next four years, Duck took the work he could get, riding on one drive and the next, from Lago Verde in the north to Tranquilo in the south. Riding, as it were, in the opposite direction of the progress that was turning Coihaique from a village into a town that, in Duck's estimation, felt like the very center of the world. And the more Duck rode, the better he became. With a handmade hatchet he fashioned yokes for oxen. He made chaps from goatskins, and from a *coigue* branch sewed into bull skin he made the traditional riding crop, or *rebenque*. Duck was exceptionally talented even among the gauchos, who normally had one strong point and bought the rest of their tack from someone better than they. He could take two solid blocks of *lenga* and turn them, in three days, into two stirrups, long and triangulated and intricately decorated to look like the ancient riding boots of the *conquistadores*.

Then, when Duck was eighteen, he joined the army. Two years of military service were mandatory in Chile, and Pinochet had taken care to expand the force in Coihaique by several times, which greatly heightened the rate of growth and modernization in town. In the army, Duck's desire for what he had never had grew. He has never forgotten the way that the rich kids and the sons of Chile's growing middle class looked at him like an animal. Or what they called him: *huaso*. That's when he realized that the officers were using *huaso* ironically. They were calling him something he could never be, and, by doing so, letting him know what he was: gaucho. Other.

In 1985, Duck got out of the army and began working as a carpenter in the rural villages that were opened by Pinochet's Southern Highway. It was not work that Duck particularly enjoyed, though, like cowboying, he was good at it. In fact, he was very good, owing to his natural talent for improvisation, and he worked all over Aisén, wherever the arterial roads went to connect the impacted, nearly uninhabited valleys with Coihaique.

Duck found a new kind of pleasure in the mountains. He was comfortable in the villages because he was from a place that had been a big village itself twenty years before. But he was also someone else; he was an outsider, and he came now on a truck and with tools. Duck spoke the village dialects and could also mix into his sentences the slang he'd picked up from the middle-class kids in the army—the language of the Center, to which Duck made the villagers feel connected. For the first time, his dual personality suited him. Not to mention that the women in the villages eyed him as a potential mate for their daughters. Which is how he ended up sipping *mate* and eating *sopapillas* one day at a little yellow house in Tapera.

The woman who lived there was named María. She was a strong woman with unnerving gray eyes like a husky, who had left Coihaique when she was very young. She was the cook at the school in Tapera, and she was illiterate, and she was not about to have her daughter Edith grow up to move around from *puesto* to *puesto,* having to ask someone what the new signs along the Carretera said, or what two kilos of salt cost. In Duck, María saw a new life, not just for Edith, but for the children Edith would eventually have.

The year before, Señor Mansilla's bus had begun coming to Tapera from Coihaique, and María had sent Edith there to find her grandmother and to enter one of the public junior high schools. Edith had lasted till the beginning of the winter, which is to say she lasted one month. "If I wasn't throwing up," Edith said while she told the story and Duck looked on, "I was wetting my bed. Or getting the dirt knocked out of me for being a hick. All the kids I was with came from the same kind of families. Their fathers were gauchos like mine, and they would grow up to be the same thing. But let me tell you, there's a difference between a country redneck and a slum redneck. Those were some *blood*thirsty sons of whores."

María was crushed when Edith showed up back in Tapera, and she never let Edith hear the end of it. And then one day there came Duck.

"Jesus," laughed Edith. "My mother invited him in and I hid in my little place behind the stove, catch it?"

"Most *huasa vieja* I could have imagined," giggled Duck fondly.

"He was *todo nuevoche*," all new*che*, said Edith. "I thought he was wonderful. I was absolutely terrified of him."

CHAPTER FIVE

The Man from Campo Grande

Alfredo Eagles was five feet six and bowlegged. On the afternoon Duck and I arrived at the nothingsummer, he moved around outside of his *puesto,* gathering his saddle and blanket and bridle with the aloof economy of a grazing deer. Duck and I were riding past as he did this, making for a wall of stacked, dead trees three meters high and ten meters long, behind which Duck and I would make our camp. We were less than two hundred feet from Alfredo, though none of us gave the slightest indication that we were aware of the other's presence.

The bowl in which Alfredo's cabin sat was surrounded on all sides by the burned remnants of forests that, when they were set afire, were in their third or fourth century. To the east, there was a fenced area of three hundred acres, and, still farther east, another fenced area of five or six thousand acres. The fences—or, rather, walls—were made with dead trees that had been stacked horizontally with the help of oxen and horses. Some of the fence-trees, despite having withered by half during the fires, were twenty meters long. The destruction, at any rate, was nearly absolute. All that remained were two trees between which the camp wall had been built, two tremendous and unscarred *coigues,* which had somehow survived the fires.

Standing at the wall and looking southeast, you could see a hundred or more kilometers into Argentina. You could see where the smooth grade of the *pampa* of Chubut province gave way to the remaining forests of Aisén just below the continental divide. It was like looking at a fault line, and Alfredo had grown old, and was likely to grow much older, in the very place where the causal relationship between men and land had created the Chilean gaucho from the Argentine.

I walked over to where he was saddling his horse, a beautiful, heavy-chested buckskin gelding with ebony points, tail, and mane. Buckskins were the only breed that he and his brother Tito would ride, and the one for which they could be recognized at long distance, for this was not a common breed in Cisnes, where bays were the norm and blacks and Appaloosas were coveted. Alfredo untied the hitching rope from the headstall. He hobbled the horse's front legs and then he stood on a stump and brushed the horse's coat with his hand. He laid the blanket on the horse's back, followed by the saddle pad and the saddle, moving each of them slightly forward and back as though testing the calibration on a delicate machine. Alfredo had a *boleadora* with him—three ten-foot horse-hide thongs united in a woven handle, each of which had a baseball-sized stone attached to its end—and he coiled the *boleadora* neatly and tied it to his saddle. He did not look at me.

When I was three feet from him, I could see whole histories, it seemed, in Alfredo's face. The Roman nose of the Argo-Italians; the high Tehuelche forehead, wrinkled like a desert sandscape; the cavernous Sevillian or North African cheeks sloping into thin lips; the expansive, dimpled German chin; and the small, close-set gray Yugoslav eyes; all presided over by bushy, dark eyebrows, and divided by a mishapenly manicured black mustache. Alfredo wore pin-striped wool trousers and white chaps and a faded denim jacket, under which his chest was naked despite the cold. On his feet were a brand-new pair of white faux-Adidas sneakers with royal blue stripes. His hair was a clump of graying black curls that spilled over his ears and forehead. Instead of a hat, Alfredo wore a stunted gray and black cat, which, aside from the horses and dogs and cattle, was his only company for months at a time. When Alfredo mounted up, the cat rose, circled his head, and lay down once again on the bed of curls.

I said, "Hello."

"Goodbye, Christian," said Alfredo, and put the horse forward.

*　　*　　*

I walked back over to the wall to help Duck with camp. We unsaddled the horses and heaved the *chiguas* to the ground. They were the size of suitcases and made of horsehide strips woven together like wicker and attached to frames made of *coigue* branches wrapped in hide. We undid the half-hitches with which Duck had closed the ties and we laid the bags open.

I asked Duck where Alfredo was going with the *boleadora,* and he said Alfredo hunted red stags, a member of the deer family only slightly smaller than an elk, for meat for his dogs. Duck said Alfredo would either run the stags into preset lines of snares or, in this case, run them down and swing the *boleadora* above his head like a helicopter prop and that, if he threw accurately, the three thongs, propelled by the centrifugal force of the rocks, would wrap themselves around the stag's neck or a leg—perhaps breaking it—so that Alfredo could lacerate the incapacitated animal's heart.

Duck said, "You get the feeling he acts around people the same way he acts alone." There was a kind of respect in the way he said it. "He won't come to the fire tonight, either."

Other than during the four cattle drives a year, the only time Alfredo had any contact with anyone was when he rode the day-and-a-half-long trip down to Tapera every couple of weeks to see his mother (who was pushing a hundred, by Duck's estimation) and to buy cigarettes and *mate*. "I guess that's where he gets those crazy shoes he likes to wear," said Duck. "We'll wake in the morning and get the bulls and leave."

There were sharpened wood stakes driven into the floor of the basin at even intervals, and I watered the horses at a creek and tied the lead of each animal to a stake and left them to graze. The ground was soft and bouncy, like tundra. When I came back to camp, Duck had a fire going.

Duck said, "Are you sorry you came all the way up here for a look at him and no conversation?"

I said, "I'll keep coming back till he talks to me."

"I'll keep bringing you," said Duck.

*   *   *

I'd asked Duck as we'd ridden to the nothingsummer if he could tell me anything more than he already had about Tito or Alfredo's life. But Duck had said only that no one, most of all he, cared. Then, as though the facts surrounding those men's lives were somehow synonymous with something deeply untrue, Duck said he hated the "legends" of the *viejos,* by which he meant the lies. How the *viejos* always managed to survive no matter the odds levied against them.

It was a criticism that I would hear Duck and Edith repeat many times in the next six weeks. This despite the fact that Edith, when she talked about her own life, often conjured a varied cast of larger-than-life characters, most notably God and the Devil. Duck, on the other hand, was loath to talk about anything that was not happening in the present; when he did, it was invariably presented as a listing of facts. Except, that is, when he'd been drinking.

That first night at the *veranada,* Duck and I shared a bottle of *pisco* that he'd carried with him in a saddlebag. *Pisco* is, like Scotch to Scotland, Chile's defining drink, a sort of rude, yellow-green eighty-proof brandy made from the husks of grapes. What separates it from anything I've ever had, aside from *tequila,* is that just about the time you begin to feel its effects, a *pisco* buzz takes on a kind of violent, narcotic edge. Far from slowing you down, it makes you progressively, maddeningly, more alert.

Which was not, considering Duck and I had only one bottle between us, something I expected to be a problem. Nor was I expecting him, halfway through the bottle, to admit that there was one "legend" that mattered to him. It mattered, he said, because it was the truth. "The story of Black Carl," said Duck, and then he began telling it.

"There was a man who lived in Campo Grande, on the other side of the mountains of Ñirehuao. His people had been there for some time. I don't know. It doesn't matter. You seem to think everything matters, Nico. In any event, it doesn't in this story.

"This man, he was an older gentleman, in his fifties, let's say, and he owned his ranch, though it was the worst kind of land. But he had some money, and one day he packs the horses and he rides to Coihaique, *che.* He had business to do there. In those days they put their money in their boots for safekeeping. One boot they put the money to drink away when they came to town, the other boot for the business they want to do. And because they don't ever take their boots off, that money's as safe as a buried rock, *che.*

"It's three weeks on horse to Coihaique. No roads, not anything like it is now, where it would take just a week on horse. Town isn't anything like what you're used to, either. There's hardly anyone there, looks more like Tapera than anything else. This is in the nineteen sixties. Soon as he gets to town, *che,* it's time to drink a boot's worth, which he does. Then the next day he rides up to a house on the outskirts of town. A yellow house, *che.*

"There's a little girl playing in the front yard and an old woman drinking *mate* inside the house. The man goes in and drinks *mate,* but not much. He's in a hurry. So he pulls off the other boot and he says to the old woman, 'This ought to be enough for a new house.' He's got a cargo horse and two saddlehorses, and who do you think is on the second saddle horse when he leaves? The little girl. We'll say she's twelve years old.

"So three weeks back on the trail to Campo Grande, him and the little girl. And there wasn't a day that passed when he didn't rape her. They get out to Campo Grande, to this cabin in the middle of nowhere on ground not suited for a goat, and he tells her he's the Devil. He says, 'Don't ever leave me, because I'll fucking find you, *che,* and when I do, I'll kill you.' Then, because he knows she'll be thinking of leaving first chance she gets, he plays tricks on her. He tells her he's riding out to go buy more stock and then he comes back in the middle of the night to say he had to turn around because he heard her thinking of leaving. Then sometimes he really is gone for weeks, but by then he knows he's got her trained, *che.* Understand?

"So. There's this other gaucho, this famous man called Black Carl. And when he passes through Campo Grande, he sleeps on the floor at this man's house, the one who now has the little girl. Only, the little girl isn't so little anymore. Now she's old enough she's had a child by the man. Two children. She might be sixteen.

"And Black Carl, one day he rides through and finds this girl alone with her children, *che.* And the girl strikes a deal with Black Carl: if he'll take her with him, she'll be his.

"Black Carl had some shortcomings, but religion wasn't one of them. And every morning, *che,* he gets up and says to God, '*Che,* I shit on you.' But when he's not drinking, he's one of the gentlest around. So when he gets the chance to help this girl—and have a companion out of it at the same time—he does it.

"And where do they go? Tapera. He sets her and the children up in a house in town. A yellow house. And Black Carl takes a job gauchoing for the Estancia near Tapera. He goes back out on the plain and he lives in his little *puesto* and he doesn't get back to town much; like any old gaucho, he's just wandering here and there and checking his *patrón*'s herd and he can't be counted on too much. Not because he's a bad man. He's got his jobs.

"So one morning he wakes up in that outhouse he lives in and he's still got half the hatchet in his head. There's a bottle of *pisco* next to the pile of skins he sleeps on and he finishes the rest, to try and keep the headache away a little longer. And he walks over to the stove and takes his *mate* from the shelf and fills it anew. On the wall behind the stove is everything he owns, *che:* chaps, poncho, lassos, a side of meat, all of it hanging from nails in the wall. And next to that is a tea kettle and a pot and a frying pan. But he doesn't see the pan.

"Black Carl gets a good fire going in the stove, and then he goes out to the creek to fill a pot with water, and he comes back and he pours the water into another one on the stove to heat. Only, the water comes streaming out of that one in eight directions and puts the fire in the stove out and fills the whole cabin with smoke.

"Black Carl looks at the pot and there's four entrance wounds and four exit wounds, *che:* someone's shot the thing full of holes. He looks behind the stove, and there's the frying pan on the floor and there's a hole in the middle of it, too. Black Carl reaches for his revolver. But it's not in the holster. It's lying on the table in front of the window. Which is when he remembers what happened the day before."

Duck pulled his jacket up close into his neck and rocked forward toward the fire. It was getting colder, and a flurry of snow had started. I handed Duck the *pisco* bottle. There was a quarter left. Everywhere around us and around the fire snow whirled like ashes.

"The day before," said Duck, "Black Carl had ridden to get his horses and put them in the corral. He was going to Tapera to see the woman, and he needed three horses for the trip, two to switch off riding and one to carry his packs, and he wanted all of his horses to be in the corral so he could choose at his leisure when he was ready.

"Black Carl had a six-shooter. 'I keep seven of everything, *che,*' says Black Carl, 'so if I get drunk and start shooting the horses or the dogs, I can't kill all seven of them. Now if I only have six horses to begin with, or six dogs, then where would I be? Fucked is where!' I swear, *che,* I've known him twenty years and I've never heard him say it otherwise. And the best part is, he can't count! I've seen him ride with ten of each.

"So. The previous afternoon, Black Carl had gone to round up those horses. And he'd been drinking. And every time he gets the horses to the gate of the corral, poof! They scatter like chickens back to the *pampa.* Five times, *che.* So he says to God, '*Che,* I already shat on you this morning. And you, Lucifer, if you're no better than a turd yourself, help me get these bastard horses in this corral.'

"Every one of those horses lined up like Indians waiting for bread, and pranced into that corral. Black Carl didn't have to lift his finger. And he latches the gate and thinks no more about it and goes inside to get drunk.

"He's sitting there in his cabin when from far out on the *pampa* there comes a horseman. A while later, Black Carl looks up. Only now, he doesn't see the horseman. But he hears a sound, one he'd never heard before. It's the clink of a metal bridle, *che.* Now, gauchos are too poor to use anything other than hide for the reins and bridles and hackamores, Nico. Only one man is rich enough to use metal. Black Carl knew who it was that was coming. His dogs ran yelping into the cabin. Then he sees Him. He sees his black chaps and black *botas de potro* and a black poncho and beret, and his horse is a black stallion. The reins and stirrups are made of silver and all the rings of the saddle, *che.* And the clinking doesn't stop till the horse puts his muzzle through Black Carl's open window.

"It's the Devil, Nico. And Black Carl looks at his face, only there isn't any face. What he sees there where the rider's face should be is like polished black stone, so clear and sharp that Black Carl sees his own face in it.

"This isn't a lie, Nico, nor is it the first time it happened, to Black Carl and lots of others. And the reason it isn't a lie, *che,* is that the story is always the same.

"And when the horse tries to bite him, Black Carl puts his pistol to the horse's forehead and pulls the trigger. Only, nothing happens, *che.* Black Carl sights along the barrel and finds the Devil's face and he sees his own again and he cocks the pistol. And: nothing. Then Black Carl just puts the gun on the table and sits down.

"But the Devil, he pulls back on the reins, and his horse withdraws its head, and the Devil turns and rides slowly away, *che*. As they pass the corral, Black Carl's horses break through the fence chest-first and scatter back onto the *pampa*.

"The Devil doesn't follow his backtrail, though. Instead, he rides south, toward Tapera. Black Carl looks at the pistol there on the table, and when he does, it fires all six cartridges; four hit the milk can, and another the frying pan and drops it from its hook, like a bird shot out of the air."

Duck looked at his feet next to the fire and wiggled his toes. The snow had quit falling. Duck said, "My hooves are cold." When I looked at him expectantly, he said, "That's the story, *che*."

I said, "Who was the man and who was the woman?"

"The woman," said Duck, "is Edith's mother, María. The man," he said, shaking his head, "I don't know who the man is. All I know is Black Carl takes Edith's mother from Campo Grande, and next thing Black Carl knows, the Devil comes looking for something at his *puesto*. Then, when He doesn't find whatever that thing is, he rides toward Tapera. Those are the facts."

Duck looked at the *pisco* bottle, but it was empty. Then he picked up a stick and turned a log on its side, so that the fire would have new fuel.

*   *   *

I lay awake for much of the night at the *veranada*. Alfredo let his dogs run free after dark, and they shadowed Duck's dogs until a fight broke out. Duck and I were close together for warmth, and each time the dogs rolled one another in the dirt at our feet, Duck would jerk and stop snoring, but he didn't wake up. Then he would gargle in his sleep, and, as though it were some cue to the dogs, they would pace and circle and lie down again, waiting for the next fight.

I wondered that night how Duck and Edith had ever found themselves at Santa Elvira. All I knew was what Duck had told me as we rode toward the nothingsummer—that a year and a half after he showed up at María's house in Tapera, Duck and Edith had been "married," which consisted simply of his saying to her, "*Vamos.*"

This one-word proposal and ceremony has been, according to the journals, a gaucho tradition for hundreds of years, and a sort of small act of rebellion against the notion that things need to be somehow officially sanctioned— whether by baptisms or marriage licenses or birth certificates—in order to be "real." Particularly when all of it is mandated by a government and a church that has for so long ignored the gauchos. Chile is an overwhelmingly Catholic country. The gauchos, though, with rare exception—and Edith is one such exception—are irreligious. The Judeo-Christian God, like the law (both legislative and theological), is an outsider in Cisnes. Only Don Satanás is firmly placed on the Inside, and gaucho lore, from as early as the eighteenth century, is filled with Faustian meetings between gauchos and "the dark stranger."

In any event, after their "marriage" in Tapera, Duck and Edith had gone to live an hour outside Coihaique, where Duck was cowboying on a ranch near Lago Polux. "Ooooh," said Edith when I asked her, "that was just a time. Just constant," and she made a motion like knocking against an invisible door, and blushed and whistled. A year later, she said, Patricia was born to them, and, flush with some money from Duck's job and wanting to raise their new child in better surroundings, they moved to town. Duck found work in construction, building Coihaique into the place that would, in a few more years, make tourism its primary business. They lived in a slum not far from Duck's mother and brothers, who were also carpenters.

Black Carl, too, was living in Coihaique at the time. He'd had a stroke when Edith was eleven, and ridden to Tapera, where María nursed him for three weeks before he was strong enough once again to ride back to his *puesto* at the Estancia. In the two years following this first stroke, Edith said, Black Carl—as though his dependence upon María during those three weeks had made him hate her—had only come back to Tapera when he was drunk, and he'd done terrible things to her. He talked constantly, said Edith, about the Devil—that it was the Devil that was making him act this way—though Edith refused to say what things she had seen him do to her mother. Then, while Edith was living at Lago Polux with Duck, Black Carl had another stroke, this one more massive, and Señor Mansilla brought him to Coihaique, as Edith told it, to die, though she would not, out of spite for the things she'd seen him do, go see him.

Not long after she and Duck had found a place in a slum of Coihaique, Duck began coming home drunk late at night and sleeping through work the next day. Then he would disappear for a week at a time, and when he came home, he would speak in voices that Edith didn't recognize, deep voices thick with booze and with something else that she didn't understand, and he'd put his knife to her face as he talked. Edith never told me what Duck said, exactly, and I didn't ask. I assumed that I would someday find out.

One night Edith ran to Black Carl with Patricia following one of Duck's episodes. Living with Black Carl was in many ways a blessing for both of them. They were, she often thought, quite a bit alike, and now that Black Carl was too old to be threatening, he was entertaining. He'd even stopped drinking, and, more surprising still, converted to the Evangelical church. Edith was happy to care for him and to try and reshape her relationship with a man she had never really known.

Then, for some reason, Edith had decided to go and speak with Duck's mother. She'd wanted to let Duck's mother know that her son was a drunk and that Edith wasn't about to subject herself to the same thing María had endured. Edith was sure that the man from Campo Grande had been the Devil, and that he'd come to Black Carl's *puesto* looking for María, his lost love. And when Black Carl looked into the Devil's face and saw his own, it had changed him. Then she wondered if Duck hadn't seen the Devil's face in Coihaique.

Duck's mother had said in response, "It's only beer and wine Duck drinks. Drunks drink *pisco*." Duck's mother had always believed anything Duck and his brothers told her. Edith heard that and thought: "Good riddance. You're all crazy."

The next week, Duck had come looking for Edith at Black Carl's, and he pleaded with her to take him back. He said he'd quit drinking, and that they should move back out to the country, back to what they knew, where there were no people and no booze, and they could make a life for themselves and a family. And to prove it, Duck had even gotten a job gauchoing out in Cisnes, not too far from Amengual. All they had to do was get on that bus.

As the weeks went by, Duck refused to give up his repentance. He came over all the time, and Edith began to soften. And as she began to soften, the words of

Duck's mother came back to her. Maybe, thought Edith, Duck wasn't an alcoholic after all. Maybe, as long as he limited himself, he'd be all right. Even Black Carl began to wonder if Duck didn't deserve a second chance. What's more, the longer Edith lived with her father, the more one thing frustrated her: she could not, as hard as she tried, tell Black Carl she hated him for what he'd done to her mother. Edith would go to say something, to start the fight she needed to have with Black Carl, and her mouth wouldn't work, as though it was she who had had the stroke.

Perhaps Black Carl sensed this. Perhaps he, too, was as anxious for Edith to be gone as he was for her to stay. In either case, he'd said to her one day, "A woman must be with her man, not her father."

A week later, Edith and Duck and Patricia got on the bus that had brought them a year earlier to Coihaique. They went north once again, following their backtrail in the direction of the Ruin, where their lives had initially crossed one another.

*   *   *

Early that morning at the *veranada*, the sun lit the border, first vaguely, and then by discernible stages as the light spread along the facing slopes of the Chilean *cordillera*. The clouds above the peaks were faded tattoo oranges and pinks and blues, and only the deepest valleys were still confined in semidarkness. The horses lurched to their feet and paced and nodded and stretched their legs. It was miserably cold, and Alfredo would remain at the nothingsummer for four more weeks.

Duck said, "Are you okay?" I'd not heard him sit up in his sleeping bag. He said, "I forgot to cover the wood last night." He went to the wall and reached inside a knothole in one of the trunks and brought out kindling that had been there since the last drive, three months before; the kindling had stayed dry within the tree. Duck kicked at the damp wood and spread it to dry along the sides of the coals, then teepeed the dry kindling in its stead. "There you are," he said, and the teepee burst into flames.

We drank *mate* and ate from the shoulder we'd roasted the night before. When the dampened wood was dry, we set that on the fire. But before it had caught, Duck was up and packing the camp. I watered the horses and watched as

Duck saddled them, trying to remember the sequence. The bulls were bellowing in the holding corral. A pair of them butted heads and steamed in the sun, and they worked around one another with their back legs pumping. Alfredo came out of his *puesto* and skipped across the creek and began saddling his horse.

"Come on," said Duck. He would ride Happy Slim today, and Happy Fat was fitted with the packsaddle and the *chiguas*. She looked up when he said this and then she cropped grass. "Bring Fat, Skinny," said Duck. Then he rode Slim toward the corral.

I put Marión forward to where Alfredo was saddling his horse. He looked at me and tightened the girthstrap. Then he reached in his jacket pocket and pulled out two cigarettes and handed one to me, straight-armed and looking directly away from me as he did so.

I asked him how the hunt had gone, for I hadn't heard him come back the night before. "I put a herd to sleep," he said, meaning he'd watched them bed down for the night. He climbed into his saddle and, as we rode toward the corral, he told me that as soon as Duck and I left, he'd take his dogs to where he'd seen the stags, and his dogs would cut one away from the herd so Alfredo could run it down a trail he'd laced with snares, which he called *guaches*—the same word, given new meaning, from which gaucho might have evolved. His accent was like none I'd heard in Chile, and he changed the letter "s" to "h" and added a "p" to the end of many words and finished them drawn-out, as in Italian.

When Alfredo and I got to the corral, the bulls were huddled against the gate. The dogs sat panting behind them, and each time one of the bulls turned to retrace his steps, the dogs trotted toward him and circled one another, looking about, with their tails raised like spraying skunks. Alfredo opened the gate. He came wide around their number, and he and Duck pushed the bulls ahead of them through the gate. We rode as far as the seeps on the plateau, and the bulls pushed ahead, stumbling and leaving the marks of their dewclaws in the mud. We watched them cross the seeps, and then Duck and I put our horses forward.

Duck said, "Well?"

"Six weeks?" said Alfredo.

"With luck," said Duck. "I'd hope to be back here sooner." He said, "It'll get nasty up here, *che*."

Alfredo nodded. Then he turned and rode with his dogs toward the saddle two kilometers distant where the stags were bedded.

*　　*　　*

Duck and I nooned in the dappled shade of virgin *coigues* that grew a hundred feet tall, and we listened to the midday rock 'n' roll show on Radio Santa María, and made mutton soup. The sun was out, and we slept there with the horseflies crawling on our faces till the heat had passed and then we rounded up the bulls and drove them till dark. In the morning, we passed the place where we'd seen the herd of wild horses, and we looked for them in the shadowlines of the trees but they weren't there.

At noon of that second day, we passed through the two rocks on the ridgeline above the Moro and looked down into the bowl where the river flowed. It was raining hard. Duck said, "We can wait for the sun or not." Then, his decision made, Duck rode forward and whipped the last bull in line and he climbed up on top of the next. The line moved tentatively down onto the lip of rock and stopped. Duck hit the last bull again and they moved cautiously forward and stopped. "We can't turn them now." Duck smiled. "I'll go first. Keep Marión from biting Fat," he said, and he put Happy Slim down onto the lip.

For two hours we inched along, and when the bulls stopped to rest, the horses sat on their haunches with their forelegs spread before them to keep from sliding down the rock and mud. When we started again, the bulls would vent themselves, and the horses slipped in the vomitous, acrid droppings. The talus-covered mountain rose in three dimensions above us, with the rounded depth of the sky higher still and the bowl below. The scrub in the bowl was tiny, and the river, too, and the splendor of it was nearly enough to make me forget about the possibility of my horse making a fatal misstep.

We passed through the bowl and gained the switchbacks on the other side. At the top of the ridge, we looked once again onto the faultline where the *pampa* began and the mountains swerved east. We hopped down off the horses to readjust the saddles and tighten the girthstraps. Duck said, "Let's push hard and make Rock House. That puts us two days out from the ranch. After that, we're out of meat, Nico."

It was nearly nightfall when we got to Casa Piedra. Duck put the bulls to pasture on the plateau; he fixed their halters with lead ropes and tied them off to trees. A freshly dead fire still smoked weakly in the cave, and the logs we'd left had been replaced by someone with two new, bigger logs, and these lit quickly. When Duck came back up across the road, we unpacked the *chiguas* and made our beds under the cliff.

For two days, the bulls had labored dismally through forests to which they were ridiculously unsuited. They'd stopped to stare at systems of fire-falls that even the light and agile dogs had trouble crossing. And as the dogs grew impatient—as we all grew impatient—they would nip at the bulls' testicles, driving them chest-first through the debris. I was amazed that none of the bulls or horses or dogs had yet broken a leg, or eviscerated themselves on the sharp wedges of limbs that stuck out at all angles from the fallen trunks.

Duck took off his boots, and I did the same. Calluses had started to form on the tips of my toes, where my boots rubbed the stirrups, and on my rear end where the second girthstrap rubbed under my jeans. The aching in my legs had, after growing worse all day, begun to subside. With only two days left, and all of it a straight shot on the road before we made the nothingwinter, I felt sure we'd come through the worst of the allhell.

*   *   *

At one o'clock in the morning, Duck sat up in his sleeping bag and looked across the top of the fire, through the vibrating air. Down the road, from what seemed like far away, came the steady rhythm of a horse's slow gait. There was something oddly muffled about the sound. Country Dog and Sheep Shearings were standing in front of their nests. When the soft clopping stopped, they whined in unison.

"Quiet, *mierda*!" hissed Duck, then added as though talking to himself: "The horse is unshod." He said, literally, that the hooves were peeled.

"Just one horse?" I whispered. Duck nodded. The horseman was coming from the west; the closest homestead was two hours away. "Why don't the dogs go?" I said.

Duck shook his head and unsheathed his knife. The clopping began again. This time it was right in front of us, somehow much closer than I'd thought. For two seconds, the form of a man on a horse moved forward from where there had been nothing—black on black, a receded image all but hidden against the outline of the *cordillera* traced by the first sliver of a newing moon.

"*Hola,* gaucho!" hailed Duck, but there was no reply, and we listened to the sound of the horse's unshod footfalls until the sound died out.

"He wasn't very friendly," I said finally.

"Cattle thief," said Duck. He was looking across the fire at the road and he had the knife in his hand.

I said, "Are you sure?"

"No."

*   *   *

That night, Edith had made supper early. She'd done the dishes in the last of the day's light and let the fire die in the stove. When Mariana asked to light a candle, Edith told her to go to bed. Then she closed the cabin's two doors. She put the sofa in front of one; against the other she wedged a chair. She pulled the curtains, slid a knife between the mattress and the frame, and climbed into bed with Oscar. Patricia was at school back in the village.

At two in the morning, Edith sat up, wide awake. From somewhere outside came the gentle swoosh of hooves in the grass. Edith could not understand why, if Duck had come home, she didn't hear the barking of the dogs. Nor could she account for the hour and the sound of only one horse. When she heard the light chink of tack, she knew who it was. She unsheathed the knife and held it to her chest. Then she heard Duck speak to the horse. "Duck!" she called; to her amazement, the children continued sleeping. "Duck!" she yelled again. Then she heard him walk onto the terrace and stop in front of the window.

Edith rose with the knife and flung back the curtains. There, clearly etched in the moonlight, stood the barn and the slaughterhouse and the empty pasture.

Salmon

Unlike many commentators, [the nineteenth-century linguist Frederick Mann] Page recognized the formative influence of the gaucho's marginal socioeconomic status and noted that the gaucho could have become a "superb specimen of humanity" had he but received the assistance required to make the transition from traditional to modern life.

—*Richard W. Slatta,* Gauchos and the Vanishing Frontier, *1983*

We woke at five-thirty in the morning. Duck lay in his sleeping bag and listened to the bawling of the bulls on the plateau below us while I fanned the coals into flames. Duck sat up and listened closer; he pushed the unzipped hood of his sleeping bag back and stared off into the fog, which was thick over the plateau but would not cross the road. When a new round of bellowing started, Duck said, "They're not all there."

We went running to where the horses were tied and then Duck went around counting the bulls. Marión's rope was lying in the wet grass; she was gone, and her tracks led west. Duck and I met on the middle of the plateau. I said, "And the bulls?"

"Six gone," said Duck. His breath steamed in the cold air. "Run that way," he said, "and don't stop till you reach the next hill." Then he took off in the opposite direction.

A kilometer later, I still hadn't reached the crest of the hill, but I knew that the plateau hidden somewhere below me had run itself into the canyon wall. I looked at the dirt under my feet for fresh horse tracks, but there was nothing save thousands of sheep and cattle marks. If Marión had not backtracked to come onto the road behind me, she was somewhere on the silent plateau below, moving through the trees.

Looking closer at the dirt, a diorama made to tiny scale rippled into being: a ring of *cordillera* in each cloven sheep track; a vast and dark sea in the exhausted scuffs of Herefords. I studied it closely because I was suddenly overcome by the fact that I had no idea what to do. I still did not know how to saddle a horse or ride with anything approximating confidence. I'd lied to Duck about everything to get him to take me on the drive and assumed there would be no problems to call my bluff, and now there were problems. So I sat there a long time watching the hoofprints for some kind of clue that I knew wouldn't appear. Then Marión came running at me out of the fog.

I rose from my heels and walked into the middle of the road and stretched my arms to the sides. Marión slid to a stop ten feet short of me. Her flank quivered like a deer that knows that you're waiting in the tree above for a chance to take the safety off. I said whatever came to mind—in Spanish and English—and I tried to keep track of which grunts and phrases made her tremble and which did not. I was three feet from her. To have gotten my hands on Marión's halter would, I felt sure, erase all my doubts about the ludicrousness of my situation. Then Marión spun her back hooves into the dirt, changing the entire landscape, and trotted back down the road, disappearing from sight.

When I came down to our camp, Duck was mounted and the dogs were circling anxiously. Marión was tied to a tree alongside the cave; next to her, Happy Fat waited in the packsaddle. Duck said, "The bulls headed back into the mountains." He said he'd followed their track a long way back up the road, then decided to come back for the horse. Happy Slim was spinning under him as he spoke; Duck beat Slim about the haunches with his *rebenque*. "When they come down the road," called Duck. . . . But I didn't understand what he said next. Then he was galloping away, and the only sounds for a long time were that of Happy Slim's hooves against the road and Duck's crop against her haunches, all of it ricocheting off the canyon walls.

*   *   *

I went into the cave. It rained and then it stopped and then it started again. The fog was burned off by turns until the mountains on the other side of the river were visible in three strips, each separated from the other by hundreds of vertical feet. Later, the road came into view. The only thing still hidden was the river, though it was not to be ignored as it fell and broke against its bed and it was, along with the roaring fire, the only audible thing.

I walked over to Marión. When I reached out to her, she withdrew her muzzle from my outstretched hand so forcefully that she broke in half the branch to which she was tethered. I caught her up at the reins and leaned against her bucking, and when I looped the reins around another branch she grew quiet and docile, and the change made me feel her disdain and the sickening isolation all the way down into my knees. I wanted to hit Marión in the face with the handle of a whip as hard as I could. Instead, I looked at the pieces of the saddle strewn about next to the tarp.

A Chilean saddle, to someone who does not know anything about horses, is a fairly complicated thing. There are five separate parts, none of which are attached to one another until the end, when you've cinched and knotted and yanked them into a single unit. First, there's the blanket, and, above that, the saddle pad. Then comes the saddle tree, which is held on with a separate girth-strap. Once that's in place, there's a sheepskin that has to be folded just so, over which is placed the second girthstrap.

I'd gotten as far as trying to figure out how to cinch the first girthstrap when Marión stamped and pulled the bridle off her head. She took off to my left, and I got her around the neck and hung on as she pulled me toward the road. When I got around on her forward side, she began nosing the trodden grass, with me all the while hanging from her neck. I pushed her flanks until she was near enough to the dangling bridle that I could untie it and still be standing between Marión and her escape route.

As I did this, the first pair of bulls came lumbering down the road, saw the cave, and broke into a trot. I let them go. First, because I hadn't gotten the bridle back on Marión. And second because the only thing I knew for sure about the bulls was what Duck had said the previous night: that if we woke up and saw that their tracks moved toward Santa Elvira on the road, it was because they knew where they were going. He'd said that we would simply pick them up on the way. In my gut, I knew I'd made a terrible error. Seconds later, another bull shuffled into view, descended onto the plateau above the gorge, labored back onto the road, and rumbled off to the west. He was followed by two more, who sparred and roared as they passed.

I'd gotten the bridle untied and was trying to figure out how to get it on Marión, who snapped her long teeth at my fingers each time I tried to get the bit into her mouth. Finally, I put the reins around her neck and looped the bridle over a stout branch, and went to the cave to smoke a cigarette and drink *mate*.

I was still there when the sixth bull came down the road and stopped briefly to watch me before running in the direction of the other fugitives. A little while later, Duck galloped up and sat his horse in front of the cave and looked down at me. His face glistened with sweat and muddied streaks of water.

"The camp?" he said, looking at the half-packed *chiguas* that he'd left on the ground two hours before; the camp looked, suddenly, like a disaster area. I tried to say that I hadn't known if he'd want some *mate* or food before we left, but I couldn't remember a word of Spanish.

Duck rode over to the steep embankment to count the bulls. "Nico!" he yelled. "Nine!" He turned Happy Slim and rode over to the cave. "Nine," he said quietly, breathing deeply. His chaps were covered in mud. "The others?"

I pointed down the road.

Happy Slim was panting and opening and closing her mouth on the bit, straining her neck forward. Each time Duck's hand was jerked with it, he unconsciously jerked back harder. "Nico*che*," he said, "I can't believe what a fucking mongoloid I am." He said it casually, almost deprecatingly, the way you might tell a friend that you'd made a poor bet and lost money. He said, "What an unbelievable, ignorant, foolish cunt I am to have brought along a fucking dumb-ass gringo that I fucking knew didn't know the first fucking thing about any of this." When Happy Slim again jerked his hand forward, Duck pulled back and left so hard that she nearly went to her knees and threw him. "If idiots like you could fly, Nico, the sky would be cloudy every day."

I began piling things haphazardly into the *chiguas*.

"Look at that," said Duck. Marión had cleared her bowels with great precision so that my saddle tree was covered in a giant, steaming pile of manure.

Duck hopped off Happy Slim and rolled his shirtsleeve up. He picked up the saddle tree and, in one motion, cleared the pile off with his forearm. He tossed the saddle tree to me and said to go clean the rest in the spring. I did it, but the whole time I was wondering what thirsty gauchos might come along to the cave in the near future and drink from the spring.

After I handed the tree back to him, Duck arranged the pieces of the saddle on Marión's back. He threw the sheepskin over the saddle tree, and then the second cinchstrap. Just as Duck was about to tighten it, Marión took a deep breath. "You asshole," said Duck, and I was unsure whom he was talking to until he kneed Marión in the ribs as hard as he could to clear her lungs and, in the same motion, yanked the girthstrap tight. "Asshole," he said again as he walked away. This time, he wasn't talking to the horse.

I rode down onto the plateau to herd the nine remaining bulls and drive them up onto the road. Duck had tossed me a bullwhip, and I used it liberally, as much to vent my frustration as a means of showing Duck that I was learning, despite what he thought, how to act the part. And the more guilty and disgusted I became with myself for imitating behavior I found somehow appalling, the harder I whipped them.

Duck was coming from the camp with the packhorse. "I'll herd them," he called. "You have the faster horse—get up the road two kilometers where the next plateau is and stay there so the escaped bulls don't get on it." I put Marión forward at a canter. "Gallop!" ordered Duck, and Marión, as though she'd understood, went tearing up the road, her hooves clacking.

What I reckoned to be a kilometer passed, and then another, and Marión would not be slowed. I sawed back on her with the reins, and she only bent her head at the neck and galloped sideways, like a fleeing crab. The gauchos use chain bits, which are very painful, and they rely on punishment to train their horses. But the chain bits give the horses very hard mouths, so that the more accustomed a stubborn horse becomes to the pain, the less it minds the rider. And the less it minds, the more pain is meted out. I reined Marión so violently to her offside that she spun around and skidded to a halt.

Duck advanced from the east, out from under the sun, stopping every few meters to lean down out of the saddle and try and differentiate the tracks of the escaped bulls from the dozens of thousands of other marks in the road. He was two hundred meters away, and he motioned to me to come to him.

"Take the packmare," he said, and handed me the rope. He pointed to the wall of rock that shouldered the road on the inside. Seeps of water glistened against the wall, and the horses rubbed their noses in them. Duck pointed above us. "The bulls are up there."

We backtracked a hundred meters to where a ledge of rock ascended from the road along the wall. Where the ledge started, it was as wide as a car, and it tapered as it climbed until it was just big enough for a bull to pass onto the top of the wall with one shoulder rubbing the rock and the other nearly hung over the killing fall to the road below. Duck pointed up. "See that broken leaf?" There was an enormous leaf hanging down over the ledge that had been broken at the stem. "That's where they passed," he said.

Sheep Shearings and Country Dog went padding up the ledge and sniffed at the broken stem. Then they ran onto the top of the wall, into the forest. "Take the bulls and the packmare," said Duck. "I'll meet you down there where another trail just like this one runs back down into the road. Stop short of it so the bulls when they come down don't turn back this way. Don't get ahead of them or they'll run back and we'll have go chasing them again, *che*." Then he put Happy Slim calmly up the ledge.

A kilometer up the road, there was a mirror image of the place, just as Duck had said, and I took advantage of my time alone to write notes on a spiral pad I carried in the saddlebag. At the end of half an hour of recording the events of the morning and reading the notes of other conversations we'd had in the past few days, it occurred to me that Duck had not once asked me what I was doing in Patagonia. I'd tried to tell him several times, and each time he'd cut me off and say, "It doesn't matter. You don't need a reason to be welcome here, *che*." I wondered how losing half his *patrón*'s bulls might affect his opinion.

But when the fugitives came ambling down the trail, Duck smiled, and we fell in behind them. Before starting out again, we watched as they butted heads and jostled amongst themselves, to see which would lead the herd the rest of the way down the road.

*   *   *

At ten o'clock that morning, Duck and I stopped to rest next to a brook that ran through a clearing at the steepest part of the road, from which we could see almost all of the Middle Cisnes valley. Five kilometers distant, a red Mercedes truck came into view and creeped along a straightaway and then disappeared, along with any sound at all, aside from the cropping and licking of the bulls. "No shit," said Duck. "We might have some good luck yet."

A while later, the truck was audible again just before it came wildly around a corner a hundred meters away. The driver braked and killed the engine, and Duck rode up to the cab and sat his horse; the driver opened his door and stood on the cab step, regarding Duck. "Nico," he called, "ride up here and meet the source of all things good in Cisnes."

It was Red Duck, the man I'd ridden with on Señor Mansilla's bus from Coihaique. Red Duck made his business running anything he could sell—whores and lumber and booze and pistol cartridges—between Coihaique and Tapera. He was drunk and smoking a cigarette. His big blue eyes were watery and red, and his chin whiskers had begun to challenge the length of his drooping red mustaches and thick eyebrows. His fair skin was freckled.

Three other men were crammed in the cab with him; one of them was the man I'd seen Red Duck talking to in Mañihuales, and he studied Duck and me with his good eye. He was called Loco, and he and the two others were heading to a logging camp in the mountains, where they would stay for three months, until they grew crazy with the isolation and the rats and walked the three days to Tapera and never came back.

I rode up and looked at Red Duck closer. He held an open box of The Brothers Carrera chardonnay. His hands were big and white, and the fingers were short and strong and covered between the knuckles with clumps of red hair. He took a long drink and handed the box down to Duck; then, as an afterthought, Red Duck stepped down onto the front tire and looked behind the truck before regaining his seat in the cab. The three of us drank from the box.

"Good!" said Red Duck. "Good good good." He passed it to the men in the cab, and each of them took his turn. The men smelled like roasted mutton and *pisco* and mildewed cotton. One of them was no more than eighteen, and Loco and the third man were in their forties. We finished the wine, and then Red Duck tossed the box out the open door. He listened as it clattered down into the canyon, and, satisfied, he reached under his seat and pulled out another. Then he said to Duck, "So, eggo, how many cattle have you stolen?"

I said, "The drive was going fine till I lost half the herd, *che*." I said it in the gaucho accent, half-Argentine and half-Chilean, all *campesino*. I'd been imitating in my mind the things I heard Duck say, and now, with the easing of the wine in the early morning, I'd suddenly begun imitating them out loud. It was the first of many times I was conscious of having done this, and in all the months I lived in Patagonia, it never escaped my attention, nor did it fail to leave me wondering if I'd succeeded in setting myself apart further or bestowing on the people around me a kind of compliment.

Red Duck said, "Gringo fucked all kinds of shit up? Maybe the bulls didn't understand Argentinian."

"Oh," said Duck, "nothing more than what's natural, considering he'd got a crazy horse breaking his nuts every ten minutes. He's all right." He looked at me. "We're having a good time, aren't we, Nico?"

The horses shook their heads and shifted beneath us, and Duck shooshed them and we passed the wine again. The bed of the truck was high—the lip was nine feet off the ground—and three other men stuck their heads up over the lip, one, two, three, and stared down at us from above the cab. They were young and dirty and had long hair and strong Indian features.

Red Duck leaned out of the cab, looked up at them, and tried to hide the battery of wine behind one of his legs. "Get back down in there!" he yelled. He might have been speaking to a group of dogs scavenging a cookfire. The three men ducked back down into the bed of the truck and were gone. "Too many mouths to feed on the ship," said Red Duck. He had the wine again, and he looked at it and raised his eyebrows pensively.

Duck fished a clear plastic Nalgene bottle from his saddlebag; a tourist had given the bottle to him one time along the road. Duck unscrewed the cap, and Red Duck fished a fresh battery out from under the seat. It was labeled "120 Merlot." There was a single star next to the number, and Red Duck sliced the nipple and poured it unsteadily into the Nalgene bottle while Duck held it. "You owe me," said Red Duck. Then he smiled and nodded distractedly and we moved the horses off to the side of the road as he drove away.

Duck and I rode behind the bulls, passing the bottle and eating leftover pieces of mutton that Duck pulled out of his saddle bags. Each time he took a drink, Duck would let loose a long, satisfied sigh, and say, "Good luck, I think, Nico. That was good luck." Then he would screw the top back on and put the bottle back in his saddlebag, and, a few minutes later, fish it out again and we would drink. When the wine was half-done, he unscrewed the cap and put that in the saddlebag and kept the bottle in his rein hand. He said, "Why are you wearing the shirt and the poncho, Nico*che*?"

I said, "What?"

"You don't wear it like that. You wear shirt-sweater-poncho, *che*. Or shirt-jacket-poncho. But never shirt-poncho."

I shrugged. I said, "It's warm, so I could almost be wearing just the shirt, *che,* but . . ."

"No! You can't just wear the shirt, *che*. That'd be like . . . wearing no hat." He shook his head. "That'd be weird."

"Right," I said. "And so the shirt wouldn't be enough, because the wind is chilly. But shirt-sweater-poncho, that's too much."

"That's why you wear shirt-sweater. Forget the poncho."

We rode awhile without saying anything. The dust on the newly dried road swirled and stuck to our skin, like makeup. Like we were pretending to be something we weren't.

Duck said, "Why are you wearing your poncho with the neck opened vertically, *che*?" He had the bullwhip propped against his thigh, and his hand sat casually atop it; the tail of the whip fell along Happy Slim's flank, and every time the dangling tail brushed up against her, she would start. Duck pointed toward me with the whip in his hand.

I strained to look down at the neck of the poncho. Roughly in the middle of it, a slit had been cut, through which you put your head to get the poncho on. I was wearing it so that the slit was perpendicular to my shoulders. "You wear it with the opening horizontal, not vertical," said Duck. "The way you have it, it's going to slip all over the whoring place, *che*."

He handed me the bottle and our horses veered into each other's paths and our legs bumped off one another. Duck reached over and took my poncho with his free hand. "Do you mind?" he asked. Then he spun the poncho so the neck hole was parallel to my shoulders. Marión stumbled slightly and pulled back to her side of the road. "There it is," said Duck. He smiled. We both were smiling.

I said, "I'm sorry about the goat-fuck I caused you this morning."

"The only problem," said Duck, "was that I was nervous."

Aside from the herd and the occasional flock of lapwings squawking overhead, there was no movement anywhere. There were no deer and no hares and no coyotes. There were no songbirds. There were all these tracks in the road, but there was no indication anywhere that the stock that had made them truly existed—no certainty, even, of their origin or destination.

Duck said, "What had me by the nuts this morning was something that happened up on the road. I didn't say anything when you told me that the bulls and Marión were gone. But I assumed we'd been robbed. I can't tell you how it would have happened, because I was up all night after that rider passed. But for bulls to have run off back toward the mountains, that isn't right, Nico. Cattle know to head for the valley this time of year, not back up to where it's cold. I thought, 'Well, that Indian must have somehow stolen them.'

"It turns out the bulls' track went up off of the road, and the horse marks kept the road, *che*. So when I came back down from where the bull tracks were, I got it in my head to follow the horse marks. And I did. I saw that he had moved easily, just like you and I are moving now.

"Now let me ask you: How is it when he passed last night these dogs didn't tear his dog up?"

I said, "I don't know. It was like they didn't even know the horseman was coming, *che*."

Duck said, "There was no dog. And this morning when I followed the horse tracks another kilometer into the fog, they just stopped."

"What do you mean they just stopped?"

"No more tracks, no more anything, *che*. I know a peeled horse track. It stands out like a flag in the dirt. I guess I started wondering if we ever saw a gaucho last night. How could he see to ride with no moon?"

I said, "Does the Devil have a dog?"

"Devil rides alone," said Duck. "Always."

"Then you're saying it was the Devil."

"I don't believe in the Devil."

I said, "Who else can see at night and travels without a dog?" We each reined the horses and sat them and looked around. The dogs sat in the dust and yawned, and the horses stretched against the bits.

"He isn't a man," said Duck. He rubbed the mask of dirt on his face, and pinched between his fingertips the dust that had clotted at the corners of his eyes.

"What is he?"

"A boy," said Duck. "A neighbor." And with that, he whistled and the dogs rose, and we kept moving.

*   *   *

Behind Edith and Duck's cabin was an area of waist-high grass and crabapple trees framed by two long lines of cottonwoods, which stopped abruptly, thirty meters from the back door, at a fence. Beyond that, a shambles of degenerate *coigue* and *calafate* grew in patches on a burned-over hillside. The hillside ran for several hundred meters steadily upward toward the continental divide before being interrupted, a quarter-mile from the house, by the road—close enough to hear the trucks that occasionally ground their gears on their way somewhere, and far enough away that you could see neither them nor the dust they trailed behind them like jetwash.

To one side of the yard was another fence, this one a sturdy wood slat job with a rickety gate that leaned off its wire hinges like a drunk. This was the gate to the chicken yard, a muddied and balding area with a plank thrown across it, which dead-ended at the outhouse. The plank and the trodden tufts of grass and the mud spots were all covered with black-and-white finger sausages of chicken droppings in all stages of ripeness and decomposition. A blue plastic barrel, the kind used to carry gas, had been halved, and handles had been cut into the sides, and it sat most of the time in the chicken yard next to the water pump. This was a multipurpose vessel that served, depending on the day, as washtub (when coupled with a wooden washboard), bath (when filled with stove-heated water and squirming children), and chicken toilet.

The outhouse, a two-seater, had a corrugated tin roof. Its walls were made of long, lean, roughhewn boards. Next to that, the chickenhouse was in a sorry state of repair. The windows were covered in yellowed and dusty and torn plastic sheeting so that the view was not much obscured and the air flowed freely in, though it was a heavy and dank place, almost cold on even the hottest days. In one corner, several planks were laid together to make a kind of floor; and eight or ten feet above this, a faux chrome nozzle poured glacial water. The chickenhouse was also the showerhouse.

It was from here that Duck emerged into the sunlight, clean-shaven and doused with cologne, on the afternoon that we reached reached Santa Elvira with the bulls. He was barefoot, and he skipped toward the cabin in jeans and without a shirt. "Sunday-wash day," he sang, sitting in a chair and tuning his guitar.

"Water's ready," said Edith as she carried a steaming cauldron to the center of the room and dumped it into the plastic tub. ("Water's ready," sang Duck, and he began a steady, melodic riff that he punctuated by tapping the head of the guitar with his fingers, like the clopping of hooves.) Edith brought another cauldron of water from the stove and dumped it into the tub, then filled the cauldron with cold water from the sink and added that to the tub until she was satisfied with the temperature. Then she reached for Oscar, and he for her, and she swung him, naked, above the halved blue barrel. ("Ouch! That's hot!" sang Duck, and he ran his fingers screeching up the neck of the guitar.)

When Edith lowered him, Oscar kicked water at her and screamed. She raised an eyebrow and looked first at him and then at the Oscar-sized cauldron full of frigid water at her side. He looked from one to the other. His pizzle receded at the thought. He smiled. "Are you going to stop the kicking?" Edith asked him. Oscar laughed, and she lowered him into the bath. ("That was the right decision," said Duck, nodding his head to the rhythm. "Cold water sucks. Hot water: good.")

That afternoon, Patricia would be going into Amengual for the week, to the little school there, and she was feverishly folding the few clothes Edith had just ironed—a hand-me-down school uniform, a pair of underwear, jeans, her only two pairs of socks—and putting them carefully into a plastic Fred Flintstone knapsack. Mariana sat on her usual perch, a wooden footstool in the corner behind the stove, from which she could see all that approached her. She wore a pink and orange shirt and green leggings under green shorts, and on her feet were Duck's rubber rainboots, each of which was a third as tall as she. She was upset that Patricia was leaving for the week, and would not be bothered to speak with anyone.

Chile has an excellent state-run public school system, and education is mandatory until the sixth grade. So it was that even the one-hundred-fifty-person village of Amengual had had a school for ten years, and it was attended by some twenty children, well over half of the known youth population of Middle Cisnes. The students ranged in age from five to twelve, and they were taught in two rooms—one for those whose ages were in the single digits, one for the double-digiters—by an eighty-year-old woman who had been country-teaching since, as Duck liked to say, "Indians shot farts with slingshots."

Traditionally, the children were brought on horseback by their parents or rode in alone and spent the week in the village. The children were separated into those who lived too far from the nearest village to make schooling feasible and those who did not. Even after the road, things didn't get much easier, because very few gauchos had trucks, and waiting all day for one to pass (a truck driven by someone you didn't know, moreover) was out of the question. Had Patricia come of school age just two years before, the distance from Santa Elvira to Amengual by horse—three and a half hours—would likely have prevented her from being educated at all.

It was something Duck and Edith never had to worry about, though, because in 1997 a man in Amengual began making trips up and down the Argentine Road in his pickup each Sunday during the school year to bring the kids who lived the farthest from the school into the village. And while there was still nothing to be done for the eleven- and twelve-year-old boys who were already living with their *patrones'* herds at *veranadas* as remote as Alfredo's, it was nonetheless a revolutionary development. At ranches like Santa Elvira, which were relatively close to the road, the man would even drive right down to the cabin. And the best part of it was that the state paid him to do it.

None of which made what happened once the children arrived at school any easier. It was, for so many children who had been raised at a complete remove from anyone outside their immediate families, a very difficult thing, suddenly to be away in a village, whether or not, like Amengual, that village was rustic in every way. It was probably easier for Patricia than for any child in the valley, because the fly-fishing lodge had at least allowed her to see other people, if not actually speak with them. Still, Patricia had cried without stopping for the first two weeks she'd gone to school, and refused to let anyone touch her. Now, in her second year, things for Patricia were, by that measure, a cinch.

She stuffed a shirt into her backpack, and said, "I hope that shit-eater Carlos doesn't bother me again this week."

"I didn't iron it for you to mess it up like that!" hollered Edith to Patricia from the floor, where she scrubbed Oscar's hair into a shampooed mohawk. Patricia took the shirt out and laid it on the table and began folding it along the creases left by her mother's stove-heated metal iron.

"Every time I go to the seesaw," continued Patricia, "he comes over and pushes me around. He's like a dog that sees a horse in the yard—he runs right over. Like a red-dicked dog, *che*. Just the same, I feel sorry for him because he has the whore's tongue."

I asked Duck what this meant. "Stutterer," he said evenly, all the while strumming his laconic tune. "He can't get the first word done before he's already thinking about the second."

"Listen, daughter," said Edith, raising her pointer finger, "that's all well and good. But that little rooster won't ever respect you till you pull the crest off his head. Don't ever make fun of him: clobber him. Once he respects you, *che*, you'll be friends." She wrapped Oscar in a towel and sent him to Duck for drying. "Next!"

Patricia and Mariana stripped down and hopped into the tub. Mariana took the soap bar and washed her sister's back. She squeezed shampoo into her hand and washed Patricia's long black hair, smiling as she did this. Edith sat Oscar on her leg and combed his hair and rubbed his brown body with white lotion. She fixed him with a cloth diaper and leggings and canvas sneakers and a little lamb's-wool sweater that still smelled of sweet lanolin.

When she was done, Edith mixed the remaining cold and hot water into another cauldron, and each of the girls stood and was rinsed before they climbed from the barrel. Duck wrapped them each in a towel; Edith put towels on their heads, like turbans, while Oscar took advantage of the distraction and ran to the cabinet, where he smeared his hair and face with handfuls of flour.

"No, you asshole!" roared Duck, slapping the guitar; and everyone, including him, laughed out loud at his sincerity—most of all Oscar. Edith brushed Oscar off and lifted his sweater and picked him up and dipped him by the feet into the tub, like an apple having the caramel applied. When she had him dressed again, and Patricia was dressed in crisp school jeans and a work shirt and boots, Edith sidled up to Duck and sat on his lap.

Underneath the window, Mariana sat on the throne with her legs dangling above the floor. With one hand she ran a comb slowly and lovingly through her wet hair; with the other, she held the severed sidemirror of a truck. She'd found it one day on the road, and it was the only mirror in the house. It was called El Nissan.

Duck watched her. "Let's get out of here," he said, gently pushing Edith from his lap. "Let's get outside."

It was raining lightly, and the sky was blue here and gray and moving there, and the tall grass was wet and the backs of the horses, and the sun shone above the family as they walked toward the river through the green grass. Bamboo grew thick and exotic along the banks, which had been left high and exposed by the receding waters of early autumn. The Cisnes here was glacial and scoured and a freestone stream, and the rocks that had been immersed and black a month before now stood baking and gray and with balding wisps of dried moss clinging to them.

The family followed the trail upstream, toward the rapids. Oscar rode his father's shoulders, and Mariana rode her mother's, and Patricia walked ahead, alone. They crossed a dry streambed that came in from the south, and they passed the corrals. At a break in the wall of bamboo, the family stopped and looked down into the stream. "Salmon," said Duck. The truck from Amengual would be there in a few minutes.

In the lee of a boulder, two king salmon, a buck and a hen, cruised and circled the break in the current as though in an aquarium. They were going white along the spine and black along the flanks, and their heads appeared hydrocephalic at the front of their depleted bodies. They were falling apart as we watched.

"They come every year," said Duck. "Must be the same ones."

I told him Pacific salmon die once they've spawned. He looked at me. I said they'd keep falling apart as they migrated, until there was nothing left.

"They're beautiful," said Patricia, taking Edith's hand.

"They're ugly," said Mariana.

"You can't eat them because they stink," said Edith.

"You mean," said Duck, "that they'll go all that way—all the way to Tapera, for example—for nothing? Just to die?"

I said, "They'll mate and the hen will lay eggs somewhere along the way, or maybe up at Tapera. The river's small up there, and the young'll have a better shot at survival." I said, "Down here, the river's too fast. There's no nutrients."

"If they make it," said Duck. "That's a big if. Up there, too, there's any number of problems waiting. Cormorants, eagles. Any number of bloodthirsty Indians wanting to have their way with them, *che*." He said, "That's . . ." but then he stopped speaking and listened instead. From a long way off came the sound of a car horn; the truck from Amengual pulled into the pasture in front of the cabin.

"Time to go to school," said Edith, and she let go of Patricia's hand.

"That's a long way to go for nothing," said Duck.

My grandfather used to say: "Life is astoundingly short. To me, looking back over it, life seems so foreshortened that I scarcely understand, for instance, how a young man can decide to ride over to the next village without being afraid that—not to mention accidents—even the span of a normal happy life may fall far short of the time needed for such a journey."

—FRANZ KAKFA

The Village

PART TWO

Messages

The Virus That Walks

For the first three weeks following the cattle drive, my life with Duck and Edith settled into what was, for the most part, a pleasing pattern. Every morning I would walk to their cabin from my tent, and the three of us would take *mate* and eat whatever meat and bread was left over from the day before. Then Duck would go to the temporary sawmill—a tarp tent with an electric circular saw that ran off a generator—that Carlos Asi had set up two hundred meters from the cabin. While Duck worked, Edith and I would divide the house chores between us: one day I would watch the children and make bread while she cleaned; the next day she would make lunch while I did the laundry. All the while, we would share *mate* and tell one another stories about our lives. Duck ended his day after lunch, which we ate together in the cabin, and after that we would all sit around and talk. On Tuesday nights, I cooked dinner; on Thursdays, Duck cooked. All meals, with the rare exception of pasta with mutton, consisted of mutton with onions and garlic.

Until the sawmill had been set up, Duck had had, by his own admission, little to do, and he welcomed the new diversion. Cattle and sheep take care of themselves for the most part, and for Duck the seasons had been divided between a few weeks of intense, often very dangerous work—midwinter calving, the long drives between Santa Elvira and the *veranada*—and plenty of time to sit around. What Carlos Asi was doing not only created more work in the short term, but it would also create more in the future, because with the money he made selling the wood in Coihaique—where both the slums and the downtown were being built up as fast as trees could be cut—Carlos planned to buy more cattle to graze on the newly opened land.

The only way that ranchers in places like Cisnes could hope to compete with Argentina and Brazil, where better road systems made ranching less expensive and more efficient, was by bringing larger numbers of cattle to market at once. The upshot was, in a way, that *latifundismo*—fencing the land into immense *estancias,* the thing that supposedly ended the gauchos' way of life—was just now coming to Aisén, a century after it had come to Argentina, because the more money men like Carlos had, the more land they would buy and fence. And Cisnes was full of uninhabited, unowned land.

Another way of looking at it was that ranchers in Aisén were making a second go of the idea of *industrias,* only this time the strategy was not to burn the forests, but to log them. The laws that governed the "settling" of Aisén had stayed largely the same since the time of Ibáñez, when anyone who could fence the land could have it. The lone exception was a 1997 law demanding that a small tax be paid to the government, a law that was to the advantage of the wealthy "industrialists," who were the only ones who could afford the tax.

In the rainy environment of nothingwinters like Santa Elvira, a second-growth *coigue,* which looks much like an oak, might need thirty years to reach one hundred feet tall and thirty-six inches around its base. Carlos had hired a logger from Coihaique, a man called Tequila, to fell as many *coigues* as he could on the west end of Santa Elvira. For the task, Tequila had a chain saw and a brace of oxen, which, because they have such soft feet, do not do well on the rocky soil surrounding the freestone Cisnes, ground that is also often very muddy, due to the springs that feed the river. When Tequila felled a tree, he would cut off the top—meaning the last eighty-five feet—because only the trunk is used to make boards; then he would use the oxen to drag the logs the mile or so to the mill, one log at a time. Though Tequila tried outfitting his oxen with hide booties to protect their hooves, they were constantly ruining their feet, which meant they had to be slaughtered and replaced. And this was only the beginning of the inefficiency of Carlos's—and many other—logging operations. By the time you added in the kerf waste (useless sawdust that piled up from the chain saw cuts and, later, from the circular saw as it cut the logs into boards) and the fell waste (those trees ruined when they collapsed under the fall of a neighboring tree) only about ten percent of the trees made it to market.

Despite all of this, the amount of boards that Duck had cut in the last year was somewhere in the tens of tons, and he stacked the boards into neat piles, using stickers—one-inch-by-one-inch wood squares—to separate the layers so that air could circulate through the stacks and dry the wood. It bothered Duck deeply, he said, that in the hundred years since the *industrias* had come and gone in Aisén, the only lesson that had been learned was that it was more financially sound to log than it was to burn. Duck was sure that as soon as Carlos could figure out a way to get a reliable road built into the *veranada,* he would start logging there, as well, and expanding his holdings in earnest. In the end, though, said Duck, it was none of his business. What could he do, aside from whatever he was told?

And all of it, frankly—Coihaique, the second coming of the *industrias,* even the road itself—seemed far away as Edith and I would sit and listen to the buzz of Duck's saw across the pasture. It seemed far away as I rode west on Carlos Asi's property and saw an unrelenting panorama of billowing forest in every direction, one that seemed to defy to the point of absurdity the efforts of two men and an unlimited supply of expendable oxen and a generator that was forever running out of gas.

But as far away as it all seemed, Duck was close, every day, to one undeniable truth: that he was cutting, at a snail's pace, the wood that was being used to expand the Center, a place both he and Edith wanted to go, but could not—not only because of the difficulty in getting there, but because the very lives they'd tried to build there for themselves four years before had all but fallen apart.

*   *   *

In order to break things up, Duck and I, when the weather was good, would take the afternoons to ride the trails that crisscrossed Santa Elvira's thirty-five hundred acres. He showed me hidden gravestones where people had been buried decades before, and he taught me to gallop and to jump and to canter. He showed me how to use a knife and a wooden mallet to shave the fractured horn from the toe and sidewalls and quarters of a horse's unshod hoof, how carefully to file the buttresses smooth, and how to slide the knife into the space between the sidewalls and the frog and remove the mud and dung that fills the space and comes away on the blade of the knife like a pancake. He taught me how to arrange weight along a packsaddle, and how to tie off the *chiguas* with a horse-hide strip forty feet long that he wrapped in a figure-eight knot and finished with a diamond hitch. Then, satisfied that I'd learned all that I needed to know in what Duck called my "week of gaucho training," he gave me Happy Slim to use whenever I wanted.

I had finally succeeded during one of our rides in getting Duck to hear me out on what I was doing at Santa Elvira. I told him it was important that he know because I couldn't quote him or write any of the details of his life unless he said it was okay. When I was finished explaining, he smiled. He seemed to think it was all a little silly, though he said I was free to write anything I wanted about him, then admitted it would be fun to have a "project," as he called it, helping me translate things and taking me along on upcoming cattle drives. When I told Edith, she said that she, too, had nothing to tell me that couldn't be shared as I saw fit, though she followed this with a comment that was much more pointed: she said, "Skinny, you're looking for the fifth leg on a cat," by which she meant I was wasting my time.

I wasn't sure on what she meant I'd be wasting my time until I added that, in order to get to know Cisnes better, I needed to start making rounds of the various neighbors who lived within a half-day's ride of Santa Elvira. Duck, who was sitting there when I said this, insisted that no one I found would be willing to talk to me. He added that it was my lesson to learn, though, and over breakfast from then on out, he would draw me simple maps depicting the points at which unnamed creeks met trails that, from there, climbed to ridges and disappeared into forests, and, several kilometers later, dead-ended at cabins.

When I got to one of these cabins, I would ride into the yard and clap, which is the accepted manner of announcing one's presence in Patagonia, though when anyone was home, the stamping of the horses and the barking of the dogs was usually enough to bring the occupants to the window. Sheep Shearings and his mother, a cattle dog called La Vieja, followed me on these trips, and they would set their haunches next to one another and pop their teeth at the circle of dogs around them. If there was a man in the cabin, he would call off his pack, and I would call off my dogs, and we would in this way be introduced to one another.

Then he would say, "Dismount," and we would go inside and sit on skins next to an open fire in the middle of the floor—Duck and Edith's cabin, alongside most in Cisnes, was very modern—and take turns going to the spring outside to fill the tea kettle.

They were tests of manners, these first visits to a hidden cabin in the mountains, and I wondered each time somebody stood there looking at me from the doorway if Duck would be proven right. It was not considered proper to ask someone personal questions until a relationship had been formed, and the relationship invariably grew from silence. If we spoke at all, it was about the weather and the herd, conversations that were routinely depleted within a few sentences.

But I would keep coming back, and in time the men I visited—seven of ten adults in Cisnes were men, by my count—would ask me to call them by their nicknames. Uncle Ya Ya and Tío and The Cripple were a few whom I visited regularly. And each of them eventually developed a nickname for me, as well—Brother-in-Law (a moniker the gauchos, because they didn't believe in marriage, used ironically with one another, and one that, considering my status as foreigner, they adopted in doubly ironic fashion) or Money (because I came from the "Funded States") or The German (because I'm tall and blue-eyed). Or, as Uncle Ya Ya called me, Mangi, which comes from the Italian verb *mangiari,* to eat, and translated as something like "necessary sustenance." ("Mangi" was Ya Ya's word for *pisco,* mutton, the female genitalia, and the only "neighbor" who ever visited him. I chose to take it as a compliment.)

Whatever the nicknames, the men and I would at some point thereafter begin talking about how we'd found ourselves together in a cabin in Cisnes. I would ask where their fathers and grandfathers had been born and what word they applied to themselves: gaucho or *indio* or *huaso,* Chileno or Argentino or, simply, *nada.* Sometimes we would have horse races (I was, by then, fond of riding to the point of near-obsession), or, in the case of Uncle Ya Ya, ride farther into the mountains together, to the claim shack where he'd been born, and to the grove of cottonwoods where misspelled gravestones marked the passing of three generations of his family, one of them his sister, who had died seven decades before, exactly one year after she'd been born.

Just as often as I found someone sitting in a cabin, though, I would peer in the windows to see that the *puesto* had been vacated long before. When I asked

Duck and Edith about this, they claimed always not to know why. They could not imagine, they said, where the inhabitants had gone. I knew Duck, particularly, was lying, because he would smile when he said this. When I pressed him about the inhabitants' whereabouts, he would say, "In the earth or to heaven, who knows?" then add that he couldn't be sure because he didn't believe in God. When I lost patience and said I wasn't concerned about his religious philosophy, but about what, if anything, had killed the people, he said plainly that it was hanta virus. "That or witches."

Hanta virus—or, as the gauchos called it, *el virus anda,* the virus that walks—is a microbe that incubates in rodent feces, urine, and saliva. From there, it uses air particles as vehicles to enter the human body, where it lodges in the lungs and is then—no one knows exactly how—replicated as it is carried throughout the body and back to the lungs. The symptoms while all of this is occurring are banal, and they normally do not arise until three or four weeks after infection. Once the symptoms set in the chances of survival are fifty-fifty, assuming immediate medical attention is sought. Which, if you're a gaucho in Cisnes, is next to impossible.

No matter who you are you're initially convinced you have the flu—headache, nausea, vomiting. Within days, though, the virus once again attacks the lungs, this time causing the capillaries to leak and causing death by drowning in one's own body fluids. Ironically, it's as simple to kill hanta virus as it is to die from it: though there is no cure, sunlight, fresh air, and bleach are its worst enemies. And, of course, developing antibodies, which happens to those who have been exposed, yet fail to develop anything more than a couple days of nausea and headaches.

For the gauchos, the virus, like the Devil, was an actual living and breathing entity. And it was the radio that, in a manner of speaking, gave hanta its voice. It's probable that until November 1997, when the Chilean Ministry of Health in Santiago and the Centers for Disease Control in Atlanta sent scientists to study hanta virus in Cisnes—and perform blood tests, which, according to a paramedic in Amengual, found nineteen of the hundred and nineteen people to be immune or infected, a statistic that, if you extrapolate it onto New York's seven million inhabitants, would come up just shy of five hundred thousand—none of the gauchos had ever thought much about the disease. Had you asked a man in

1996 or 1906 or 1886 what hanta virus was, the answer would have been the same as if you'd asked him what staphylococcus was. Once the virus had a name, though—and, more to the point, once *el virus anda* was established as a dominant character on Messages—its power became implicit.

For Duck and Edith, hanta was both one more reason not to remain in Cisnes and one more thing that kept them there. The virus that walks did not arrive from the Outside—although, according to the radio, it was rampant from Coihaique to Bariloche, Argentina—it emanated from the home, where it killed the gauchos for doing the most culturally characteristic things: getting tack from a musty storeroom, or taking refuge for the night in an abandoned *tapera*. As such, *el virus anda,* like the Devil, lurked in their minds, always a step ahead or a step behind, and always unseen. If the gauchos moved, the virus moved, too, and it became a kind of cautionary tale that no one could avoid: how *could* a young man decide to ride over to the next village without being afraid?

Neighbors who had at one time been happy when the swollen river began to ebb in the spring started wishing that the barrier would remain in place, so that those who were known to be infected would not visit. To be infected was to be *huaso,* which in this case meant unhygienic, and the hypocrisy of people's biases was as much of a plague as the disease itself. Duck and Edith, for example, wanted less than ever to have anything to do with Don Tito, who had spent six weeks in the hospital in Coihaique and was the only gaucho I'd heard of in Cisnes who had survived the infection, even though Duck himself had tested positive for immunity—meaning he, too, had "seen" the virus without being "caught."

Nor was I above having biases, and it was for this reason that I never stayed the night in any of the cabins I visited. It was also one of the reasons that, for the six weeks following the cattle drive, I resisted Duck's continual offers that I move into the storeroom of his cabin. If hanta was everywhere inside, I preferred to stay out.

* * *

In order to keep the bulls from trampling me while I slept, I had pitched my *puesto,* as Duck called the tent, next to the lodge, which was surrounded by a fence. If you looked from Duck's cabin toward the lodge you saw my aqua-green, two-man The North Face Leapfrog. The more Duck saw it, the more strenuously he insisted that I move into the storeroom of his cabin.

Hanta virus aside, I was not sure how much I trusted Duck and Edith. Or, rather, I wasn't sure how much I trusted myself to keep from making some kind of intolerable gaffe without even knowing that I'd made it. Add to this that I was in Patagonia to get a story which required both the ability to infiltrate Duck and Edith's lives as well as the ability to maintain some kind of distance, and remaining outside—even as I was dependent upon Duck and Edith to get the story—became an increasingly difficult line to walk.

There's a sort of debilitating uncertainty about everything in Patagonia. More people believe—and believe profoundly—in witches and in the Devil than believe in God. On a moonless night, you cannot, try as you might, see to put one foot in front of the other. It's so quiet at times that the sound of the horses and of the river are disproportionately loud. The wind howls downvalley, then is, ten minutes later, dead silent.

What's far more frightening than the idea of witches is the thing that people do to those who are suspected of being witches. There was a woman who lived deep in the mountains near Argentina with her two sons, who were twins in their forties, both mentally retarded. It was rumored that she had, by mothering the children of the Devil, wagered her sons' health in order to be a witch. Everything that went wrong in Cisnes—a death from hanta virus, a bad fall from a horse, a drunken knife fight—was blamed on her.

When I asked Duck how to get to the woman's cabin, he said, "She's not there." I asked where she had gone. "Looking for her body, I guess." He said a man whose brother had died of the virus that walks had gone to the woman's cabin and decapitated both her and her sons, and hung their heads in a burlap sack in the doorway. Then he buried the bodies a long way off so that, should they disinter themselves, they would never be able to find the heads, which were necessary to give the witch and her sons new life. When I asked Duck how he knew all this, he said a neighbor had stopped by one day while I was out riding and told him and Edith. He said the neighbor was the same one who had done it, which meant that it could have been any one of the people with whom I'd spent many hours. It could even, theoretically, have been Duck himself.

As the first two weeks passed, and fall began turning to winter, Duck spent less time at the mill and more time in the cabin. Sixteen hours a day in a single room with four other people—Patricia was at school in the village during the weeks—could, at times, be crushingly monotonous. The shelf-life of my Spanish-speaking ability normally deteriorated after the first eight hours, which could suddenly put all of us in a bad mood—me because I would, without warning, forget how to say the simplest things; Duck and Edith because they couldn't understand how I could go half a day speaking without pause, only then to be muted by a throbbing headache.

None of which was as bad as the feeling that Duck and Edith and I all shared: loneliness. No matter how much time we spent together listening to the news of the Outside on the radio, or catching glimpses of the neighbor across the river riding his horse, there was a constant, pressing urgency to the isolation. The radio programs invariably ended, and the neighbor invariably rode off into the forest and was gone from sight, leaving us with the disconcerting feeling that we had been left behind, alone, even as a whole, invisible world went somehow along its way.

Duck and Edith, in fact, lived closer than just about anyone else in Cisnes to the nearest cabin. Pork Rind and Juana (unlike men, women in Cisnes are rarely given nicknames) lived just twenty minutes away by horse, on the north side of the river, behind a grove of cottonwoods. They had three children, all of them girls, and all of whom had tested positive for exposure to hanta. The youngest daughter, whom Mariana referred to as Dumb-Dumb, was six years old and could not yet speak in complete sentences. Pork Rind also had four sons by another woman, all four of whom were, at that point, out of the house. The nickname applied to the most famous of those sons was John of the Cows; he was, as Pork Rind had been before him, a cattle thief, though John's legend had far surpassed that of his father.

John of the Cows was, during the austral fall of 1998, living at a *veranada* ten kilometers north of Carlos Asi's. John was another of the people in the valley who offered himself as an excuse for anything bad that happened, although so far he had been, alongside the murdered woman, much luckier. He did his stealing, according to the rumors, always in Argentina and always at night, and he sold the cattle to a woman in Tapera called Olga the Cheese Lady, who was herself a feared witch.

The thing that kept John alive, aside from being reclusive, was that he stole from the Argentine *patrones,* which is to say he stole not only from the wealthy, but from wealthy foreigners. Olga, in the same way, was considered okay because she had not been known to cast any spells beyond those that furthered her business—selling stolen beef—and that business did not affect Cisnes. It affected the Argentines.

Three weeks or so after Duck and I got down with the bulls, John of the Cows came to visit Pork Rind, and I rode across the river to introduce myself. I was expecting, as usual, an uncomfortable couple of hours spent sporadically talking about nothing—a couple of hours that would, if repeated often enough, convince John of the Cows that I could be trusted enough for him to answer questions, first about himself and his life and, with luck, about his stealing. What I got, right off, was much more. When I rode back across the river, I didn't waste any time getting to my tent to make a recording on my dictaphone of the conversation with John.

No sooner had I begun recording than I heard the gentle patter of feet on the grass all around me and the catching breath of little girls trying not to laugh. A minute after I started talking into the dictaphone, Mariana and Patricia began beating on the tent with bamboo limbs.

Patricia said, "Uncle, what are you doing?"

I said, "Talking to the machine."

Mariana said, "Uncle has shit in his head. Uncle talks to things."

"Uncle," giggled Patricia, "what are you saying to the machine?"

"I'm saying things your Uncle John said. And things he did."

"Like what?" said Patricia.

Mariana said, "Uncle of the Cows doesn't do *any*thing except drink *mate* all day and steal cattle!" Their laughter was cast backward, then forward as they looked to the house to see that no one had heard this. Mariana said, "Uncle, what are you *really* doing?"

Patricia said, "I'll bet he's doing something dirty in there."

Mariana said, "Patricia, Uncle doesn't do shit either except smoke cigarettes and take *mate*! Then he rides around on his horse."

"Uncle! Uncle! He's a brute!" they chanted, keeping time against the tent with their bamboo limbs.

Finally, the drumming stopped and I opened the rainflap and peered out. The whole family was standing there. Edith had Oscar in her arms, and Duck had Mariana by the hand. Patricia was standing between her parents and they looked, through the gray mesh of the tent's mosquito-proof zippered "door," like a black-and-white portrait of a family.

"What are you doing?" said Duck. He let Mariana's hand fall and hitched his thumbs in his belt loops.

"Oh," I said, "just telling the machine some stuff I heard John saying."

"Like what?" said Edith.

"Well, nothing really. It's more the way he said it, *che*. Like he was admitting something without admitting it."

They looked at one another. "Huh," said Duck.

Edith said, "Well, that isn't much of a story to be telling the machine."

"About stealing cattle?" said Duck.

I nodded. I said, "About the stealing. Only, it wasn't about the stealing. See what I mean?"

Duck said, "It sounds to me like you're piling shit up like a stallion."

Edith said, "How come?"

"How come what?" I said. I was getting defensive, though I tried not to show it. I said again, as nonchalantly as possible, "How come what, *che*?"

Duck said, "How come you're stuck on that? And how come you're not talking now, *che*?"

I said, "Because you're making me feel like an asshole because you're standing there, *che*."

Duck bent down and pulled back the flap and looked in the tent the way you'd look at a dead person—with a kind of unwilling interest. He said, "Either way, how come you don't get out of that Lago Nicolás and come inside the house, *che*? I mean, really," he said. "This place is a mess."

Duck also called the tent Lago Nicolás because I'd lined the floor with sheepskins that had needed only a week to build up a critical mass of humidity from the leaky ceiling, from the rains, and from the low dewpoint in the pasture to become a constant, soggy mess. The whole tent smelled like wet coals.

Duck unhitched his thumbs. He said, "I swear I don't understand the first thing about you, Nico."

The next day, the thought that I would ride out to visit the neighbors seemed suddenly to offend Duck, and he insisted we go together. He would, according to his plan, conduct an interview of questions I had prepared for him; all the while, he posited, the "machine" would be hidden in his shirt pocket. When I refused, he became indignant.

Duck knew as well as I did that the people I visited would never talk to me with the machine on the table in front of them. It's for that reason that I never took the Dictaphone with me, but preferred instead to write things down or record them when I got back to my tent. In addition to fear of hanta and a desire to understand Duck and Edith better before I slept within arm's reach of them, I knew that I'd never get anything written or recorded if I moved into the cabin. Living with them, I feared, would limit my ability to function as a journalist in another way, as well: it would make me just another member of the family. In the same way, I knew that if I started taking Duck with me on the daytrips, it would invariably make us the "team" that he wanted us to be.

Duck referred to whomever and whatever he didn't like—Tito and Alfredo, a brace of stubborn horses—with the only two words of English he knew: Team Fucking. He and I, on the other hand, were El Team*che*. It seemed impossible to tell him that, although we often spent sixteen hours a day together and were getting to be good friends, none of this made us a unit.

The key to Duck's "hidden machine plan," as he called it, was to show me how reactionary and "barbaric" "the neighbors" were, and, in this way, to foster some kind of solidarity between Duck and me. Duck was dying for a concrete incident to justify his dislike of the *viejos*. It would make it much easier for him to leave Cisnes if I, as representative of the Outside, could be shown, in front of Duck, the oppressively *huaso* world in which he was trapped. If Duck could get the machine and a *viejo* and the Outside all abutting one another in the same *puesto*—if he could wield the very thing that the *viejos* found intolerable—El Team*che* would finally rise above El Team Fucking.

What I hadn't realized was that, once I was in his world, my own survival was dependent upon the inverse of what Duck needed: I had to have the Inside as an ally—for the morning directions, for the horse I needed to follow those directions, for Duck's intimate knowledge of the people and the slang that they used, and that I needed, daily, for him to help me translate.

It was sunny on the afternoon I came back from John of the Cows', and when the family walked back across the pasture to their cabin, and I was again alone in my *"puesto,"* everything in the tent stood out in stark contrast. The white sheepskins, the dark brown sweater I'd bought from Julia, the pedestrian-yellow Walkman I listened to at night before falling asleep—all of it showed up in the aqua-tinted light of the tent like things seen through expensive sunglasses.

But what stood out the most to me was that hanta virus had all along moved invisibly through Duck's and my relationship, carrying with it the perfect and unseen metaphor. For Duck, Cisnes was like the virus that walks: all around him, though its effects had been forever unseen. And unnamed. Now, there was a name—El Team Fucking. Mario, the doctor in Coihaique, had told me that as soon as hanta was named, it became a "cultural epidemic," by which he meant its perceived power was increased tenfold. Duck had clearly wanted out of Cisnes long before I showed up. What was still unclear was whether, like hanta once it enters the bloodstream, my presence would circulate and, after a few days or weeks, be tolerated by Duck. Or whether I would come to represent for him everything he couldn't have—if the idea of the Outside, seen through me, would make Duck drown in his own desire for change. If that was the case, I wondered what Duck might do to rid himself of the infection.

*   *   *

One day while Edith and I were having *mate,* I said, "What do you think of, *che,* when you try and imagine New York?"

"Well," she said, "things I've heard about on the radio. Not so much how the city looks, really; more what goes on there. I imagine, if you'll catch this, the unimaginable. I imagine everything I've never known to be in one place, one small place, the size of a holding corral or something. Which is to say I don't *see* anything, because what's unimaginable is unimaginable. Catch it or don't catch it? Like, it's more of a feeling I get when I think about it."

I asked her if she would want to live there. "No," said Edith. "I mean, I've never been there, *che.* I've never seen it. How could I want to live there?"

I said, "In the same way, how could you know you *don't* want to live there?"

"That's a good point," she said. "But I do know. It's part of the feeling. It's a feeling like excitement for something I don't want. Something I would watch but wouldn't want to . . . enter."

I said, "Like a movie."

"Like a movie. Only, because I haven't seen many movies—maybe a half-dozen, and half of them animated—I don't know what that means, *che*. You know, life is the same all over. That's what I really mean to say," she said. "People are the same and life is the same, *che*. There's the same elements. So I can imagine a feeling that's the same feeling *I* have *here,* in Cisnes, because it's not really just the same shit, different smell. We say you wouldn't give a drunk the keys to the bodega. Where is that *not* true?

"Do I want out of here, Nico? Jesus yes. Do I want to go to New York or Santiago or Puerto Montt? No way. I don't know where I want to go. Coihaique, I guess. The world is going on all over. Everywhere but here. Just leaving here is the trick, Nico. I don't know. Sometimes I hear Duck say that, and I tell him that's wrong, too," she said. "Sometimes I feel like I've lived too long already."

Edith drank the *mate* and held it casually in her hand, wrist bent like a movie star with a cigarette. She smiled. "Did I ever tell you the story of how I had Oscar?" she said, slurping the last drop from the gourd. "That's how I know I'm half witch."

I could see Mariana through the door; she had taken a detour on her trip to get wood and gone to the middle of the pasture to stare across the river. She turned a somersault; perhaps she wanted someone to notice this. I shook my head as I watched her, and Edith began her story.

"So, two years ago, *che*," said Edith, "in the late winter, we have this rain. I mean: but did it *rain*! Days and days. Every centimeter of those mountains," she said, pointing at the wall of the cabin with her cigarette, "melted. And that *mountain* slid in pieces into this *valley* like God was peeing on them, or somebody had taken a giant hose," and she made swishing sounds and moved her hands back and forth, laughing. "And with that mountain and all that mud came trees, boulders, cows, sheep—you name it. I saw a *cabin* come sliding down that mountain! And all the rock they left from blasting that road, in case we don't have enough shit pouring off.

"And me, I'm eight months pregnant, *che*. And let me tell you something else," she said, patting Oscar on the head and raising her eyebrows, "this little goat is *ready*. He wants out. So Duck says, '*Che,* you're going to Coihaique on the next bus, and no questions asked. We're not going to invite Luther to give mass,'" she said, which in Chile is a common way of saying that one should avoid obvious trouble.

"Well, I didn't like that idea, catch it? The last pregnancy, Mariana, had been hard. I'd had bleeding problems, and had to stay on for weeks afterwards. Now with the stock just calved and falling in the holes, what kind of time is that to be gone, *che*? What if I have to stay in the hospital again like the time before?" she said. "And never mind if something happens to Duck while I'm gone. The girls would starve to death. But Duck won't let up. He keeps saying, 'You're not going to lose this child. *We're* not going to lose this child.'"

I said, "And what if you'd had bleeding problems out here? What then?"

"Well," said Edith, "that's a good question. And the answer is that there was another motivation for not wanting to go. I'm scared, *che*. I'm scared because I've never taken the bus to Coihaique alone, except that time when I was thirteen and my mother made me go to school there. I mean, Coihaique's a long way away, catch it? It had been three years since I was in that place. My father could've been dead. And if he was, I'd have never heard about it."

Mariana came in with a load of wood and went to her seat in the corner behind the stove. Edith watched her. She said, "I mean, you get on that bus and it's like the whole world is passing by, *che*. I get a few kilometers out of here and one horse trail looks like the next, and I say, 'Excuse me, but have we already passed Don Tito's?' and the woman next to me says, 'Oh! That was way back there, *señora!*'" It reminded me of the day I'd come to Santa Elvira to find her and Duck: it had been three years since the last time I'd been on that road, and, as soon as Señor Mansilla's bus had passed Mañihuales, I felt like I didn't know where I was. Everything had looked the same.

Mariana came over, and Edith put her arm around her. She played with Mariana's hair, and Oscar tried to slap the hand down. "Shhh, child," said Edith quietly. She began braiding Mariana's hair. When she'd finished, Edith inserted her finger in the braid and pulled it straight down, as though gutting a small bird. Mariana said, "Ow!" and looked at her mother. Her hair hung as it had before.

"So. To resume with the soap opera: We all one day file up the trail to the road, me and Duck and the girls, me waddling like a duck myself, fat, fat, fat. And we wait in that fucking rain for the bus, and the bus doesn't come. I find out later Mansilla hardly made it out here for the dead animals blocking the way. Finally, about four in the afternoon, here comes Trusty Mansilla. I got on the bus, sat down next to this old squaw, and she took a look at me and my tummy and crossed herself, and God on a Wednesday if that didn't make me feel good.

"But off we go. A half hour later it's practically night, or more like a long, long dusk—that's what it was like in those days, every day a long dusk it seemed— and I'm looking out the window feeling nauseous and looking for any clue, anything I can see that places me in the world. Late that night we got to Coihaique. And I went up the aisle of the bus to Trusty and I said, 'Sir, I came to find my father, and he lives up in such and such slum, could you take me there?' 'Of course,' he says, and let me down at the very door I came looking for."

"Just a minute. Sorry," I said, "but what do you mean, 'such and such a slum,' *che*? What's it called?" I wanted to know where Black Carl lived, so that I could go find him one day.

Edith said, "Nothing escapes you, does it?"

"You're not normally one to avoid details, catch it? Unless," I said, "you want to."

"I catch it," said Edith. "You catch it, too." Then she pretended I'd never asked her. She said, "I don't know why, but it's always late at night when I come to my father's house—wherever that is, *che*—and he about had another stroke when he saw me standing there. We marched straight to a cousin's down the block and she put me in her bed with her, and starting then I didn't sleep for two weeks. All day and night she and I sat at the table smoking cigarettes and listening to that radio. One minute, the death toll is rising; the next report has Cisnes unapproachable but, miraculously, with no reported deaths. Those birds didn't know *what* was happening. They were probably getting crazy calls from every gaucho out here with a radio telling of God knows what. I swear there was one who tried to build himself a boat, like Noah! Or at least that's what the radio said.

"So I just said to myself and to my cousin both, 'I'm going back.' My cousin said, 'You'll give the light en route, woman,' and I said, 'I'll close it off. I won't let him come out till after I see everything's okay and I get back here.' I knew it was the will of God.

"So two weeks after getting to Coihaique," said Edith, "I went to Mansilla's house. He looked at my stomach and told me he wouldn't sell me a ticket. Besides, he said, he'd barely gotten past Amengual on the road the week before, and he wasn't taking a woman from Coihaique to Amengual to have a baby."

Edith was running her fingers through Mariana's hair, and, although Edith couldn't see it, Mariana was trying hard not to cry. It's then that I realized how wrong I'd been about something. I'd always thought that Mariana and Patricia, even Oscar, failed to understand much of what they heard and saw in the cabin. I had thought that the extreme close range of events had to make it a bit blurry to them, had to come to them myopically. But life in a single room is painfully focused, right down to the smallest details. And there was never an attempt to shield them from the arguments or the stories or the fights or any of the things that came out of two people's attempt to change the very nature of their lives. How could it be any different? Where could they go to avoid seeing their parents' lives in absolute detail?

Mariana caught the breath in her throat, trying not to let out a sob. "Shhh, sweetheart," said Edith. "Everything I've ever done was for you and your sister, child. I'd do anything in the world. Don't you see that?"

That, I think, is precisely what Mariana saw, and the pressure of it was too much.

Edith said, "So I say to Trusty, 'Okay, I'll go to the other bus driver's house, the one who passes by Amengual on the way to Puyuhuapi, and he'll take me. And then I'll wait in Amengual for a jeep going past Santa Elvira.' 'Well, now,' says Mansilla, 'that'd be crazy! You won't find a jeep headed in there! That's insanity, *señora*.' 'Well,' I say, and I know by the look on his face I've got myself a bus driver.

"So back we come, *che*, me and Mansilla, and there isn't another soul on that bus; and I'm thinking, 'Ha! Me in my limousine! Imagine that!' And I think hard about this because the only other thing to think about is night's coming.

"Now. I haven't gotten to a certain point yet I was saving because now it's important. Not only do I need to fix my teeth, Skinny, I've got cataracts. I'm more bat than *mujer, che*. We say, 'Blacker the night never was for a man without calluses on his hooves.' That means when a man not used to traveling finds himself in unknown territory he's in trouble, *che*. Finally, Trusty calls back to me. He says, '*Señora,* we've arrived.' I look around through the windshield and all I see is blackness, and a fence running along with the headlights that disappears on up there a ways. I say, 'You sure?' 'Santa Elvira, *señora.*'

Then he looks at me and he says, 'I won't let you out of this bus. That gate is locked, and you don't have a light and I'm taking you to Tapera. If the weather's good, we come back tomorrow. There can't be anything here at this hour a pregnant woman can't live without, *señora.*' Dirty bastard. And he reaches to put the bus in gear, and I say, 'Oh no you don't,' and I grab that door thing and swing it open and waddle down the steps. Before he can stop me, I'm over the fence, God knows how, I'm surprised Oscar didn't come flying out of me right then and there.

"Now I can't see shit, but I go down the trail and I stand there wondering what to do. After a while, Trusty gets down out of the bus, and he's yelling at me to get back in for God's sake, you crazy woman. But I'm a hundred meters down the trail, and he can't see me, and I don't say a word. He probably thinks I'm in the cabin by the fire, and pretty soon he drives off.

"I was standing there in the pitch black, not moving because I knew something was wrong. So I take a step forward and a voice says to me, 'Wait.' I take another step and the voice says, 'Wait.' And I asked the voice, I said, 'This the right trail?' and he just says, 'Wait.' *Bueno.* I say, 'Could you maybe give me an idea about how long?'

"And that's when I see this light coming. 'Holy Christ,' I'm thinking, 'here He comes. The Devil himself. That's whose voice it was! That's what I knew was wrong! The Devil's in this place!'

"So I turn around, but I can't see any better in that direction, and I'm stuck, and I look back and here comes the light, and the horses start huffing and stomping.

"I get down to my knees like a blind beggar and start looking around for something, a stick or a rock, anything. And when that light gets closer, I hear a voice and it says, 'Who's there!' 'Duck?' I called. 'Duck?' But he goes around me wide, and then he's standing next to me and he says, 'Woman, you're more stubborn than a one-eyed horse—what are you doing here?' I say, 'I'm standing here in the cold because I didn't want to take another step,' and he gives me a hug like he never has and never will again I don't think, and he shines the light ahead of me, and there, taken right out of the trail, is a hole must have been seven, eight meters deep. Even *I* could see it with the help of the light."

Edith patted Mariana on the rear end and got up and handed Oscar to me. She said, "So that's what I mean about feelings versus seeing, see. Sometimes I get a feeling about going to Coihaique."

Oscar and Mariana watched her, waiting.

"I think of Duck and me sometimes," said Edith. "I think of that night, *che,* and those holes in the road. Sometimes, no matter who you are, not in a thousand-thousand years would you ever see what you were walking into."

CHAPTER EIGHT

El Colo Colo

The hens had been laying, and we had, for the time being anyway, a few eggs. Edith fried them in a pan, and cut *lomo*, thin slices of mutton taken from the loin, and rubbed the hot surface of the stove with ewe fat, cooking the *lomo* in the grease. The fried eggs she then served on top of the meat. It was a special delicacy called "poor man's loin."

And it was the very fact that I was—that we all were—so happy to have some eggs to break up the strict diet of mutton and bread that made me very uncomfortable. Duck's monthly wage was divided between cash ($120) and meat, he was allowed to slaughter one ewe per month, free of charge. Any extra food that the ranch manager brought from Coihaique—pasta, hot sauce, tomato paste—was automatically deducted from the $120. It was costing Duck and Edith a good portion of their wage to feed me. For one thing, Duck now had to slaughter a ewe every three weeks, and the ranch manager was charging him the difference.

As often as I thought it would not be offensive, I had offered to pay for my meals, though Duck and Edith both refused. But money was still a constant presence, and for every conversation we didn't have about it, there were ten on the radio talk shows we listened to all day. The context was always the same: that while the Asian crisis was pummeling the Chilean and Argentine economies, the United States was not only flying above the turbulence but with its seemingly inexhaustible capital, was producing bombs to drop on Iraq. I knew as well as Duck and Edith that the connection between me and the "Funded States" was irresistible. They never said anything about it—and many gauchos that I visited often did, normally by proclaiming Americans, me included, to be "shitting silver"—which almost made it worse.

After eating the eggs that day, Edith finally said, "Skinny, Duck and I were talking last night, and we're ready to take you up on your offer." She smiled. "Maybe if you start paying, you'll shut up about it."

She said they'd figured it cost $3.50 a day to "keep me alive," and then she walked over to the cabinet, where she kept a notebook of their monthly finances and showed me her calculations. "I was wondering," she said, "if you could pay in dollars. The radio says that's better because of the exchange rate."

I said I'd be happy to.

"Not on drives," said Duck. "On drives I'm taking you to work for me, assuming you won't lose the herd and I have to pay for it, and that food's paid for. Deal?" We shook hands and then Duck changed the subject. He said, "Now that the hens are laying, we might get a brown one. In that case, we throw it under the lodge, *che*."

"That won't do any good," said Edith. "It'll *still* be us that have to kill the Colo Colo. There hasn't been anyone in that lodge in weeks. You're long on plans and short on good planning, *che*."

Many times I'd heard people in Cisnes refer metaphorically to brown eggs. I said, "What's all this brown egg business?"

Duck said, "You haven't heard the story of the Colo Colo, Nico? It's the most famous story in Chile. There's a Chilean soccer team named for it."

"It's not just a story," said Edith.

"Well," said Duck. "This story comes from the central valley, near Santiago."

"I don't know what kind of people name themselves after this," said Edith.

"Seems there was this couple living in the country," said Duck. "And one day the wife or him or one of them goes to the chickenhouse and comes back with a brown egg.

"He says, 'The rooster laid a brown egg.' 'Like hell the rooster laid an egg,' says the wife. So they're looking at it, and they don't know what to do. Do they eat it? Because a poor man's *lomo* might be nice to eat. But the more they look at it, the more they know something isn't right."

"It doesn't take the president to know a brown egg out of a rooster's ass isn't right," added Patricia.

"Right, *che*," said Duck. "So they throw it away. Only, they throw the thing under the house.

"And pretty soon, things start going bad. Nothing anyone can put his finger on. They get bored with one another. Just sort of general unhappiness. Then things really go to hell. Fighting, all kinds of things. And then they start to wonder if it wasn't the egg that's responsible. And they fight about that, too.

"Once they get in their heads that the egg is the cause of the problems, they start blaming one another for the decision to put the thing under the house. Meanwhile, there's something happening down there. Because under the house, that egg has hatched this monster. It's a snake, see, the Colo Colo, and it's growing under there like a cancer. Actually, it isn't just a snake; it's more like all things bad wrapped into one. It even has wings, though I don't think it can fly.

"But here's the thing: it doesn't grow by killing. It grows on their unhappiness. They can hear it down there moving at night. They can see the floor of the house moving as this thing moves.

"Now the arguing starts in earnest, *che*. Or, what really happens is, they don't even talk to one another anymore, which is much worse than arguing. No one'll leave the house for fear of getting eaten by the Colo Colo. And here's the worst part: they know they can't kill it by themselves. They have to kill it with the help of the neighbors—same as the shit they tell you in church, that you can't get it done alone. Only, in this case, it's true."

"How do they know that?" I asked.

"I don't know. Maybe there had been another Colo Colo before under someone's house, and they knew because of that. Maybe they found out in a dream that this was the way. I don't know; what matters is they still think the problem is with the monster, not with them.

"So. One day the man can't take any more. He just can't right himself. He says, 'I'm going for help.' And the woman couldn't care less. She'd just as soon have the man dead, because of the terrible things they been doing to one another."

I said, "What kind of things, *che*?"

Duck looked at Edith and looked away. "I don't know," he said. "Just bad." Edith took Oscar up into her lap and held him there, like a shield.

Duck said, "So this gaucho makes a run for it. He doesn't even have a horse to go get help. They ran off a long time back, along with the chickens and the cows and the sheep. Everything gone, gone, gone, *che*."

"What have they been eating?" I said.

"One another. Feeding on themselves, on their unhappiness. Just like the Colo. So he makes it past the cabin and past the fence and out to the trail, and he's thinking, 'Shit, *che*, I ought to just get the hell out of here and never come back.' He's so relieved to be out of that cabin, man, he doesn't ever want to go back.

"So he decides he'll go to the neighbors' place and borrow a horse, and off he goes. But, see, he can't take the guilt. Now that he's outside, all he can think of is what's back there still on the inside.

"The neighbor tells him they have to burn the cabin down to get the Colo Colo out, *che*. When the Colo runs—or slithers, or whatever he does—they have to kill him with their knives and hoes. If they miss the Colo—and he's fast—he'll end up under the new house they build. They basically have one chance.

"So, they round up some other neighbors and go back to the cabin the next night with their torches and their knives and hoes and lassos."

Duck stopped there and leaned back and crossed his legs. He played his fingers against the *mate* and then he passed it to Edith. The story, it seemed, was over.

I said, "So what happens?"

"I don't know," said Duck.

"What do you mean you don't know?" I looked at Edith. "What does he mean he doesn't know?"

"No one knows," said Edith. "It depends on the family. Maybe they got the woman out and burned the house and killed the Colo Colo. Maybe she wouldn't come out and they burned it with her in there, to keep the Colo from getting her in the end." She said, "Maybe it escaped, *che*."

Duck said, "There isn't one end, Nico."

"Yeah," I said, "but there's an end to *this* story, and then maybe another one to another Colo Colo story, right? There's a different end to each one, right?"

"We're so poor," laughed Duck, shaking his head, "we can't afford an ending."

✿

An Altar in the Headlights

The lodge had been locked up since late February, though its presence was not unfelt. It seemed to dominate the landscape, silhouetted against the river and the glaciers and the shifting walls of fog that moved in and out of the valley. We felt it every time we walked through the rain across the yard behind Duck and Edith's cabin to take a freezing shower in the chickenhouse. Just before dusk, the sun shone like a headlight on the lodge's black roof and dark-honey sides, and it reflected in the white-framed windows before disappearing behind the mountains.

The lodge was only a hundred meters from Duck and Edith's cabin, though even when it was open, they rarely, out of embarassment or envy or dignity, ventured there. Its interior and its workings were, like those of distant Coihaique, largely invisible. And all the more compelling.

When Duck and Edith and I one day heard a car engine stop and then start again up on the road, as though the driver had gotten out to open Santa Elvira's most distant gate, we all looked at one another. When we heard the engine coming closer, we rushed to the window in time to see Rex coming through the second gate at the end of the pasture. He had, indeed, after a monthlong dry spell, gotten a last client for the year. His truck bumped through the pasture, and Duck and Edith and I watched as he went. He waved, but he didn't stop.

We sat down again. We didn't say anything. The door was open, and we listened to the two men's voices as Rex unloaded the client's bags and the food they'd brought for the week. I wished that Luisa, the lodge cook, had come with them, because she liked to pass the time in Duck and Edith's cabin when she wasn't working, where she felt more comfortable, more among her own, than she did in the lodge. Her presence would, I figured, lessen the shock of the Outside suddenly coming to Santa Elvira. But she'd not come—there was no reason to have a cook for just two men.

Duck said to me, "You bored?"

"No," I said, though he and I knew better. We were all bored. The weather was getting bad in the mountains, and Duck was anxious to go back for the rest of the herd before it got too dangerous. That, too, was a source of contempt, for Alex, the ranch manager, had to give the okay for the drive to begin, and he was intolerably irresponsible. Duck tried daily to raise Alex on the radio to tell him that it was getting too late in the year to bring five hundred head of cattle back down through the pass. But Alex was more concerned with "maximum yield" from the grass, and he either disregarded Duck's requests or failed altogether to answer the radio.

"Yes you are too bored," said Duck.

I didn't say anything. I had, despite the day-trips to the neighbors and the fact that I slept in my tent, been a constant guest in their cabin for four weeks. Yet Duck had also begun to be less willing to tell me where neighbors lived so that I could go visit them. He seemed, in this way, to want me around more, instead of less. I supposed that these trips served to remind him that I, at any point, could hitch to Coihaique and, if I so chose, leave the country altogether.

I had no intention of doing that. What I wanted more than anything was to walk over to the lodge and see Rex, who was a friend of mine and who, more to the point, was someone with whom I might, for just ten minutes, speak English, thereby reestablishing my connection with a place and a time—the United States and the twentieth century—that I'd been away from for what seemed a very long while.

Mariana was asleep on the couch. With the failing light of the short Patagonian fall, she'd begun sleeping fifteen hours a day. I looked at her, and looked away. I didn't want Duck to see me do this. I was surprised when he said, "Why don't we go and have a big time in Amengual tonight, Nico?"

"What's in Amengual tonight, *che?*" I said.

"Shearing's over for the year," he said, "and there's any number of Indians in the schoolhouse tonight, booze and dancing, *che.*" He looked at me. He said, "All we have to do is get there."

I knew he'd not mentioned the party all week because he'd not wanted to ride the four hours on horseback to get to Amengual. And hitchhiking was not a good option because traffic on the road, following the summer (when it might exceed three or four trucks a day) had been reduced to three or four trucks every week. Now here was a truck just across the pasture. And I knew the owner.

Duck said to Edith, "Do you want to go? We'll take the kids."

She shook her head again. The thought seemed to scare her. I didn't want whatever it was to cause a rift between him and Edith. But the only thing that was clear was that, if I refused—and I didn't want to for any number of reasons—it would be very uncomfortable. Twenty minutes later, Duck and I were zooming along the Argentine Road toward the village.

Duck picked up a Gipsy Kings cassette off the floor and put it in the tape player. Stands of second-growth *leña* and *coigue* floated above the road and rocked in the evening wind; their leaves turned in the photochromatic light and flickered first silver then green then black and silver again. When the music started, Duck played time against the dashboard with his fingers, and said, "Gallop!" I pushed the accelerator. At the blind turn just above Don Tito's cabin, I downshifted. "No!" hollered Duck, "don't slow down at the turns. Speed up!"

At the confluence of the Southern Highway and the Argentine Road, a new green road sign bordered in reflective white marked The Crossing, as it was called, and listed, absurdly, the distances in kilometers from that anonymous point in the middle of the mountains to places that were, by sheer virtue of their immense remove from The Crossing, far more inconsequential: Coihaique, 110; Mañihuales, 40; Santiago, 1,000; Arica, 1,600. Next to the sign, an elaborate wooden altar sat housed in a conspicuously well-tended wickiup made of hand-rubbed wood. The altar was covered in tens of tens of candles and empty bottles of beer, and the candles had been lit by the passing gauchos on their way to the party.

Duck buttoned the collar of his shirt ceremonially and checked his hair in the side mirror. The anticipation was intense. We crossed the stream below Amengual, and fog rose from it, as it likely did at that moment for all the miles of its course and the varied courses of its tributaries, which ran like circuit cables through the uninhabited area of the mountains the gauchos called the Inside. Fog stuck to the trees and the hills all around, and we climbed the long, winding approach to the village. Duck said, "This was a great idea, *che.*"

When we got to Amengual, Eulogio, the village idiot, was seated in the window of his mother's house, just as he'd been a month before when I'd passed through in Señor Mansilla's bus; Duck and I turned left at the stop sign onto the 100 block of Calle Miguel Opazo, where, as yet, there were no houses. Opazo was Amengual's main street, and it was configured in a rough circle. All other streets in the village began and ended there, each carefully marked with signs.

As we came around toward the school, dozens of horses, some still saddled and dragging their reins along the ground, wandered through the dim beam of the headlights. In the haze, hovering inches above the little soccer field in front of the church, loomed several tarp tents and a brace of Toyota pickup trucks. A generator hummed and spit, filling the school with light. I pulled onto the soccer field, and, before the engine of the truck had stopped thumping and shaking, Duck was out the door. We smiled at one another. There was nothing in the world like a party, it seemed, to change the course of things.

*   *   *

The smell in the doorway of the schoolhouse was like a wall of damp wool and wet hair and long trips on horseback. The townswomen were making *empanadas,* fried meat cakes, in their cabins and bringing them through the back door on trays as fast as they could, and the intense, pleasing familiarity of the smell was like a memory blurred in your head that had become suddenly and overwhelmingly clear. The movements of the crowd, the smell, the lights—even the steps of the men dancing, and the rise and ebb of their collective voice in that little room—all of it had been choreographed like any party, and yet it was like none I'd ever witnessed. After not having seen more than a couple of people at a time for so long, the effect of so much movement in one place was disorienting.

An impromptu bar had been set up in the first classroom; a three-man band, two guitarists and an accordionist, stood in the corner playing Mexican *ranchera* and Colombian *cumbia,* high-pitched tunes at which the guitarists picked in tandem, stalking the whining accordion and overtaking it and riffing and then falling back in its wake.

In the back classroom, dozens of bowlegged gauchos sat at tables and at children's desks. All week, they had been quietly arriving in Cisnes. They'd come on horseback down from the nothingsummers, and they'd come from Argentina, riding alone or in pairs or five or six abreast and pushing hundreds of sheep ahead of them in a fog of dust and the dissonant padding of hooves. And, at the same time that they sheared the sheep in sneezy, crowded *galpones,* they had peeled back the layers on their own lives, for many of the gauchos had families in Cisnes and in Coihaique and across the border, and the young men and boys that worked in those barns and were now at the party were their sons whom they'd not seen in years, and maybe never.

The men and boys alike were washed and red-cheeked and unshaven. Some wore new-shorn mohawks, and others wore their hair to the shoulders, and none but the smoothest-faced teenagers were without a mustache. They wore chaps of every color and hide—cocoa-brown-and-white Hereford calfskin and mahogany, curly goat, and some in mixed sets of butchered coltskins, Palominos and Bays and skewbalds. There was one man who was not five feet tall, and his nose had been splattered across his face by a kicking bull and never reset. The uppers of his boots came up over the thighs in the style of the conquistadors; he'd decorated the borders with intricately woven locks of horsetail that jigged and swayed. Some wore boots cut from foal hocks, stained brown here with age and bleached there with watermarks from river crossings. They had wide brown belts under which they hid their "necessaries"—money and matches and small-arms cartridges—and under these they wore woven wool cummerbunds tucked into pants of pinstriped wool. A man who patiently watched the others from a corner and sipped his *pisco* wore a shirt of purest indigo, and he set his glass on the table and sat down and fell asleep on his crossed forearms.

The women arrived a few minutes later. Until then, aside from the cooks bringing *empanadas,* the party had been all men, and the new arrivals came carrying babies and holding the hands of little boys already bowlegged from having learned to ride at the same time they'd learned to walk. The women wore jeans and riding boots, and some of them wore long black skirts and bright, multicolored ceremonial ponchos. Most of them lived in Amengual and raised the children of men whom they saw only once or twice a year.

The band played its way out of the corner and moved to the improvised dance floor, and the music stopped; there were chairs and little desks against three of the walls, and the gauchos sat down in them. A door was opened onto another small, well-lit room to the left of the bar. This room, too, was filled with chairs. Two dozen women and girls went into the new room and sat down. When the music started, a group of men went in and offered their hands. The number of men was five times that of the women, and those who had not risen waited patiently in their chairs and passed batteries of wine.

The dancers formed two lines separated by sex, and stood waiting while the band members conferred and wiped their foreheads on their sleeves, and the accordionist knocked his heel against the floor. At the fourth jangle of his spur, he filled the instrument with air and squeezed it easily together and played for several seconds before the guitarists deftly joined him in a rousing, quick-fingered fugue.

The dancers took short, stuttered steps, and they were light on their feet, and the men approached the women and the women approached the men and they did not touch. They were inches from one another and they danced in place and then they retraced their steps backward and came together again and again in a ritualized imitation of a rooster courting a hen. When the music stopped, the women retreated into the side room and sat down. At some unseen signal, a new batch of men rose and lingered briefly in the women's room before emerging arm in arm and taking their places, as had the men before them, in a line across from their partners. Duck was among them.

So, too, were three tall young gauchos who wore their hair short and black. They had steep, open faces into which were etched feline eyes like perfectly symmetrical seeps in a cliff. Their cheeks were red with drink, and they might have been brothers, though they gave no indication beyond the similarities in their faces and mannerisms, which were languid and fluid. Next to them, Uncle Ya Ya hobbled in a circle, testing his old legs for the dance, or like a dog about to make its bed. Duck nodded to me from the middle of the line as though to say, "Watch this." The music started.

It was clear from the outset that the chemistry of this group was decidedly more derelict than that of the previous set. They stutter-stepped forward and came in for a landing. But then two of the boys twirled about in front of their partners, and so taken were they with this move that they were late in completing the backward steps from which the separate lines were formed once again. Not to be outdone, Duck bent his knees and crossed his arms in front of his chest and did a Russian jig.

Halfway through the tune, the rules had disintegrated altogether and the lines swayed like algae in a river. The women blushed and smiled, and the three tall young men grabbed other men's partners and spun them around, and now it was clear they were brothers who had long ago danced together in the same shack to music on the radio, and had developed a characterizing set of steps. It was clear, too, that they had not seen one another in some time. With the dance, though, they grew familiar and they egged one another on by sticking out their chins in time to the sharp cuts of the accordion. They high-stepped backward and came forward once again. They stalked around the backs of the women and looked down provocatively at their backsides, and Ya Ya clapped his arthritic hands above his head. "Ya ya ya ya ya yaaaaah!" he called, then brushed self-consciously at his white mohawk.

Duck, to my delight, was the best of them all. His was a motley amalgam of many dances and none at all, Russian and Mexican and Irish and Jewish and disco. In his starched denim, the shirtsleeves rolled up haphazardly and the collar buttoned like a priest's, and his white tennis shoes, he was like an emissary from some other planet or some other time, and he made himself not only welcome but the absolute focus of the party by clearly not giving a shit about anything in the whole world, neither the one he occupied nor any other. The three young men surrounded him and clapped and jigged in place and backed off, and one of them imitated Duck's steps while the others just watched him go, there at the center of their undulating circle.

*   *   *

I went into the back room. It was quieter there, and the men sitting around at children's desks and at long tables of wood looked up at me. They were playing a card game called Trick, in which the winner, generally speaking, was the best liar.

A young man called to me from where he and three others sat in their chairs with their arms rested across the backrests. There was a bottle of *pisco* on the floor between them. They were all four tall and thin, and they wore their hair long and black so that their height and wiriness were enunciated more clearly still. They might have been Sicilian were it not for their eyes, which were dark-rimmed, like Egyptian figures on the walls of tombs.

The leader—who, at eighteen or nineteen years old, appeared to be the youngest of the group and wore his hair braided with horsehide, like an Indian—reached down and handed me the bottle of *pisco*. I profoundly felt that I had never before seen them; I was sure of it. But I was also somehow sure that I had. It was easy, in Patagonia, to get caught between what was familiar (where is the smell of frying food or the offer of drink at a party as a means of introduction not ubiquitous?) and wanting to feel kinship in a place that was as far from familiar as I could imagine.

I said, "Where do you come from?"

"East*che*," said the leader, as though, wherever he went, he were the absolute center of the world.

"All of you?" I said.

He looked around, smiling and nodding. "*Todos*," he said. "Tehuelched the mountains," he said, by which he meant they had, like the nomadic Tehuelches who had been long before wiped out in Cisnes and neighboring Chubut, Argentina, wandered through one of the many passes.

I said, "Do I know you?"

We sat there, drinking *pisco*. I remembered my grandmother and the smell of fried catfish in the summers and the faces of her three brothers, all of whom were dead.

"Do we know *you*?" He smiled.

*   *   *

Although John of the Cows had not come, one of his uncles had, and he, too, was dancing. He was called The Cripple, and he was the finest shearer in the valley. He had a man's torso and a big head, and his ropey, simian arms hung much of the way to the floor, for his body below the waist was that of an eleven-year-old, and his legs were deeply bowed. He wore rubber boots with the pants tucked in, and the boots came nearly to his thighs. With this incongruous quilt of a body, The Cripple could shear two sheep for every one that another man could. It was as though he'd been genetically engineered for the task, for the passer would slide a ewe his way and The Cripple would sit on her heaving flank, and his bowed, foreshortened legs were just long enough that he sat her like a bike. And with his boxer's forearms and massive hands he worked the manual shears with startling precision. Then he'd take the ewe and rise on his little legs, and grab her by the shorn scruff of the neck and slide her out from under him, one-handed, to be harried back onto the *pampa*.

I sat against the wall, and the quiet man in the indigo shirt who'd long before passed out onto his forearms and woken up sat down next to me; we watched The Cripple pull himself onto a table and dance, flailing his arms like a terrestrial Man-o-war. The man next to me was called The Black, and his skin was the color of an Atlanti olive. He wore navy-blue wool pants, and over these the flour-cured ebony skins of a wild boar. I'd seen him only once, and no one seemed to know where he lived, because he would pop up here and there to work for a time and then disappear again. He'd worked once for the Frenchman up above the Río Moro, who, after escaping the Nazis, had flown for the RAF in World War Two and then emigrated to Patagonia and bought a ranch. From the Frenchman, The Black had taken in payment the headgear for which he could be recognized at a distance: an aviator's leather helmet lined with wool. He passed me a bota bag of white wine mixed with crabapple *chicha* and said he'd ridden from Río Mayo, Argentina, with a string of colts he'd put to graze in the churchyard, though he didn't say why or when, and I didn't ask.

The man whose nose was smeared across his face drunkenly parted the dancers and stood in front of me where I sat. He wore a big mustache, one side of which appeared shorter than the other because of the grotesque miscentering of his nose. His face was squat, like a frog's, and his cheekbones curved deeply along the sides of his head.

Several times he started to say something, and burped and screwed up his face as though in pain from indigestion. He closed his eyes tight and nearly fell over backward and opened them wide and nearly fell over frontward. I looked at the The Black. "Be patient," he said dryly. "It must be something important."

When finally the man did speak, he slurred his words so severely that I didn't know what he'd said. I looked at The Black for a translation, and the man leaned down and rapped on my head like you'd rap on the door if you were not expecting whoever was there to want to answer. Then the man wiped his nose and mouth and mustache and chin with his whole palm and knocked once again, harder, on the crown of my head. When I offered the bota bag to him, he shook his head.

"What does he want?" I said to The Black.

"Whatever you do, don't stand up."

I had heard from Edith and Duck on several occasions about the specialized choreography of knife fights. How the gauchos would wrap a poncho around their arms, to deflect blows, and how they could wave scarves or handkerchiefs with the covered hand, to draw attention away from the knife, and how, often, killing blows were not considered, as Edith put it, "elegant." It was more a form of dance, she'd said, and the first man to score a laceration against his opponent—the more prominent the mark and the more artful the move made to produce it the better—was the winner. I also knew that, by standing up, I would be tacitly agreeing to fight the man standing in front of me.

The man was wearing a heavy black-wool three-piece suit, and his shirt was buttoned up under his flaccid jowls. At his neck was a long kerchief. Duck stopped dancing and came over toward us just as the man began unknotting the kerchief. Duck came in a circle around the man so he wouldn't see his approach, and he stood there at a remove, tightening his belt and loosening it and tightening it again. The Black took out his knife and shaved the nipple from a battery he had hidden under his seat, and he passed the battery to me and nodded toward the man that I should offer the first swig to him. The Black had not resheathed his knife, and it now lay crossways on his chaps.

This time the man took my chin and the bones of my jaw in his one hand and held them tight while he hit me over the head with the other. I didn't wonder why he was challenging me. What I wondered was how long it would be before he deemed my unwillingness to stand up as an act of aggression itself.

Duck walked up and put his arm across the man's shoulders like an ox yoke. When the man tried to face Duck, Duck, who was much bigger and less drunk, squeezed the man to his side. He said, "How are you, Tea Kettle?"

Tea Kettle Without a Spout, Julia's disappeared husband of late, said, "Oh, pretty good, you know. Just . . ." and he slurred off. Duck asked after his family and the herd. He wanted to know where he'd been the past months, and before Tea Kettle could get too far into the explanation of his whereabouts, Duck interrupted him and pointed to me.

"This rooster here is my friend Nico," said Duck. Tea Kettle looked at me and tried to raise his left arm, and Duck squeezed Tea Kettle tighter.

I offered Duck the battery, and he drank from it expertly and with one hand. Duck then held the battery in front of Tea Kettle, like a carrot, and eased his grip slightly to let Tea Kettle drink. When he was done drinking, Duck winked at me and escorted Tea Kettle through the dancers like a child through a crowd at a ball game, and seated him in a chair on the far side of the room. Then Duck spoke to Tea Kettle, evenly nodding and without pause, and put Tea Kettle's hands in his lap and walked back onto the dance floor.

The Black was smiling, and so was I. He reached over with his thumb and wiped blood away from where one of Tea Kettle's fingernails had punctured my skin. "I have seven sons," he said, "and they've never seen one another."

I asked The Black where his sons were, by which I meant where they lived.

"Here," he said. The whole time, he never took his eyes from the dance floor. I said, "In this room?"

"Dancing," he smiled.

The players were playing furiously, and people stood around them clapping and keeping time against the floor with the spurs on their boots. There was such a din of voices that they seemed all to be one voice, and then a stray word would fly out and the din would intensify. Don Tito came over and sat with us.

The Black asked me if I had a mother. I told him I did. What I didn't say was that much of what I knew about her I'd gleaned from the family photo albums that my maternal grandmother meticulously compiled through the years. My grandmother had been educated to the fourth or fifth grade before leaving Ebo, Missouri, for St. Louis, and in the margins of the photo albums, she narrated the pictured events in her perfect and misspelled cursive. The notes said things like, "In Calgary and so hapy." To read them, you'd never have known that her husband, a dark Irishman called Jimmy Finnegan, had left her alone with two small girls, nor that my grandmother had spent all of her life fighting the odds levied against her by the decision she'd made as a teenager to leave everything she'd ever known and come to the city.

My grandmother meticulously monitored the appearances of her things, even her private albums, in hopes of suggesting exactly the opposite of the truth: that all was well, and that the world in which she found herself—one that rejected misspellings and divorced mothers who pronounced Missouri as though it ended in an "a" instead of an "i"—was not the one that rejected her, but, far to the contrary, the one in which she belonged. I wondered, if Edith and Duck ever made it to town, what they would do to cover their tracks.

I looked at the scattered lines of dancers moving back and forth on the floor like sine waves. Life, as Edith had said, *was* going on everywhere. And though the details varied, the events were welded together of a piece. Human beings, simply, were human beings, and they feared living lives gone before them, and they feared and beckoned to the lives that awaited them, and they left what they knew and came to one another and loved and destroyed each other's lives.

The voices in the crowd rose and fell and then they were silent. The music ceased. The crowd moved to the walls. The only dancers left were the three short-haired boys I'd seen dancing next to Duck earlier in the night and, lined up in front of them, the four long-haired gauchos with whom I'd shared the *pisco*. Their seven languid, lanky bodies were held rigid, like they'd been frozen. The boy with the Indian braids addressed the crowd, though his head didn't move, and it was unclear what he was saying. The Black took a step forward, and Don Tito hopped up and put a hand on his shoulder. Then The Black walked onto the floor and stood between the two lines.

These were his seven sons, and they had never seen one another before that night, and they were about to fight. The band stood their ground like cattle mulling the intentions of approaching riders, and then they, too, moved off toward the walls. Two rumpled policemen on hire from La Tapera looked from one gaucho to the next, subtly grinding their molars. Then they went outside into the rain.

Across the room near the door the crowd parted, and I saw Tea Kettle climb on top of a table in the corner. It was the table upon which The Cripple had been dancing, and Tea Kettle pushed him out of the way. Tea Kettle raised his arms. The seven sons turned to look at him and then at one another. It appeared that the fight would begin, like a drag race, when Tea Kettle let his arms fall.

But he did not let them fall. Instead, Tea Kettle Without a Spout yelled something unintelligible and stopped; the audience waited. He began anew, and yelled and flailed and mumbled and stamped his boot heels. As he neared the denouement, he suddenly, in midsentence, finger raised to make a point, passed out cold and fell face first onto the table. Had his nose not been already flattened, he would surely have crushed it in the fall.

In recognition of this one absurd fact among many, the players began playing, and the crowd roared with laughter and converged on the sons. It swept them up in a kind of benevolent, bifurcated wave, and moved them, like currents parting at a rock, to opposite sides of the room, harrying the sons once again into the stuttered steps of the dance.

The Black and I hugged one another. Don Tito passed the wine to Duck, who waved with both arms as five men carried Tea Kettle, spread-eagled and unconscious, above their heads. They took him through the open door of the schoolhouse and tossed him unceremoniously into the bed of a Toyota pickup and covered him with a tarp.

One of the policemen came over and stood next to us, still dripping with rain. The Black regarded him and said, "When it's good, it's good, *che*. And when it's bad, it's bad."

*   *   *

At four-thirty in the morning, the party was still going strong, though Don Tito and The Black had long before passed out onto their arms at school desks in the other room. Duck, too, was passed out in a chair. His hands were clasped in front of him and rested on his lap, the fingers woven together. His head was bowed, and he might have been praying, but he was stone drunk.

It took me a long time to wake him. He kept mumbling in a dream. Finally, he looked up and rubbed his eyes and bounced to his feet as if all of it had been a ruse. I said, "We have to go. Either that or we spend the night here, *che*."

We walked out the door and went past the truck where Tea Kettle was passed out. Rain pelted the tarp, which moved up and down with his deep breathing. Duck and I climbed into our truck. Only the dark road lay ahead.

I looked at Duck, sitting in the passenger seat with the back of his hand against the window, his head rested in the palm. I asked if he'd had a good time.

He shrugged. "So-so," he said. "It's the same people all the time. It's not Coihaique. I want Coihaique."

We neared The Crossing. There was no moon, and the sky was dark, and the only thing darker was the silhouette of the mountains that ran around us, tomb-like, in all directions. The shrine showed in the dim headlights.

I said, "You want Coihaique?" I wanted more than anything in the world right then to get out of Cisnes and, distracted by the thought, I didn't stop the truck till we'd nearly run through the altar.

Duck seemed not to notice. He said, "Where's the music?"

"In the tape deck. It's in the tape deck, remember?"

"I remember," he said, pushing Play.

The shining green sign announced the possibilities. Coihaique: 120 kilometers. Santiago: 1,000 kilometers. "You want Coihaique?" I said again.

"Quiet," said Duck. Then he turned the volume up.

✳

Peeled Hooves

[Gauchos] are indifferent about any thing that is beyond

their reach, and set no value on that which is hard to be

acquired.

—*Sir Edmond Temple,* Travels in Various Parts of Peru, *1833*

When Rex went back to Coihaique at the end of the week, I went with him. It was Good Friday, and I told Duck and Edith I'd be coming back to Cisnes with Señor Mansilla two days later, on Easter Sunday. Edith was disappointed. Duck had just slaughtered a ewe, and they'd planned to have a special, surprise meal: a soup made of stuffed tripe and the congealed marrow of the leg bones, which are cooked hoof and all.

But the temptation of thirty-six hours in Coihaique was too much, and Rex and I and the client got in the truck and left. Early on Easter Sunday, I went to Señor Mansilla's house to take the bus back to Cisnes. Red Duck, too, was on the bus. He'd rented his Mercedes two-ton to a pair of drivers from Lago Verde, who'd taken the truck to Argentina to pick up a load of timber; Red Duck was going to Tapera to get the mail jeep he kept there at Olga the Cheese Lady's house and drive it back to Coihaique. ("I can't be without fucking wheels, eggo," he'd told me on the bus. "No wheels: no puss.") I'd wanted to see Olga, in hopes of better understanding how she ran her rustling business, so when Red Duck invited me to Tapera and said that he'd drop me at Santa Elvira on the way back to Coihaique later that night, I'd accepted.

Olga, who is tremendously fat and has warts on her nose, was in the kitchen frying dough in ewe fat. Olga turned the *sopapillas* and watched them bob. Her lover leaned against the wall. He was much younger than she and was skinny and mustachioed. He was called Monkey, and his black hair was long and stringy; he seemed always to be loping about town like a cattle dog, looking over his shoulder as though expecting an unseen hand to swat him from behind. Presently, he walked outside and disappeared.

"Long trip, Witch," said Red Duck to Olga. She looked at me and looked at him. Red Duck said, "Don't worry about him. Is it in the back?" Olga looked at me. Red Duck shook his head and got up. "I told you," he said, "the gringo's fine. He's with me—he isn't going to tell the cops anything."

He went through the little door at the back of the kitchen and looked into another room. Flies poured in and out through the doorway, as though they'd been just at that moment created out of thin air. There was the smell of fresh kill, and in the room was a white table, and on it a skinned beef with the head stuck straight out, rigid as a plank. John of the Cows had been at it again. Red Duck whistled. "How much?" he said.

Olga shook her head. "Think I'd know with this fucked-up market? It's not like I'm a witch, *che*."

"The weight, Witchy, the weight," said Red Duck.

Olga shrugged. "Two fifty, three hundred kilos," she said. "I don't know. Small." She ladled the *sopapillas* one by one from the fat and watched them drip before dropping them onto a plate and laying a square of cheese on each. She offered forth the plate. She said, "The grass up there is no good. All the stock's shelled this year."

"I'll be back in a few days," said Red Duck. He made toward the door and checked his keys in his hand before turning. "How'd you get that thing up on the table?" he said, but Olga's mouth was too full to respond.

From Olga's house, Red Duck and I had driven straight to the general store, where he'd bought three bottles of *pisco,* four boxes of white wine, and all seven packs of Belmont cigarettes on the shelf behind the register. He got back in the jeep, opened the *pisco,* and did a U-turn in a swirl of dust. A police jeep piloted by two sunglassed men in military fatigues glided smoothly out from behind the general store. They followed us ten or twelve car lengths back, which in a village with two cars makes you feel like a mouse being toyed with by a cat. Red Duck put the *pisco* bottle between his legs and screwed on the cap. He crashed it against the metal floor till it stuck precariously out from under the seat. Then he rummaged through the junk piled about the stick shift—papers, bags, bottle caps, .38 cartridges.

In front of the hospital, a rotund nurse held the hand of a grinning mongoloid. Horses trotted ahead of us wearing the first of their winter coats. We climbed a hill in low gear and looked down at veined ravines where shacks clung precariously to the parched earth. The police followed. We stopped in front of a tiny cabin on the southern edge of town. It was the last house before the *pampa,* a scale-model dwelling silhouetted against dark hills so far distant they may have been a sea or they may have been nothing. The police pulled to the side of the road and killed the engine.

Red Duck stepped from the mail jeep and hitched his pants above the girth of his belly and shot them a glance, mumbling to himself. "Halloo!" he yelled merrily. Three little boys appeared in the lone window of the cabin and disappeared, and then a woman stood uncertainly in the open door. A flock of white and brown geese waddled and flapped across the dust, herded by the pair of nodding, roan geldings that followed. "Gimme the fattest!" called Red Duck.

One of the boys appeared with a lasso and quartered the gaggle while his brother shooed the horses and outflanked the cackling birds. The first boy lunged and made a perfect throw and waited for his unlucky target to flee, and, in doing so, ensnare itself by its neck and wing. There came the muffled crack of hollowed bone. The goose looked at its broken wing and then at the gaggle, and the boy reeled it in like a fish, waddling and tripping and, finally, sitting down as though to lay an egg. The boy undid the lasso and hoisted the goose by the neck.

I'd not noticed the third brother, who was standing inches from me at the open window of the jeep, until he said, in English, "Hello." He was perhaps seven years old, the elder of the bunch, and he wore his black hair in a swarm of curls; his face was the color of my own, and his eyes were blue. "Hello," he said again, blushing, then added, in Spanish: "Trouble with the *pacos?*" He looked over his shoulder at the indiscreet jeep and the crossed rifles on its doors.

The woman handed Red Duck a burlap sack, straight-armed, so as not to get too close to him. Red Duck took the goose from the boy, and it pedaled against the sack with its big yellow feet. Red Duck shoved the goose's head inside three times before he got the mouth of the sack tied tightly. He handed the woman some money and threw the sack into the back seat; the little boy walked alongside as we pulled away, saying, "Hello! Hello! Hello!"

We drove past the police jeep and they turned onto the street, and the only two vehicles in Tapera again traveled one behind the other. At the general store, they pulled back into the alley at the side and shut off the engine. We passed the empty yellow house where Edith had grown up and we passed the trail where Black Carl used to ride into town off the *pampa*.

Red Duck rubbed his belly and pressed the accelerator to the floorboard. He said, "You know what the problem with Chileans is, eggo?" I shrugged. "I work my ass off is the problem with Chileans. You know what I work for, eggo?" He looked over at me; I watched the road. He said, " 'Shit' is the correct answer in this situation, eggo. I drive this road day fucking in and day fucking out bringing these animals what they need, and it's for shit, eggo. I work hard, and because this is such a poor country, I can't make any money." He skidded around a corner. "I used to be well-off. My father was wealthy. But the government doesn't value work, eggo." He rooted around the stickshift. "Get some cups," he said.

I turned in my seat. The goose had succeeded in exploiting with its bill a small tear in the sack; it looked behind itself as though its head sat on ball bearings. It fixed its right eye on me. "Honk! Honk! Honk!"

"Shut! The fuck! Up!" said Red Duck. The goose withdrew its head, shuffled about inside the sack, and was still. "Lazy," said Red Duck, reaching for the cup I handed him. "Lazy and untrustworthy and losers. The poor are poor because they don't work. All they do is wait for handouts. Me, I'm honest and I can't get a decent job." He poured *pisco* in the cup and put it between his legs and filled my cup. He said, "Asian crisis? Killed us. The other Duck, your friend, the guy you live with, let me tell you: he's a friend of mine. Don't get me wrong. But: classic loser. He wouldn't ride across the river for a job. He'd rather sit around and not bathe. And do you know what the alcoholism rate is among these Indians?"

The jeep breached a rise in the *cordillera* and came rocketing down the other side. Several hundred vertical feet below us was the valley and the river and, though we could barely see it in the failing light, a small ranch. The road worked its way painfully into the valley across a long series of switchbacks. A half-hour later, we were breasting the invisible, burned-over swells of land that surrounded Uncle Ya Ya's cabin somewhere in the pitch blackness. The grade of the road and the darkness and the speed at which Red Duck drove made my stomach move up and down in my body. He leaned forward on the wheel and looked over and said, "Uncle Ya Ya must be asleep, the old rooster."

In his youth, Uncle Ya Ya had ridden all over Chilean and Argentine Patagonia with Black Carl and Don Tito and Alfredo Eagles. Now, he was the lone entrepreneur of Cisnes, the *dueño* of an unadvertised, well-known, and completely illegal amalgam of businesses, impressive for both its ingenuity and its eclecticism. The shed behind his cabin was the only place in the sixty kilometers between the villages of Amengual and Tapera that you could buy booze, a fact that everyone everywhere seemed to know. It was also the only place in the two hundred kilometers between Mañihuales and Argentina where you might get a good discount on truck tires, the bicycle pumps used to inflate them, fan belts, cigarettes, gas, oil, goats, geese, animal skins, chaps, whips, puma skulls, wild boar teeth, and .38 and .44 cartridges.

Red Duck, who was one of Uncle Ya Ya's primary suppliers, held the *pisco* bottle up to the windshield, where it was backlit by the jeep's one working headlight, and checked the level. We'd finished half of it already. Red Duck and I lit cigarettes. Then he said, "What do you think about Pinocchio?"

With regard to Pinochet, to whom Red Duck was referring, there's only one thing upon which all Chileans will agree, and that's that Chile is split—some will say evenly, some will say unevenly—between those who think Pinochet is the Savior and those who think he is the Devil. At first glance, it's hardly possible to know which side any given person will fall on. Should you have the unfortunate luck of being asked about Pinochet and then be foolish enough to answer the question, you are simply taking your chances, which is something I made a habit of never doing. I said, "I don't think about Pinocchio."

"Hmm," said Red Duck. "What you're saying, eggo, is that you don't think about a man who killed thousands of people in cold blood in order to fuck things up further than they were already fucked up. And let me hasten to add: this business about three thousand people 'disappeared' is horseshit. He killed at least ten thousand. So what you're saying," said Red Duck, "is you don't care."

I said, "I didn't say I didn't care."

"No?" he interrupted. "You said you didn't think about him. Which is to say you have no opinion, affirmative or negative? Affirmative." He punctuated the syllables of his sentences by hitting his palm on the steering wheel. "To have no opinion is to fail to care, is it not?"

It was a priceless trap. Any way I tried to climb out of it, he'd make an easy shot. "Well done," I said.

"Is there any excuse for killing innocent people?" I said there was not, in my opinion. I fumbled in the dark for a seat belt, but there wasn't one. "So then," said Red Duck, "what do you think about Pinochet?"

A while passed. I'd ridden that road at night before, when it was so dark that I couldn't see Sheep Shearings and La Vieja trotting ahead of Happy Slim. I only knew they were still there by the tik tik tik of their paws on the stones, and because they would yawn and murmur amicably in their throats when I said their names. I didn't like to ride at night, but sometimes when I went to see a neighbor I'd feel uncomfortable about having to leave in the face of repeated invitations to spend the night, and I'd extricate myself slowly, only to get on the road again far too late. When the trucks came, I had to use their headlights quickly and decisively to locate the widest side of the road, and spur the horse onto it before the trucks, which ran at night more than in the day and never slowed down, killed me.

I took a long drink of *pisco*. I thought, "If Red Duck goes off the side, it's better not to have a seat belt. At least that way I might get out of the jeep and grab onto something before the jeep falls all the way into the valley." I poured us each another couple fingers.

Red Duck said, "I'll tell you right now that Pinochet didn't kill anyone that didn't deserve to be killed. Would you like to know," he asked rhetorically, "what it was like in this country under Allende and his master plan of destruction? You couldn't even get bread. The lines were to be *told* you couldn't get bread. People were running in the streets demanding that something be done. There was a civil war brewing, eggo." There was also a pothole in the road that Red Duck made no effort to avoid and the axle slammed so hard on the uproad lip of it that I thought the floorboards had cracked.

For some reason, this seemed to calm Red Duck. He exhaled. "People are stupid, gringo. You take a guy off the shitter, he doesn't know if he should go left or right. Pinochet was the only hero this country ever had. Only thing he'd have done better is killed ten times that many."

In the headlight up ahead was the fence surrounding Santa Elvira. We pulled off the road and I hopped out to swing open the gate. The vague shapes of horses stood huddled in the weak beam with their eyes lit. A cold wind blew downcountry and moaned in the fence wire. Red Duck shut off the engine, and the headlight went dead, and the horses and trees and the road all disappeared from sight. "Come here," said Red Duck. He got out of the jeep.

"Come here," said Red Duck again. I kept the hood of the jeep between us. "Listen," he said, "my only point is this. And I hate to say it, because Duck is my friend. He really is. But what's wrong with Chile is that the poor need to learn how to *work!* They don't respect work. Pinochet respected work. And all I can do, all I'm relegated to doing, is what I can: running shit back and forth on this shitty road.

"When we go in there, eggo, don't say a word about what we've talked about. I know you're not as ignorant as your people, gringo. But don't say anything about Pinochet. Duck doesn't understand. I'm sorry to say it, gringo, because he's my friend, but Duck's a drunk."

Red Duck pulled through the heavy gate and I latched it behind us. We came around the corner, and in the distance was the little cabin and the twinkling of candles in the windows. Duck stood in the door with his arms around Edith. They'd heard us coming a long time before.

Red Duck pulled almost onto the porch, reached behind the seat, and took out a bottle of *pisco* and two boxes of wine. "Hah!" he bellowed merrily, holding the booze aloft and stumbling from the jeep. "I come bearing gifts, eggos. The Red Duck comes like a savior!"

*　　*　　*

The next day, Duck disappeared. When he came back two days later, he had shaved his thin black beard—at the river, with the knife he always carried, or had he taken his razor when he'd left the morning before and not come back?—and his hair was disheveled. He might have slept the two preceding nights in the woods. He looked west through the open window, at the lodge, which was locked up for the next nine months. Everyone finally gone for Coihaique. Outside past the barn the little flock of gray-eyed sheep stood in the raked shadow of the fence.

"What do you see?" said Edith.

Duck dropped his head and pointed at the floor with his lips. He went to the sink and splashed his face several times with water and took his knife in his hands. The wood handle was worn; the rounded edges shone dully from years of being handled by fingers smeared with mutton grease. Duck put the flat of the blade against the palm of his hand and raised an eyebrow. Then, as though her words had finally reached him across a great distance, he looked at Edith. There was a look on his face that I can only describe as deeply, calmly violent. Then he walked outside into the blinding afternoon sun, crossed the pasture, and disappeared from sight.

"I have to leave before he kills me," said Edith. She looked at Oscar as he fed at her breast. "That's it, my little king," she whispered. "You'll be a big boy."

*   *   *

Two more days passed. Duck slept in the main room, on the floor on a bed of sheepskins. In the mornings, he would leave without taking *mate*. It was a mystery where he went, and not once did I hear the whine of the mill saw. One day he came back for lunch; on the next, he was gone until dinner. He did not join us at the table, nor did he speak to anyone. Instead, he would sit on the throne and remove his shoes and set them neatly by the stove and strum his guitar. Then he would pace the room and sit again. He did not eat. From time to time, Mariana would walk over to where Duck sat and study him like a painting or a sculpture. Only when she laughed—did she imagine pigeons perched on his head?—would Duck look down at her, though there did not register on his face a single recognizable emotion, not love or hatred or annoyance. In the mornings, he would put on his shoes and leave again.

Edith and I passed those days in the cabin with Mariana and Oscar (Patricia was at school in the village), making bread and cooking and cleaning. And talking, though never about her and Duck. Until finally I said, "Where does he go, *che?*"

She shrugged. "He hasn't been like this in two or three years," she said. "Just once two or three years ago he was like this for a couple days, and then he was fine. He'll be fine again."

I said, "Is this what he was like before he did whatever he did to you in Coihaique?"

"Yes," said Edith. I asked if she knew the cause. "Life," she said.

We were cleaning the floor with Brillo-covered bricks that Edith called the Pigs, because she put the bricks under her feet and rubbed them against the particleboard like rooting swine. She said, "He won't talk about it. He never talks about anything. I try to get him to, and he won't. For a while, catch it, right after Oscar was born, it was different. He won't let me help him with whatever this thing is that he's fighting. A marriage takes work, Skinny," she said, then added, smiling, "even if you're not legally married.

"But if one of you only wants to work alone on your own problems, that horse won't run. Both of you have to be willing to accept help from the other, catch? I don't know that he even knows what it is that's got him. He says he can't put it into words. Thing is, I know he's really trying, but he doesn't know what it is that's got him by the nuts. Closest I get is when he talks in his sleep."

Edith bent down and picked up Mariana's sketchbook from the floor. "Here," she said, and Mariana sat at the table and began drawing. I asked what Duck said when he talked in his sleep. "Oh, Skinny Man," said Edith, shaking her head. "He talks to someone, I don't know who, asking them not to do things. It's hard to hear what they're doing. I've never heard. Then he'll get up like he's not even in his body and go walking around the room, catch it? The next morning I'll say, 'Were you thirsty last night?' and he'll just look at me. I'll say, 'You were walking around last night.' 'Really?' he'll say. He doesn't remember any of it. It started after we went to this evangelical tent show in Mañihuales last year. I'd been trying to get him to go for some time. He said evangelicals are looking for the nuts on an ox, catch it?

"We went anyway. Devil exorcisms and people talking in all kinds of strange languages. People who couldn't walk got carried up to the preacher, and he'd heal them. We saw it with our own eyes, *che*. Then the preacher says, 'I can see a man who has seen the Devil's faceless face, *che*. You know who you are, brother, and your wife knows, too, and your children. And I'm offering to take the Beast away.' The preacher raised his hand and closed his eyes and next thing I know, Duck is up there on the stage. 'It's me,' says Duck. I was so embarrassed, and then I wasn't. The Lord," said Edith looking down, "took my pride.

"The preacher put his hand on Duck's head and beseeched Lucifer to leave this man's body. Finally, Duck fell unconscious, catch it? I thought he was dead. And you know, *che*? I wasn't sorry. I felt relieved. More for him than me.

"When we got back, all this about the dreams started. He said he was having this dream all the time. Doing terrible things in his dream. Things he wouldn't talk about. Personally, I think it had him so frightened that he was trying to get out of the bed to get away from the dreams. Trying to wake himself up."

Mariana started crying. "What do you have?" said Edith impatiently. Mariana tossed the sketchbook across the room and walked outside. Edith watched her go, and then she closed her eyes for a moment before rising to put Oscar down for his afternoon nap.

The newly cleaned floor was bathed in an oblong swath of light. Under its scrutiny, each of a thousand new abrasions glowed against the particleboard. Where the light ended at the foot of the oven, a deep shadow hid all but the corner of Mariana's bedraggled sketchbook. I pulled it out. Each centimeter of the first two pages was covered in the hieroglyphs of a child trying to learn the alphabet, and drawings of men and women in front of houses, and drawings of dogs and horses—all of it economically bunched together, front and back, for she was unlikely to have another sketchbook for a very long time.

On the third page was a drawing that caught my attention, because it enjoyed an entire page to itself. It was of a man and woman and three children outside a cabin. They appeared to be floating away from the cabin, or to have been blown out of it, for their bodies hung in every posture, upside down and looking up and diagonally, each of them at odds with the other. The eyes and noses of the faces were simple dots, the lines for the mouths almost imperceptibly downturned. Under the cabin loomed a large creature, a sort of Everymonster with the body of a snake, legs like a dog's, and ridiculously protruding fangs and claws. It was the Colo Colo. Although it made me feel like I was neglecting Mariana, I tossed the book back under the stove before Edith walked back into the room. I didn't want her to see the drawing, or to know that I had seen it.

Edith sat down in the throne and said, "You know part of it's that he thinks I'm having an affair."

I said, "Who could you possibly be having an affair with out here, *che*?" She looked at me. "You have to be kidding me," I said. "Tell me you're kidding me, *che*." Edith shrugged. I said, "Did he tell you this?"

Edith said, "He didn't have to, *che*. The last time he acted like this was when the carpenters were here fixing something at the lodge, and one of them asked Duck if he and I were going to stay together. The carpenter said he didn't get the impression we would, and would Duck mind if the carpenter moved in with me. Not that the fucker ever asked me. Not that we ever even talked. Duck told the carpenter he didn't think that would be a good idea. Then Duck just disappeared for a few days. I think he was testing me," said Edith. "Like, giving me the chance if I wanted it. I think Duck honestly wanted me to do whatever I might."

"*Are* you having an affair with anyone?" I asked.

"No," said Edith. There was something about the way she said it that made me not believe her, and I thought about what Duck had said on the drive about Edith not liking to be left alone. "I do wish he had a better sense of humor," said Edith. "Like my father. Or like Soto." Soto was the paramedic stationed in Amengual.

"So I need to leave," I said.

Edith said, "Where in the world do you think you can go? Mansilla won't be back for a week, and it would take you days to hitch a ride on the road this time of year."

"To a neighbor's."

"To a neighbor's. And how are you going to get there, steal a horse? It's one thing if Duck lends you a horse. It's another thing if you ride away and never come back."

I said, "So what happened with the carpenter?"

"I tried to kill myself with livestock antibiotics."

"What stopped you?"

Edith raised her hands and slapped her knees as though she would get up and go somewhere. She said, "Mariana's what stopped me. She was standing at the door. She didn't stop me by taking the syringe away. She was standing at the door watching." Edith paused. "It's hard to explain, *che*. Light was coming in through the storeroom window, and it was lighting her and . . . it doesn't sound right. But it's what happened. What happened is God's hand reached out from her to stop me."

"Where was Oscar?"

"I was holding him; he wasn't yet walking. I didn't want him getting into the cupboard and pulling the vegetable barrel down on himself."

"And Patricia?"

"At school."

I said, "Did Mariana understand you were going to kill yourself?"

"She's smarter than I give her credit for," said Edith.

I said, "Did you want her to see you?" I wondered if this might explain some of the contempt that Edith felt so explosively toward Mariana from time to time.

"I wasn't thinking about that. I was thinking that the only way to get out of the situation was to inject myself with that foul-smelling shit. I thought that a knife was too messy, *che*. I'd once thought about hanging myself, but, catch it, the thing is, I assumed I'd have time after the injection to put the syringe and everything back in the cabinet. That way," said Edith, "it wouldn't look like suicide."

I said, "But your daughter was watching."

"I don't claim any of this makes sense, Nico. But I didn't think about that. What I thought about was I thought her and Oscar wouldn't have anything to eat. They can't cook—they're too young. And I didn't know where Duck had gone."

I said, "Have you ever thought about killing him?"

"I've thought that I'd like him to die. Not kill him. I've thought it would be a great weight off of me were he to die. Sometimes, *che*, I think one of us will have to die to get out of this mess. Maybe a horse to throw him in the mountains. Or were he to drink and get into a fight and someone kill him, *che*. Cross John of the Cows," said Edith, "and he'd kill you."

She looked over at the corner of the notebook sticking out from under the stove. "But Duck doesn't fight," she said. "He waits."

* * *

That evening, Duck came back to the cabin just as Edith was putting supper on the table. It was dark outside, and we heard him unsaddling Happy Slim over at the barn. The horses called to one another, and the dogs barked. Duck came inside and nodded to each person in the room. He sat down to the table and cleared his throat several times. Then he said, "Could you pass the bread?" Edith passed it to him. "Thank you. I was thinking that tomorrow night we ought to have an oven roast, *che*. Have a big special meal."

Edith said, "Do we have enough meat on that ewe still hanging?"

"We've got everything we need," said Duck. He ate ravenously, then served himself and me another plate.

"What's the occasion?" said Edith hesitantly.

Duck said, "The big game is tomorrow night." He turned to me. "Colo Colo's playing. If the Colo loses," said Duck, "he's out for good."

* * *

The next night, though, Soto and Fat Will showed up from Amengual, and listening to soccer on the radio was promptly forgotten. It was Friday night, and they came in Soto's brand-new Toyota four-door truck. Patricia was in the back with the booze.

Duck acted as though all of it were a great surprise. Earlier that day, though, I'd heard him call Soto on the radio while Edith was behind the house doing the wash. Soto had a two-way radio in his office, and he and Duck had arranged for Soto to bring Patricia and a box of alcohol.

"Figured what the fuck," said Soto, playing along and opening the door to the truck. Patricia hopped down in her school uniform, her backpack in her hand. "Figured we'd give her a ride out here and have a party, eggo! Gringo," he said, shaking my hand.

Soto had perfect black hair with streaks of white, and a black mustache with hints of gray, though he could not have been more than forty-five. He wore pressed, new jeans with a leather belt, and a pink-and-green polo shirt. His eyes were hazel, and he was an altogether handsome man. He'd moved to the village the year before from Coihaique.

Fat Will was one of the two truck drivers who had relocated to Amengual from Coihaique to cater to the market that opened with the road, namely gauchos like Duck, who wanted, once a month, to buy everything from batteries to "batteries." Fat Will was an enormously overweight man who wore photochromic glasses that adjusted to the light but were always, no matter how dark it was, partly opaque. The latent aggressiveness of the glasses, though, melded incongruously with the effeminate sheen of his fingernails, which were painted with clear polish. His hair, like Soto's, was more coiffed than cut. (Neither man was missing a single tooth, which seemed itself an effeminate trait.) Fat Will wore good, black loafers, jeans, a maroon oxford shirt, and four gold chains. His cologne was like a force field; on his chubby pinkie he wore an emerald-and-gold ring with the stone rakishly tilted to the side. He'd thought me an asshole since a month before when he'd made his last run and I'd declined to buy anything out of the back of his truck.

Fat Will looked at me. He said, "My mother's cunt if it isn't *el virus* Nicolás." Then he walked inside the cabin.

Duck said to me under his breath, "Don't worry, Nico, he's not bad people. He just has to get to know you, *che*."

Each place setting had two plates—a large one and a salad plate—a knife (Duck used his *facón*), a fork, and a glass for wine. Underneath it all was a frilly white tablecloth that Alex had brought. In the middle of the table were three boxes of Hermanos Carreras chardonnay, the tray of meat, fresh bread, and the plastic bowl that doubled as Oscar's toilet and now brimmed with cucumber and garlic salad. The radio was nowhere to be seen. It was the first and last time during which I lived with Duck and Edith in Cisnes that we didn't listen to nine o'clock Messages. With the coming of the guests, we didn't have to.

"Have you heard about this Clinton business?" said Fat Will. "The radio says he gets $5 million a day to maintain his entourage on official state visits. Five million a day, eggo! Radio says in Santiago you could buy a hundred houses for what he gets a day. Now you tell me they're not shitting money up there."

"No," said Duck, seriously, "there's poverty in the United States. Nicolás will tell you. Of course there's poverty there."

"Ah, because *el virus* Nicolás says so," Fat Will said to Soto in French, which, when he and Soto had been educated in Coihaique, had still been the mandatory second language taught in schools. "Please," he snorted, "there's no such thing as poverty there."

"You're a bastard." Duck laughed. He coughed he laughed so hard.

"You're a fucking butterball," I said in English, smiling.

"I'm not being funny, Duck," said Fat Will, watching me. He was trying to match what I'd just said to the litany of vulgarisms he knew in English. "Fuck?" he said, leaning toward Soto: "*Culiar* is fuck, eggo?"

"Listen," I said in Spanish, "you hear all this stuff about Clinton and $5 million a day and you assume that he represents all of us, but that isn't the case."

"That's exactly true, eggo," said Soto. "That's precisely what people do, and it's inaccurate. Tempting, but inaccurate. Can I borrow $3 million, eggo?"

Edith laughed loudly, then blushed.

Fat Will looked at me. "What're you doing here, eggo?" he said.

"He's living here and I'm showing him things, eggo," said Duck. I'd rarely heard Duck use the word eggo much before. *El che,* it seemed, had been temporarily pushed out of the cabin. Duck said, "Nico, he's like family."

Soto said, "Let's drop it. To health, gentlemen eggos."

"See, Clinton," said Fat Will, ignoring Soto, "he can't even walk down the carpet like the other heads of state. He has to go in the back door. Then he can't eat at the same restaurant with all of them." That week, Clinton, citing security concerns, had angered the other Latin American heads of state by not parading with them publicly into the place where a summit of American states was being held. Then he'd refused to eat dinner at a restaurant named Augusto, for fear of associating himself with Pinochet.

I said, "I don't make Clinton's decisions for him, I don't ask him to make my decisions for me. What he does has nothing to do with me."

"I beg to differ," said Fat Will. "He's your leader. Leader of the eggos. Makes you like him, insofar as what he does *represents* you, eggo."

*   *   *

It was ten o'clock when Soto and Fat Will drove off, and Duck and Edith and I went back inside the cabin. Duck said, "Boy, is Fat Will ever an asshole."

"You can say that again," said Edith.

"I've met some Americans in Coihaique that would have deserved to be treated that way," I said.

"Yeah, but to come into my house and eat my food and imply that I shouldn't be serving you," said Duck. "I mean, talk about shitting on my authority. I'm sorry, Nico. I wanted to tell him to leave, but, you know, it just wasn't worth it. He's not even my friend. Soto's my friend. Fat Will, he's a drunk on top of it. Did you see the way he downed the wine?" He walked over to the cardboard box they'd left in the corner. It was still half-full of beer and batteries and *pisco*. "Nice of Soto to leave this, though," said Duck. He pulled out a liter of beer and said to Edith, "Let's leave the dishes for the morning." He opened the beer and took a sip and passed it to me.

Edith put Oscar to bed and came out and sat down.

"You know," said Duck, "fuckin Fat Will, eggo, he's what I hate about Chileans. Think every outsider is bad. With him, at least he said it to your face. Indians around here wouldn't even do that."

"Soto isn't like that, *che,*" said Edith.

"No," said Duck. "Soto's good people, eggo. He isn't like Chileans." He drank a large portion of the beer and breathed heavily. Edith made an effort not to look at him. Duck passed her the beer.

"I don't drink," she said.

Duck said, "I'm glad I'm not driving with them right now."

"Me . . ." began Edith.

"I mean," continued Duck, "they'll be lucky to get home alive. Patricia," said Duck, "they weren't drinking on the way out here, were they?"

Patricia squirmed in her seat and shook her head.

"The answer is no or yes," said Duck impatiently. "Don't be *huasa,* eggo."

In the day since Duck had come back to the cabin I'd nearly forgotten about the severe depression from which he seemed to be suffering. Now, with each drink, he was making a new fire from the smoldering coals. He couldn't stop talking, and the more he added to the coals, the more paranoid and afraid of the fire he got.

"They ought to be concentrating on the road instead of talking about us, eggo," he said.

"Soto isn't that way," said Edith.

Duck looked at her angrily. "Soto's my *friend,*" he threatened.

*   *   *

I was hopelessly drunk. Several times, Duck had asked me to sleep that night in the cabin, and each time I'd refused, I could see how angry it made him. I hadn't wanted to be in the cabin with him at all—much less sleep there—but I'd stayed because I didn't want to leave Edith and the children alone. I thought that, if I could keep up with Duck drink for drink, he'd pass out. Then, the last time I'd refused to stay the night, Duck rose from the throne and pulled the little cabinet off the wall, smashing it on the floor. That's when Edith ran into the bedroom and barricaded the door with the barrel in which she kept a fifty-pound sack of flour.

Duck and I listened as she moved it slowly across the bedroom floor. Then Duck opened a bottle of *pisco.* "Our friend, Nicolás!" he said ironically. "Señor Capel. That's true, isn't it?" It was three minutes past midnight.

"Yes," I said.

"He's not our friend, Nicolás? Is that what you're saying?"

"I just told you he was," I said. "Don't start a fight over this."

"Drink this and shut the fuck up," said Duck. "Listen, what's the best I can hope for my daughters?" He put a Gloria Estefan tape in the tape player and pressed Play.

"I don't know," I said.

"Help me. Hear?"

"Get the fuck out of here," I said.

"Thank you," said Duck. "Only friends say things like you just said. Still, despite this, you're absolutely fucking incorrect. The best I can hope for *when* I get out of here is secretary. Tops. What the fuck is that? I'll tell you, because you won't answer the question, even though you know the answer. It's worse than nothing. It's the same shit with a different smell. Might as well rot out here as in an office, no?"

He got up and put Mariana's shoes behind the stove, where he couldn't see them. They were white Nike knockoffs. On the sides were abbreviated swooshes. On the back they read "Golf."

Duck said, "Better to have gauchos in their pants than to have to doll up like whores for some office-eggo and get fired when they no longer look good. We're friends, are we not?" and he reached out his hand. For a moment, he seemed almost sober.

"Yes," I said. Rain was falling like rocks on the corrugated roof.

"Then let me ask you: you've seen my lasso?" Duck, during the afternoons a couple weeks before, had made a new lasso for the next cattle drive. It was an incredibly intricate process that had taken him nearly a week, for the cattleskins had first to be carefully selected, then soaked and scraped free of hair. Duck then cut the skins into thin strips and braided them together, constantly stretching and restretching the strips; and when he reached the end of one strip, he would have to splice it to the next series of braids. The lasso was, above all else, an example of mathematical genius, and the result was absolutely seamless.

"Yes," I said.

"How much can I get for it at the lodge?" said Duck. Rex had, for the last two seasons, been selling things to his clients that the gauchos made. Julia rode up from downriver to sell sweaters, and a man called Tano came down off the border to sell chaps and socks.

"A hundred dollars," I said.

"Fifty dollars?" said Duck.

"A hundred, easy. That lasso's the most beautiful I've ever seen." I meant it— it was extraordinary, and Duck, as the final step, had rubbed it with a new-killed eweskin so that the fat gave the lasso a high, supple shine.

"Fifty, then," said Duck. "And do you think I should sell it, eggo? You do."

"A hundred dollars is almost as much as you make a month."

"Let me tell you what happened last time I sold something at that whore-house, Christian." Duck took his shoes off. He was speaking now in a thick, nearly impenetrable accent, and he turned his body at a ninety-degree angle away from me. He waited, and then he said, "Nothing. Nothing is what happened, Christian. Shit happened. Do you understand that?"

He peeked around his shoulder at me to register my response, and when I looked away, Duck took one of his shoes and threw it against the bedroom wall. He yelled to Edith and the children to wake up before throwing his other shoe out the open window. When I stood up, he put his knife to my throat.

*   *   *

Duck breathed quickly and steadily through his nose in the same audible, aggressive manner in which Fat Will had breathed that night as he ate. One of the times Duck exhaled, he took the knife away and turned around all in one motion and sat on the throne. I turned and went outside. I just walked right out the door. For a second, I wondered if Duck had even noticed I was gone.

I had to urinate, and when I unbuttoned my jeans, my knees buckled spasmodically. I turned to see Duck move away from the window, where he'd been watching me, and I thought about stealing a horse, but even if I could find Happy Slim during one of the moments when the moon wasn't obscured by the clouds that drifted across it, it was hard to imagine I could get the hobble off and get onto her back before Duck got to me. I thought about running into the storeroom and locking the door, but I was afraid Duck might burn the cabin down. There was nowhere to go but back inside.

Duck was on the floor sharpening his knife. He'd lit three candles and set them on the floor between his chair and mine. His shirt was buttoned to his neck. He stood up and dropped the whetstone to the floor and tested the sharp edge of the blade against his thumb. "Skinny," he said in a thick, steady voice, "Duck is no longer with us. Duck is gone." He looked at his knife and touched it and touched his ear and looked to his right, offering the floor to some new speaker. On the wall behind his head was a calendar with a picture of a horse at the top. "Don Lucifer has waited for you," said Duck.

I said, "Hey Duck*che*?"

"Hey what, Nico*che*?"

"What are you talking about?"

He looked at me and blushed and laughed. He said, "Don't go, *che*. Sleep here."

Through the middle of all the debris littering the floor, Duck had cleared a bodywide space just long enough for me to lie down in without lying on top of broken pieces of plate and bottles and cans and boxes. It was at one end of this corridor that Duck had arranged the candles, so that either my head or my feet had to be within the triangle of light. I laid four sheepskins on the floor and took off my sweater and rolled it for a pillow and put that down, so that my head would be near the light.

"Good," said Duck, breathing with anticipation. He rose and went to the sink and began filling a frying pan with water. I thought he might be doing the dishes. I lay down, hoping that I could stay awake long enough for him to drink himself to sleep. I closed and opened my eyes. For a moment, I couldn't see anything. Then I saw Duck crouched over me.

He had the frying pan in one hand and the knife in the other. He dipped the knife in the water and brought it down to my face so that it rested just above my eyes, horizontally. Water fell in arrhythmic drops into my eyes and ran down the sides of my head before falling onto my sweater. Duck rocked back and forth like an autistic child, speaking in tongues, and I thought I recognized words in Spanish and Italian and Tehuelche and Arabic, though none of it, when taken together, made any sense.

"I'm Satan," said Duck, all the while carefully marking the fall of the drops. "And I," he went on, repositioning the blade to get the other eye, "baptize you." He waited with his tongue in his cheek for a last drop to fall. "There," he said.

It occurred to me each time Duck dipped the knife in the pan that I might have time to roll out from under him. But no sooner was I thinking something than it was already too late to do it: back came the knife. I tried to think of sequences of events like shots on a pool table. But there was nothing fluid about my ability to perceive the outcomes, nor even the actions themselves. For instance, in the sequence "roll, hop up, kick his teeth into his head," I would arrive at hop up and wonder what had come before. Then I thought of all the times I'd seen a dog flush a pheasant and how I'd killed the bird before knowing what I'd done. If I moved, I knew Duck would kill me more easily than if I made him think about it.

"Don't move," he coached. "I am Don Lucifer, and I baptize you in eternal darkness, Christian." Then, to expedite the process, he poured water from the pan over my face and neck.

I said, "Remember when I lost the bulls at Rock House?"

"Yes," he said fondly.

"Duck," I said. I said his full name.

"I'm sorry," he said. "I'm not in control. There's nothing I can do, Nico*che*."

I said, "Let's just have another drink, *che*."

Duck stood up and walked toward the sink. He was halfway there before I hopped to my feet and fell down again. Duck dropped the frying pan to the floor and turned around, and we watched one another. When he took two steps toward me, I stood up and took a step toward the door. The rain was beating against the roof and we were four feet from one another. I looked at the door, and when I did this, Duck shook his head. He still had the knife in his hand.

I said, "Let's just have another drink."

Duck sat down on the throne and took a long drink of *pisco* and reached to hand me the bottle. I watched his knife hand while I took the bottle from him. I sat down. While Duck tried turning on the radio, I poured *pisco* on my leg. "Nico," he said, "that trick doesn't fly." He seemed to have forgotten how the radio worked, and he threw it against the wall; when it didn't shatter into pieces, he said, "Break that fucker." Then he said, still looking down, "I'm too poor for you. Is that why you won't sleep here, because we're too fucking poor?" He turned ninety degrees away from me and said, "Because I'm a fucking secretary who makes sure that two *viejos* who can't count and who don't care what day it is can get their money on time?" Over and over again he said it made no difference to him. Nothing, he said, made any difference. His life, his desires, the people by whom he was surrounded—it was all the same shit, different smell. Then he clasped his hands in his lap and put his chin on his chest and seemed to fall asleep.

Before I'd made it to the door, Duck rose and grabbed the back of my hair. He got my neck wedged into the crook of his arm, and said, "I want you to come outside. I have something to show you."

His chin whiskers raked my ear, and I wedged the toe of my boot under the doorjamb.

"Come on," he said. With his knife hand, he pushed the back of my head farther into the crook of his elbow. He groaned with the exertion. "Christian," he said, "I'm going to cut you open and crack your spine and hang you from the ceiling."

My arms were braced against the door. Duck was suffocating me to death, and I kept thinking about Mariana and Edith and Oscar, huddled somewhere on the other side of the wall. I let my elbows give and I spun out of Duck's grip as he fell forward and planted his face in the door.

I retched and retched again, and when my eyes cleared, I saw Edith's knife on the sink and the glow of the fire in the stove. The frying pan was lying on the floor, and there was the loaded rifle he kept in the bedroom.

I said, "One more drink."

"I can't."

"I'll leave."

"Can't, *che*."

I went over to my chair and sat down with my back to him and poured a glass full of *pisco*.

"Please," said Duck.

Then he walked barefoot across the broken plates and sat down on the throne. There was blood on the floor and on the broken debris, and Duck looked at his bleeding feet. When he did this, the knife fell from his hand. I poured him a glass and handed it across. I poured him one drink after another. He made a valiant effort to keep up.

A while later, Duck crumpled in his chair and hit the floor with a thud. His face was wedged against the cabinet that housed the sink pipes, and one arm was caught beneath his body.

That was at five o'clock in the morning.

＊　　＊　　＊

I didn't want to sleep in my tent and take the chance that Duck would wake up and come looking for me, so I took a flashlight from my pocket and walked into the woods. In the light ahead was a fallen *coigue* tree; beneath it the ground was eroded, and I lay down there and fell asleep.

I woke at ten o'clock the next morning. The sun was shining, and it was very cold. Standing at the edge of the woods, I could see smoke above the chimney of Duck and Edith's cabin. I walked through the pasture past piles of my vomit and went inside. There was nowhere else to go.

Edith was seated on the throne with Oscar asleep across her lap. "My God," she said. There was no sign of what had happened the night before. The floor was scrubbed, the remaining dishes were done, the broken plates were gone, and the cabinet had been rehung.

No sign except for Duck, who was slumped at the table with a brand-new bottle of *pisco* in his hand. His shirt was open to his waist and his boots were once again on his feet. "Drink," said Duck. He was too drunk to move. He beat against the floor with his boots, groaning with the pain of the cuts on his feet.

He said, "I would like for somebody to get rid of my shoes. I would like for someone to peel my hooves."

CHAPTER ELEVEN

Brew Wheely

We will . . . in a few seconds more send Trollope to Kazakhstan and the grand library of sixteenth-century Timbuktu to Tampa. . . . In general, we will accomplish tasks so quickly that we will create enormous new wealth. That's for starters. The revolution will end by changing the nature of time itself, thereby alternating the way we live, work, seek pleasure, and gather together. We shall achieve simultaneity, ending the gap between desire and fulfillment; we shall no longer *wait.*

—*David Denby, "The Speed of Light:*

The High-Stakes Race to Build the Next Internet,"

The New Yorker, *November 27, 2000*

Eight days after all of this, my three-month Chilean visa expired. I spent all but the last two days riding a cattle drive with Duck, Don Tito, and another gaucho called Tano. We went once again to the nothingsummer, this time to bring down the remaining five hundred cattle in the herd.

Duck and I hadn't said anything to one another during the day he took to sober up. In fact, we never said anything to one another about that night. I spent most of the day in my tent making recordings on the dictaphone. I had what I'd come for. I'd seen the breakdown amidst the pressure from the Outside that I'd imagined, and I had it, like a camera shot in war, in its most violent essence. I thought that the story was complete. But I wanted, in the same way you might want another hit of a drug, to see the gauchos one last time doing the most *gauchesco* thing of all: driving cattle over a long distance on horseback. More than this, I wanted one more chance to work and ride among them. I was more sure than I'd ever been that gaucho culture as it had existed for nearly four centuries was near its end.

I'd heard from a friend while I was in Coihaique over Easter weekend that there was talk of a dam on the Río Baker, two hundred kilometers south of Coihaique, that would provide enough hydroelectric power for ten Coihaiques, a fact that would appear to lend credence to the prediction that Aisén will quadruple in population by 2010. There were plans for at least a dozen and a half more "excursion" lodges in the state, and another fly-fishing lodge was to open in 1999, fifteen kilometers south of Amengual, which, along with Tapera, was within two years of getting telephone service. None of which would affect Cisnes or the lives of the gauchos there as significantly as the fact that the army engineers were planning to pave the Argentine Road past Santa Elvira and Tapera, all the way to the border.

Back in April of 1998 when I heard about these impending changes, I knew that the pavement would have an even more profound effect on Cisnes than the road itself had. First, because it would make a more compelling visual case for heading to Coihaique—the asphalt road would stand out in much sharper contrast to the land than the dirt ever had. Men like Red Duck would descend in ever greater numbers to corner the market on bringing the herds to Coihaique in their trucks. Logging roads would be built and paved so that eventually even the drives that shuffled the herds twice a year between the *veranadas* and the *invernadas* would be done by truck.

By 1998, cattle prices in Chilean Patagonia had been plummeting for twenty years, and the reason was the very infrastructural inferiority that the pavement would assuage. Aisén, until the late 1980s, had forever sold its beef and mutton to Santiago. But as soon as Argentina and Brazil (and, more galling still to Chileans, tiny Uruguay) had built a reliable system of roads, those countries had been able to undercut prices severely, forcing Santiago to import its meat.

In lieu of this, the modus operandi around Coihaique for ten years had been for the wealthiest landowners to buy out the smaller ones in order to make conglomerate ranches, wherein larger and larger herds could be raised while employing fewer and fewer gauchos. Change in Aisén, like the road, starts in Coihaique and moves outward like shock waves. And as soon as the pavement reached Cisnes, with all of its middling-sized ranches and as-yet-unaccounted-for land, the same thing would begin happening there, too. Carlos Asi's land-clearing operation on the south end of Santa Elvira had marked the beginning.

Martínez Estrada was right that "cattle do not require populations." But he was wrong about cattle being "contrary to society." In Cisnes, cattle had resulted in the flourishing of many cabin-centric "societies," all of which, taken as a whole, defined the Chilean gaucho a full century after he disappeared in Argentina. And what kept these societies in contact with and influencing one another is, paradoxically, the gauchos' ability to leave their herds and wander unencumbered by the thought of any but the loosest of schedules.

Duck was the lone exception to this rule. As the head cowboy of Santa Elvira, he was responsible for two men, Alfredo and Tito, who saw time the old way. And Duck hated the old way as much as he hated trying to make men like Alfredo adhere to Alex's schedules. Several times, Duck had gone to the nothing-summer to get the bulls and Alfredo wasn't even there. Duck was an emissary of change—a transitional figure. Soon enough, the head cowboy at Santa Elvira would have a truck and be able to get to the nothingsummer in two hours instead of two days. There would be a wholesale change in the nature of time itself—and little difference between men like Alfredo and Duck.

And all of it was as it should be. With the pavement, the Outside would be more readily available to men and women who wanted a life of greater convenience for themselves, and education and inoculations for their children. For those who remained, too, life would get better. Even hanta virus would not be the same ace-in-the-hole killer in five years, when an ambulance from Coihaique might arrive in Cisnes hours, instead of days, after it was called. There would be solar energy and hot water. Perhaps there would even be recognition in Coihaique that people actually lived in Cisnes. Or, at the very least, that such places existed.

I went on the cattle drive because it was a final chance to ride with the gauchos on the unchanged landscape. Levied against my fear of missing this chance, my fear of Duck was nothing.

It seemed only fitting that, halfway through the drive, I was also riding against the rescheduled coming of Señor Mansilla. The night after we left the *veranada,* it was announced on Messages that Mansilla would be making his trip to Tapera early because a blizzard was expected by the week's end. The plan was that I would ride with the gauchos through the switchbacks above the Río Moro and that, once we'd come out onto the ridge on the other side, I would leave them and continue on to Santa Elvira. When Señor Mansilla passed the following day, I would flag down his bus and go on to Coihaique.

Midway through my final morning on the drive, the snow started. Marión, always sure-footed, lost her bearings and, for the first time since I'd arrived in Chile, she threw me. I landed squarely on a rock and cracked two ribs. After getting back on her, I drove the quarter of the herd in my charge to catch up the drive.

It was midday when Don Tito and Tano and Duck and I rode onto the ridge above the Moro. Duck and I had kept our distance from one another during the drive—it was easy, given that rounding up the cattle at the *veranada* had required us to work separately, and that, once the drive had begun, each man had his own hundred twenty or so animals with which to deal. At the Moro, the gauchos stopped for the night, hoping for a break in the weather.

I shook Tano's and Tito's hands. When I shook Duck's, he said, "When are you coming back?" I told him I didn't know. He was holding his riding crop, the one he'd used since he was fourteen, and he asked if I would take the crop as a gift. I did, and we shook hands again and I rode away.

Thirteen hours later I made it back to the cabin at Santa Elvira. My ribs were swollen and the skin around them was black and blue from the fall. I unsaddled Marión and hung the saddle by feel in the tack room. I didn't want to scare Edith by suddenly walking on the porch, so I stood in the pasture and called out her name. It took her a while to get the throne moved from where she'd propped it against the door. When she finally came outside, she had a candle in one hand and the rifle in the other.

She said, "Skinny, if I knew how to shoot, you'd be dead. I thought sure when you started calling the Devil had come for me." We went inside, and she and the girls and I had supper by the light of a single candle and with the curtains drawn. "Just because I had good luck once tonight," said Edith, "doesn't mean it'll happen that way again."

Three days later, I was back in New York.

*   *   *

Between June and August 1998, I sent three letters to Duck and Edith. According to Duck's orders, I addressed them in their names and in care of the general store in Amengual. Duck had said that if a letter got that far, someone in the village would be sure to deliver it to Santa Elvira. A rider headed that way, or Señor Mansilla when he passed on his Sunday trips. For a long time, I got no reply.

At the same time, I was also writing this book. And the further I got into it, the more I realized how little I knew about Duck and Edith. For every question that I'd answered between February and June 1998, there were five more that needed to be asked. Now that I had seen the changes coming to Cisnes, I wanted very badly to know how Duck and Edith would adjust to them. Then, in November, all three letters I'd sent came back. On the envelopes, right next to their names, was written: "Does not exist. Return." By Thanksgiving, I had decided to go back to Patagonia.

I could only imagine the degenerative effects that the long austral winter had had on Duck. I was afraid once the letters came back that he had killed Edith. Assuming he hadn't, I knew that I'd have to live in the storeroom of their cabin in order to prove to Duck that he was not "too poor" for me, and to have any hope of preventing him from once again trying to kill me.

For that reason, I decided to go earlier in the austral summer of 1999, when the fly-fishing lodge was in full swing. There was, it seemed to me, protection in numbers. On the night Duck told me he was the Devil he'd kept saying he was going to castrate me—the precise thing that he felt was happening to him with the coming of the lodge, which represented a world he did not, by his own admission, "have the balls" to try and get to, as badly as he might have wanted to try. To lash out at that world while it wasn't looking at him across the pasture was one thing; to do it under scrutiny was another. If Duck lashed out toward the Outside while the Outside was there to see it, it would be a blight on his pride. And Duck was nothing if not proud.

By early February 1999, I had bought a plane ticket to Chilean Patagonia for the third time in four years.

*   *   *

"I knew," said Duck, "that if you ever came back, you'd have sense enough to move inside."

He was leaning against the window of the storeroom watching me unpack my things. The storeroom was a hundred thirty square feet. On one wall were supply shelves. What little they contained mostly comprised the various foodstuffs that Alex brought Duck and Edith once every month or so: a few cans of tuna and tomato paste; three or four packages of spaghetti; a liter of hot sauce paste; a box with twenty packets of dried orange juice and another with lemonade; several unpackaged size D batteries, half of which were leaking acid. On another wall was the cabinet where Duck stored the livestock antibiotics, which smelled like iodine. On warm days, the odor drifted into the main room of the house and, if the wind was right, all the way out into the pasture.

I was worried as much as I'd ever been about the hanta virus. In the last year, the number of cases in Chilean Patagonia had gone up again; even the *New York Times* had written an article about it. There was nothing to be done except keep the window of the storeroom open so that the air circulated and hope for the best. If it was a mild year, the rats wouldn't be trying to get into the cabin until late March or even April.

Duck went to the barn and brought two sheepskins to the storeroom. I laid my sleeping bag on top of them and arranged everything else on the shelves: the Walkman and the same cassettes I'd had in 1995 and 1998, a dictionary, and a book. The ceilings of the storeroom were just under seven feet, so that I could stand up straight but had to duck to get under the crossbeam. There were nails in the crossbeam, and I hung my clothes and tack from them. Moving in took five minutes.

There were two doors into the storeroom, one from the porch and another from the bedroom. If Duck went on a binge again, I could lock both doors. If he decided to burn down the cabin, I had two escape routes: the window and the porch door.

And because the bedroom doorway was somewhat obscured from the view of the main room, I could go there under the pretense of changing my socks and write notes before anyone looked in to see what I was doing. After dinner, I could write as long as I needed to, lying on the sheepskins with, ironically enough, a ring of candles around my head.

The first night of living in Duck and Edith's cabin that year was particularly cold, and Duck built up the stove fire and opened the bedroom door. I was writing, and he stood there a moment before saying, "Keep this door open tonight, *che,* and the window, too. The stove heat will circulate in here. In the morning," he said, "time for *mate.*"

It was dark in the family's bedroom, and I heard Duck get into bed with Edith and Oscar. "May I?" he asked formally. Then the family whispered and tossed in their beds, and the wood frames creaked. They told stories about what had happened that day, about how Uncle Skinny had finally shown up again, and how Sheep Shearings had chased his tail in the pasture.

Mariana said, "I wonder if Chickenhead's asleep. Hey! Chickenhead, are you asleep?"

Duck and Edith shushed her, and then the shushings turned to giggles, and pretty soon we were all whispering back and forth to one another, two or three conversations at once in the last moments before unconsciousness.

Patricia said, "Uncle Skinny—sleep with the angels, *che.*" After that, the only audible thing was a family of five piled into two beds a few feet away, breathing deeply in and out.

*   *   *

During the winter of 1998, Duck had added a bedroom and a bathroom to the cabin, making his the only place in Cisnes, aside from the lodge, with an indoor shower and a flushing toilet. The additions had doubled the size of his home; it seemed that the cabin had been rebuilt for the long term. Not only that, he and Edith were supplementing their income by doing extra work for the lodge—Edith by baking bread and ironing clients' clothes, Duck by cooking the weekly *asado,* or fire-roasted ewe—as though they'd finally decided to make the most of their lives in Cisnes. That was not the case, however, for during that winter Duck had also resigned himself to being fired from his job. I'd been in Cisnes two weeks before I knew anything about it.

We were riding to the *veranada* again to get the bulls when Duck casually told me that if you quit a job in Chile, your employer doesn't pay any compensation. He said that if you get fired, on the other hand, the employer is required by law to pay one month of wages for every year worked. Duck had worked five years; five months of compensation was starting money for moving to Coihaique. But getting fired, he said, wasn't as easy as I might think. For the past ten months, ever since Alex had suspected Duck's intentions, he'd been waiting him out, making it harder and harder for Duck to stay at Santa Elvira. Alex was supposed to bring the supplies and Duck's paycheck every month on the fifth. In all the months I'd lived in Cisnes, Alex had never once come before the fifteenth or twentieth. And in the wake of his suspicions about Duck, he had become even more unreliable.

Just after lunch on the day Duck and I got back from the *veranada* the dogs went barking across the pasture, and Alex's red Toyota pickup came bumping down the trail to the cabin. While I was in Santiago I'd picked up a book for Edith that she'd said she'd like to have the year before, *How to Survive in the Chilean Jungle (and Learn Slang in English),* and the three of us were paging through it at the table. We'd looked at it many times, though only Edith ever added the words, all of which were Santiaguino, to her vocabulary, words like "Wendy," which meant cool, and *"esnob,"* a Latinized version of snob. Duck, when he saw Alex driving through the pasture, ran his finger along the page and dryly read the line where it stopped: "There's no wind, and the shitted toilet paper has arrived."

Alex was wearing blue jeans and a dress shirt and Italian shoes. On his head was the kind of hat worn by men who go hunting in Africa. He watched Duck and me take the supplies from the bed of his truck to the storeroom. After the seventh trip, he followed us to the cabin and stopped in the doorway, waiting to be invited inside.

Alex's eyes, like Duck's, were set oddly on his face, one slightly higher than the other. There was a kind of brutal ambivalence in them, like a doctor who is by turns amused and bored by caring for patients he considers beneath him. He would tilt his head back and to the side when he spoke or was spoken to, and look at you condescendingly, the corners of his lips upturned in a nearly invisible grin. Nor was Alex one to stay long whenever he came to Santa Elvira.

"Pass," said Duck.

"So, Don Duck," said Alex as he walked inside, "when might you like to bring the rest of the herd down from the *veranada*?"

"Well, Mr. Alex," said Duck, "as soon as possible." He got up from the table. There was a tear-sheet calendar nailed to the wall by the bookcase; above the torn remnants of past months was the same picture that had been there the year before of three blonde women in see-through white dresses standing around several Stihl chain saws, one with her hand raised as though she might be hitchhiking. Duck put his middle finger on the twelfth of April and ran it along the calendar. "Anywhere in here would be good," he said.

"I have to schedule the inspectors," said Alex. A law had been passed in 1997 stating that men working for the government had to come out to ranches and have a look at the animals and oversee certain vaccinations. Everything had to be timed so the inspectors came shortly after the cattle drive and the herd didn't spend too long in the holding corrals. It was, as far as Duck was concerned, one more thing that gave Alex power over him. Alex said, "I'm sure I can do it sometime after that."

"I'd prefer not any later than a week," said Duck. "This weather'll change like it did last year, and by May there might drop whatever amount of snow, and . . ."

"No, no," said Alex. "Clearly we don't want that to happen again." The day after I'd left the gauchos in 1998, they watched as a dozen head of cattle lost their footing on the snow-covered road and went bellowing and spinning end over end onto the rocks four hundred meters below. Tito, too, would have been killed had he not jumped at the last moment and held fast to a *calafate* bush to keep from following his horse to its death. He finished the drive nearly a week later, riding bareback and with no bridle on one of the horses from Alfredo's *cabalde*. Alex said, "I think they stayed up there last year till just the right moment. They got the maximum yield from the grass. It was just unforeseeable and unfortunate that we got weather right then."

"It's been a mild summer, Mr. Alex," said Duck, taking his finger from the calendar, "but everyone knows that means an early winter. And mild or not, May is a touchy time. Nico and I were just up there, and the herd looks better than I've ever seen. But those animals can't be chest-deep in snow and have to go for seventy kilometers. Some of them will die. Or lose so much weight and be so broken up they won't make it through the winter or calf-out."

"Of course," said Alex, "we *do* want them to be as fat as possible when they come down. Assuming the inspectors can come, we'll go ahead as you've planned. Who will accompany you?"

Duck smiled. "Nico here, instead of Don Tito. Don Tito's too old, Mr. Alex. You get him in the rain and he catches the shakes like he'll die. And when that happens," said Duck, "he just can't work like we need him to. He's dangerous."

Alex had never liked it that I was living with Duck and Edith, and he liked it less when I went on cattle drives. I'd met him in Coihaique in 1998 when I'd gone to his office, and he'd asked me very detailed questions about what I wanted to do in Cisnes. Then he'd offered to take me out to Santa Elvira. He told me to call him, and we'd schedule a day—he even gave me his cell phone number so we'd be sure not to miss one another. I called him every day for three weeks. He was satisfied to think, I suppose, that if he didn't take me to Duck and Edith, I'd never find them on my own.

I knew as well as Duck that I would never ride a cattle drive in the stead of Don Tito. I might go with them again, as I had the year before, but only as an added hand, never as a replacement for someone employed by Carlos Asi. It was an interesting and brave ploy on Duck's part to try and use this lie. Alex said, "You know I can't deny Don Tito the work." He tilted his head and said, "He *does* work for me."

"I think you ought to fire Don Tito," said Duck. "He'll get one of us killed, if he doesn't get himself killed."

"We've discussed this ad nauseam," said Alex impatiently.

Duck said, "He's an old man, Alex. He can't work anymore." It was the first time I'd ever heard Duck refer to Alex without using Mr.

"He's three years before his pension," said Alex.

"Give it to him, then," said Duck. "Give it to him early. He's worked since the Flood."

"What else would he do?" said Alex. "What else were he not working?" He was moving for the door now. "We'll talk on the radio before the drive." Then Alex walked outside. Duck followed him.

The two men stood side by side at Alex's truck. Duck ran his foot over the tire rut in the grass and nodded. Alex put his hand on Duck's shoulder; he pointed toward the river. Edith had been smoking as she watched this, and now she lit a second cigarette with the first one. Duck looked out over the river and the mountains and nodded as Alex talked. Then Alex got into the truck. He looked like he was in a great hurry. Duck put his hands in his pockets and walked slowly over to the storeroom, whistling. A minute later he came into the cabin carrying the watermelon Alex had brought as part of the supplies. Duck said, "What is it they call Clinton?"

"Slick Willie?" I said.

"Jess!" Duck laughed. He put the watermelon on the table. He said, "Well, Slick Al said to me out there, 'Why don't you quit, Duck? It's obvious you're not happy here. And you're doing some things I've asked you not to.' That's when he looked over at the river at Broken Ear."

I said, "What's Broken Ear got to do with anything?" Broken Ear was the horse that Pork Rind had lent me that year in Marión's stead; she'd been butchered and eaten the winter before.

Duck said, "Alex doesn't want another horse cropping grass meant for the ranch horses."

I'd not realized this, but it had all been part of Duck's plan. Had I known, I wouldn't have gotten involved—I'd have ridden back across the river each day that I used Broken Ear and then recrossed the river up at the shallows on foot. But now that it was over, I didn't care. I was happy for Duck. His plan had worked.

Duck said, "So Alex says, 'I'd hate to fire you and have you have to deal with the stigma of that.' I said, 'Mr. Alex, if I quit, you don't have to pay me anything, eggo.'"

Edith said, "You didn't really call him eggo."

"Almost. I said, 'I'm not quitting, *che*. That way I get my compensation.' Boy, did that turn him red."

"Wednesday," said Edith. "I wish you would have called him eggo, *che*. That would have been Wendy."

Duck said, "Alex says, 'You know, Don Duck, I'd completely forgotten. You're absolutely right. God! How could I have forgotten that?' You believe that shit?" said Duck, incredulous. "That son of a whore thinks I'm dumb enough to believe he *forgot* that little detail?" He looked down. I think he'd not meant to call Alex a name, even if he wasn't in the room. That, in a way, was going too far.

"You should have called him son of a whore," said Edith. "Couldn't have hurt your chances."

Duck looked at the watermelon on the table, and now I knew why he'd asked Alex to bring it: it was for the celebration. Aside from a few crabapples and plums we picked from the trees, it was the first fruit we'd ever had. Duck giggled as he sliced the watermelon open. He cut a thick round from one half, and then cut the round into wedges and passed them around. There was color in his face, like a fish that gets returned to the water.

Edith said, "When does the alarm go off?"

"He says he'll send a truck to move us in ten days," said Duck. "Eight A.M. sharp. Alex says he'll come, too, and we ride to Coihaique with him."

I said, "What're the chances he'll show up within a month, never mind eight A.M. sharp?"

Duck laughed. He said, "It's like the boxer story I told you last year, Nico. Losing a small battle isn't the point—we already won the war, *che*."

Two yellow jackets came zooming through the door and took a wide turn around the stove, then came in low over the table, smelling the fresh melon. They ran the gauntlet of flailing arms and seemed to move in several directions at once, as though a fourth spatial dimension was available to them. Every year in Aisén, one or two people died from yellow jacket stings.

Mariana said, "Hoo-ha!"

Edith said, "Aahhhh!" and Oscar jumped up and down on Edith's leg, galloping at full speed, his play-crop throttling her thigh.

Duck said, "How do you play baseball?" He got a wooden spoon from the drawer. He swung it and said, "Like this, no?" He took the proper stance and adjusted his imaginary cap. "Now, how's it called the eggo who throws the ball and the eggo that hits it? And what are the ways the eggo throws it: they have names, no?"

He was eyeing the two yellow jackets as they hovered near a plant in the corner of the room. Duck closed the door so they couldn't escape.

I said, "If the ball veers toward you at the last second, it's called a screwball. If it veers away, it's called a curveball." Duck described the possible trajectories with his right hand. I said, "A right-handed batter always finds the screwball hardest to hit, assuming the pitcher is right-handed."

One of the yellow jackets came on and banked right up into Duck, who stepped away and hit it with a crack. Edith smooshed the stunned bee under her slipper and left it where it lay. Duck said, "I am the screwball exception. Now, explain to me the rules of the game, *che*."

I said there were nine men conspiring to remove the batter from the playing field. The batter, meanwhile, was trying to advance through a series of safe areas called bases, of which there were three. Once he had reached one—and there were two basic ways of doing this—then his teammates would try and advance him until he had gone through the bases and come back home.

"So," said Duck, winding up to pitch and then swinging at the invisible ball he'd just thrown, "it's everybody ganged up versus the *huaso* with the bat. And he wants to leave home so he can go through all kinds of trouble trying to get back there, only from another direction."

The second yellow jacket came at Duck, and he swung and missed, and the bee hovered there and let him take another swing. This time Duck foul-tipped him into the window by the stove.

Duck said, "How's it called when you hit one so far away that it leaves and doesn't come back?"

"To run from home," I said, trying to translate.

*   *   *

John of the Cows sat making a bridle on the other side of the stove from me. Flames rose freely into the air between us through its rusted surface. A radio played from the windowsill, and a snarl of flies buzzed around it as though they would find something to eat there. Laid about John's feet were flat pieces of horse- and cow- and bullhide that curled at the edges. While he braided the hide he told the story of how he'd come to seek refuge in Pork Rind's cabin after, according to the rumors, he'd murdered a policeman in Tapera three weeks before.

"So we were running about in La Tapera, where the show," he said, using the shorthand that dropped the "was" from the end of the sentence. "There's a rodeo, and after, they showed the show. I'd ridden down from the mountain with my brothers, looking for something good to look for," he said, using a gaucho euphemism for women and *pisco*. "Some cartoony shit from Mexico like Condorito, always gets himself in trouble for this and that. I don't remember the name. And after that some action show. An American, you know, a *paco* runs around here and there in I think New York. I think Bruce Willis." "Brew Wheely" is how he said it. He looked at the hides at his feet and added, "We didn't run in the rodeo because I didn't have a horse."

John picked up a bottle of *pisco* and took a swig and formally screwed the cap back down onto the bottle before handing it to me; I unscrewed the cap, took my drink, repeated the process, and passed it back. We drank this way for some time, steadily and in silence. John was tall for a gaucho—five feet seven or eight—and unusually muscular, all shoulders and forearms. He wore brown goatskin chaps and fake-suede tennis shoes, the kind worn by skateboarders, and a black wool sweater; his cheeks were wide and high, and the color of his eyes changed with the light. At times they were olive-brown, and at others a sort of transluscent beige with hints of amber, like agate rocks in the bottom of a clear stream. He might have been eighteen or twenty-eight, and his teeth were unnaturally long and white and straight. It was difficult, when you were in a room with him, not to want to be John of the Cows.

I said, "Where was your horse, *che?*"

John had a match that he was using to cut horsehide *pitas,* or strips, from a sheet of hide tied to the leg of my chair. He bent at the waist, and laid the match on the hide and used it to guide his big knife as he shaved a long, thin strip. Liberated from the sheet, the *pita* wanted to curl, and John rubbed it back and forth across his chaps. In the hour and a half since I'd been in his cabin, he'd turned a square of cowhide into a nearly complete bridle. Now he was ready to attach a length of chain for the bit to one side of the bridle with the *pitas*. He said,

"Where was my horse, *che?*" Repeating a question was John's way of letting you understand the question's absurdity in absolute terms.

I said, "How do you know how long to make the bit?" He was making it for Uncle Ya Ya in return for a couple boxes of wine.

John said, "I saw the animal's head, *che.*"

I said, "And you remember how big it was."

"I wasn't meaning to say I'd forgotten, no." He smiled.

He took two steel rings and cut them open with the wire-cutters and closed them with pliers onto either side of the bit. Then he ran the tag end of one side of the bridle through one of the rings and doubled it back on itself and held it to his knee and eyeballed the length. He used his fingers as a measuring tape by putting his thumb on the ring and his pinkie on the bridle where it would pass under the horse's eye, and he rotated his hand so his thumb was now at the forehead of the bridle. He let out some on the doubled loop, to make the bridle longer, and repeated the thumb-to-pinkie measurement. Then he began wrapping over the doubled loop with a *pita*, just above the bit ring. If he was wrong about the length of the bridle, the next hours he spent braiding would be all for nothing. He knotted the *pita* around the doubling like a bandanna. Then he shaved two more *pitas* and affixed them to the doubling the same way, so that six foot-and-a-half-long wisps of horsehide hung like tentacles from the bridle.

"And so," he said, "halfway through this Brew Wheely show, the fucking *viejo* runs the show says come back tomorrow, and he shuts off the generator. He says the generator is done for the night because it's nine o'clock, *che.*" He ended the sentence high, as though it were a question. He said, "Brew Wheely is the nun's tits, *che,* the best. Running around shooting and jumping out of buildings. Is that what it's like out there where you come from?"

I said it wasn't. It was just a movie. He looked at me incredulously.

"Well," he said, "at any rate, after the show got called, my brothers rode back to the mountains, and I came here to help Pork Rind finish his fence."

He wrapped one of the *pitas* loosely around the doubling and ran the tag end back under itself in a whip finish. He wet it with saliva and pulled it tight. The result was seamless: no visible knots, no beginning and no end. Then he began effecting a kind of six-stranded French braid, first by weaving three strands of *pita* around the doubling and then lifting the tiny braids with an awl, reinforcing them with the fourth, fifth, and sixth strands of *pita.* It was a maddeningly slow process, one that moved millimeters at a time—lifting, sliding, pulling, smoothing, on and on and on. When he'd completed a ring of braid around the doubling perhaps half a centimeter wide, John drank from the *pisco* bottle and spit a drooling gob onto the completed section and let it sit while we drank. He screwed the cap back on the bottle, and took each tag of *pita* and pulled it until his face was red and there were white creases along the backs of his blunt hands. Then he rubbed the braid and the bridle in general back and forth across his chaps. He was ready to begin another section.

I said, "What about the *paco* who got bludgeoned to death with a *pisco* bottle?"

John said, "What about the cop who got bludgeoned," as evenly as though it were a statement or judgment instead of a question. He took the awl and lifted a loop of *pita* well back into the braided body. He studied it, seeing some invisible imperfection in the pattern. He'd not expected me to ask after the murder. "Messed up," he said, smiling.

Slowly he began undoing the braid one tiny loop at a time, pulling the spit-slick tags from where they'd been cinched into one another. It was a long time before he began the story again. He said, "The people up there at Tapera don't like us. They say we have a mafia, us brothers. After the show, there was a big fight and they blamed us. Louse and I were walking in the street to our horses, and we had a *pisco* bottle with us, and they stopped us." He studied the little loops he'd raised with the awl. "According to them, you can't drink in the streets. I might have had something to say about that."

He took up the bullhide from the floor and eyeballed it, perhaps seeing in it something he wanted carefully to slice out with his knife and add to the bridle. Then he put it down again. He said, "I guess I won't go that way." When he said this, three very different things happened at once to his face: his cheeks blushed; his lips framed his big white teeth in an eerie smile; and his bright eyes, the lids half-closed around them, reduced me to the size of my reflection in them. I wanted suddenly for him to like me almost as much as I wanted never to be alone with him outside of earshot of other people.

"Where were you born?" I asked. He pointed east with his chin. I said, "Tapera?"

"Sí."

Everything with John of the Cows had at least two meanings, it seemed. "To be born" might have meant anything—it was all a matter of putting the clues together. I'd asked him the same question the year before. That time he'd pointed vaguely to a bedroom hidden in the dark on the other side of the wall behind the stove. The wall was made of rotting wood; sides of cardboard boxes were nailed to the wall for insulation: they read Pisco Capel and Nido and 120 Merlot. The floor had holes in it, and I could see through them to the dirt below the cabin. I took a long drink from the *pisco*. A chicken that had gotten under the floorboards flashed by white underneath one of the holes. I said, "How often you go to Coihaique?"

"As often as I can, *che*," said John. "My mom lives there. I have another brother there, too, who lives with her. He isn't much good for anything, though. My *mami* went there after she left Tapera and took him with her. She works like injustice; I don't know what he does. Another brother might be there, too. And I like to get out of here, *che*. Only . . ." And he stopped here.

I said, "If the other brother isn't in Coihaique, where might he be?"

"I haven't seen that kid in a pair of years. He might be there, he might be anywhere. He might be in Argentina. Might be dead. Me and Louse and Filly have stuck together," said John.

I said, "Why don't you go live in Coihaique?"

He sat for a long time redoing the section of braid he'd undone. When he was finished, he wet the braid with his mouth, and put the bridle under his foot and pulled each *pita* till his hands puffed up red with blood under the skin. He set the bridle on the floor. "Coihaique's complicated," he said finally.

"Did you do your time in the army?" Gaucho kids, like everyone, were required to register for the two mandatory years of military service, and to do this they had to get to Coihaique. Then, when their number came up, they were required to return for service. The announcement came on Messages. Edith told me John's number had been announced many times.

"I registered," he said.

I said, "But they didn't call your number?"

He looked at me. "I haven't heard anything about it," he said. Then he walked to the windowsill and switched the radio off.

*   *   *

There's a story of the first policeman to be sent to Lago Verde in the 1890s, a village north of Tapera. The policeman arrived there from the academy in a pressed uniform, ready to bring peace to the half-wild gauchos he'd been told were living there in a state so decrepit that it was interfering with the government's best attempts to settle the area. And when the officer's replacement rode into town five years later, he couldn't find his onetime classmate. He asked about him for days. He was told only that his classmate was gone. His suspicions grew until, finally, he was convinced the man had been murdered.

One day, the new policeman went to the bar and sat down next to gauchos in sheepskin chaps and with long hair and mustaches. When the man next to him bought the replacement officer a drink, the officer looked at him. Only now, under the mustache and long hair he saw his old classmate. According to the story, the replacement jumped up and said to the man he'd long before known: "Traitor!" When the other gauchos at the bar drew their knives, the ex-policeman raised his hands and said to his replacement, "That's the last time I save your life."

John of the Cows had been a legend since he was little more than a child. At night, from where he lived alone or with his brothers at a crude *puesto* on his *patrón's veranada,* he would ride into Argentina to steal stock and drive it, right under the nose of the law, down the main street of Tapera. If police presence in Tapera was a cobra, John's brazenness served as a kind of flute, as if by taunting them to strike at him he was able to halt them in their tracks. That was the early nineties. The road was brand new and the connection to Coihaique was still static-filled. To be a well-trained, educated officer—worldly, ineluctably urban— and sent to Tapera was as much a punishment as it had been to be sent to Lago Verde a hundred years before. The very presence of a law that hardly applied reminded the gauchos of their disenfranchisement, of the meddling of a government that made a career of misunderstanding them. A thief was more their own than a *paco*—as long as John stole from the wealthy Argentine *patrones,* who cared?

In a very short time, though, the road began to take more hold. The Outside was coming like a tide. No matter that traffic on the road was limited to four or five vehicles a week—four or five was a world's worth compared to none. A new class developed, stocked with men like Red Duck, and along with them the market grew. And so grew the attention that John attracted.

To counter this, John stole fewer cattle, butchered them immediately, burned the hides (and evidence of their brands), and sold the meat, according to the story, through Olga the Cheese Lady. It was a supernatural marriage: the immovable witch and the boy who, through whatever dark covenant he'd supposedly struck, could maneuver at blind night through the mountains. The police in Tapera had a battered Jeep in which to get around. But what good was a Jeep when there was one road, and a hopelessly decrepit one at that? And what good were three frightened policemen when a man could disappear into the border or ride unnoticed into Argentina? What, for the time being at least, was a Jeep compared to a horse?

Nothing. Except that the Outside now became the flute player, and John the cobra. Seeing Brew Wheely was too much temptation to pass up. Then he committed the fatal error. Whether he or one of his brothers murdered a policeman was of no importance. Either way, the flute player had been struck, and the spell was broken. John, in a way, had gone feral—he had become both the *viejo* and the *joven.*

John fled to Pork Rind's cabin. Pork Rind's *patrón* owned the land across the river from Duck and Edith's cabin, and his land bordered the thousand-square-kilometer rectangle of land that formed much of the northeastern border of Middle Cisnes that the gauchos called the Inside. No one had ever managed to live on the Inside; John of the Cows and Pork Rind and the 120-year-old gaucho named Tío were its lone intimates, and the former two had used it for years as a place to graze stolen stock. When John of the Cows ran from Tapera, he'd cleverly elected to hide in the cabin closest to what seemed the perfect escape route.

There was no chance of interference from Pork Rind's *patrón,* a man that Duck called Mr. Quietlike, who lived in Lago Verde, two weeks north of Cisnes by horse. Mr. Quietlike was a traditional *patrón* who for all his life had worked alongside his gauchos. But now he was too old to ride from Lago Verde to his outranch in Cisnes, and his nephews did most of the work for him, which meant that they came to Pork Rind's only twice a year, first in the spring and then again in the fall.

Duck and Pork Rind's families, though they lived closer than almost any neighbors in Cisnes, were as different as could be, and, in a certain way, had been created in the very different images of their *patrones*. Carlos Asi owned a furniture and clothing store in Coihaique. He'd inherited Santa Elvira from his father at a time when there was no Argentine Road and the ranch was three weeks from Coihaique by horse. Whether he knew how to ride was open to question. On the rare occasions he came to the ranch, he would stay for, at best, a weekend, and he passed his time fishing and barbecuing. When not in Coihaique, he was traveling to the United States, to Europe, and to Buenos Aires.

While Carlos looked to the Outside—to business opportunities in Coihaique and in the rest of Chile—Mr. Quietlike was devoted to ending his life the same way it had started: as a landowning gaucho. He was focused on the old way—on the Inside. Whether Mr. Quietlike knew that John of the Cows was nicknamed for his talents as a cattle thief was unclear, though my guess is that he did know and didn't care so long as his own stock was accounted for. In the end, Duck and Edith, like Carlos, lived with their eyes fixed on the south, on distant Coihaique; John and Pork Rind stared stoically, if not opportunistically, at the mountains to the north.

*   *   *

John hung the bridle from a hook in the door. It had grown dark in the cabin. Through the open door, I could see hundreds of bright green parrots swooping downvalley, iridescent even in the failing light. John took a long drink from the bottle. He handed it to me and said: "Do you want to go with me Inside?"

I felt the liquor's heat spread from my throat to my chest, before settling in my stomach. Brew Wheely, it seemed to me, was John's brown egg. Wherever he went, it would be there, under the cabin. The police would never find him if he didn't move. But if he was driven out by Brew Wheely, John would be once again on the run. It would push him farther Inside, and he wanted to refamiliarize himself with it. I nodded. I said, "When?"

"A week," said John.

We walked outside, and Broken Ear groaned when I pulled the girthstraps tight and swung onto his back. John followed us to the high riverbank on foot, and I reined the horse to reach down and shake his hand. "Maybe we'll find something good to look for," he said, smiling at the ground. There was something in the way he said it—the shyness covered with a certain excited air of confidence—that made me think of a young boy speaking with a girl on whom he has a crush.

"I doubt it," I said. Then I put Broken Ear down the eroded bank and into the heavy river. Halfway across, I turned to look back; John of the Cows was still standing there watching, vaguely outlined against the opaque hills.

The Yellow Jacket and The Grape

All was spacious—earth, sky, the waving continent of

grass; the fierce and blinding storms, and, above all, the

feeling in men's minds of freedom, and of being face to

face with nature, under those southern skies.

—*Robert B. Cunninghame Graham,* Rodeo:

A Collection of Tales and Sketches

of Robert B. Cunninghame Graham, *1936*

The evening I rode back to Duck and Edith's after watching John make his bridle, it was announced on Messages that The Grape was to arrive in Cisnes the following day on Señor Mansilla's bus. The Grape, who was the daughter of Julia and Tea Kettle Without a Spout, was considered to be the most beautiful woman to have lived in Cisnes in a generation. But the year before, she'd moved to Mañihuales and had begun living with a man who was the father of her child, making her, for all practical purposes, married. Or, as John of the Cows liked to say, married, but not dead.

"*Che,*" said Duck, shaking his head, "there'll be a tree full of yellow jackets coming past the cabin this week. Just whatever number, Nico. You're going to see

Indians you never knew existed: Monkey, Louse, Filly—I bet even Uncle Ya Ya'll come sniffing around for this event."

Yellow jacket was John of the Cows' slang for a man (because the most characteristic part of a yellow jacket was his stinger). And because John often came to visit—mostly in the evenings or at night, to avoid being seen—he and Duck and Edith took from one another favorite bits of slang and recombined them. A yellow jacket's favorite food was what gauchos referred to as "grapes," which were actually the little plums that grew wild in the trees during the summer. To Duck and Edith and John, then, a "grape" was also a woman. Edith's favorite saying, "more dangerous than a monkey with a Gillette," was remixed with the names of two other members of John's "mafia"—Monkey and Louse—to become "more dangerous than Monkey with Louse." It seemed all the more appropriate, considering the two of them had, like John of the Cows, disappeared following the murder of the policeman.

The double-sided euphemism in this last saying, that Monkey and Louse, paired and on the run, were as dangerous to one another as they were to anyone who crossed them, was intentional. Homosexuality was, in a place where the ratio of men to women neared seven to one, considered normal, even if it was simultaneously looked upon as abhorrent. And women, because of the disproportionate gender ratio, had their pick of the hive, as they said. If a man left a woman—and they often, like Tea Kettle, did—it was not uncommon for several other men to "move in," by which was meant anything from actual cohabitation to "visits" when the spirit moved any of the parties involved.

Cross-pollination was as inevitable as it was acceptable. It was common knowledge that Julia had among her suitors both John of the Cows and his brother Louse. Uncle Ya Ya was the father of six of the children who lived with Don Tito and his woman, each of whose births might theoretically be traced to roughly nine months after Tito had decided to "move on" for a while, be it to Argentina or Lago Verde or any number of other points on the map within a month's ride.

Which is not to say that Duck or Edith seemed to share any of the same notions. In fact, they had the most traditional situation in all of Cisnes. Still, the mood in the cabin in the wake of that one five-second Message was like it had been at the start of Liberator's Cup, in which all the qualifying teams in South America would compete for the title of most dominant soccer power. Edith said her money was on Tío, who lived with Uncle Ya Ya. How could you bet, said Edith, against a benevolent hundred-twenty-year-old witch whose spells were only cast to maintain his virility? Duck's money was on Louse, who, though he'd not been seen for the last five months, Duck was sure would come calling.

"You?" said Duck.

"John of the Cows," I said. If anyone had adapted his morals to the state of things in Cisnes, it was John of the Cows.

"Good point," said Duck. "That's why mine's on Louse—John wouldn't kill his own brother, and Louse is better looking than the old Fucking J."

"Tío won't kill anyone," said Edith. "He'll just fly down and roost on her breast. No one will know he's even there. Except," she winked, "The Grape."

I said, "Julia might have something to say about all this, *che.*"

"No, eggo," said Duck. "Catch it that she's got too good a thing going starting the day The Grape leaves to be an *esnob* about things. Back to her choice of stingers, *che.*"

Duck, ever since he'd been fired, had started using more Outside slang, as though preparing himself for integration by amplifying his vocabulary. It seemed only fitting that he would be talking about Julia right then, who had integrated herself into the completely masculine society of Cisnes in an almost unimaginable way: the men there accepted her as one of their own, *un gaucho más.* Perhaps they understood her better because the way she loved Tea Kettle was like the way some men loved *pisco*: passionately, steadfastly, and irrationally—"right to the hilt of the knife." Julia was, in any case, considered more of a man than Tea Kettle because she was more useful and practical. Which is decidedly not to say that she wasn't also considered feminine and attractive. She managed to occupy two very distinct roles at once.

It was a coupling that, since a month before, had gotten much more difficult to carry off. This time, Tea Kettle had not only left, he'd gone to Coihaique and pushed the knife deeper than he'd ever before pushed it: according to a Message played on the radio, he'd sold most of Julia's animals, right down to the dogs. In Chile, even though the ranch and the stock were Julia's to begin with—because they were passed to her by her widowed mother—it had all become Tea Kettle's when he and Julia had been lawfully married. If she wanted to retain the stock Tea Kettle had not sold, Julia would have to divorce him, a lengthy and expensive process that, in the mountains, was nearly impossible. How can you divorce someone you can't find?

With the impending winter, it was a treacherous time to be without horses and dogs. Julia's few remaining stock were at the *veranada* and needed to be brought down—she hadn't even gotten the bulls she still owned down yet. Her only hope was to borrow a horse to get to them, and a dog to herd them, neither of which is an efficient alternative, given the loyalties of most animals to their masters. To have a dog run off, or, worse yet, a dog that fails to mind, in the middle of a cattle drive is to risk losing as much of everything as Julia had left.

Julia was one of the only two gauchos in Cisnes (Ya Ya was the other) to run her own herd on her own land, as opposed to that of a *patrón*. She had reached the pinnacle of success. She had cornered the market on selling produce to the lodge and she was locally famous for making sweaters and ponchos. The neighbors were doing their best to help her get things back together. Tío had given her a horse to use and he was bringing another for The Grape, who'd come home to ride the drive. Don Tito had lent her a dog. It seemed on the suface at least that there were no ulterior motives involved. Helping neighbors (so long as they weren't bad witches) was considered a sacred endeavor, though that sacredness stemmed from an ultimately and obsessively utilitarian point of view: you might need it yourself someday, if ever the Colo Colo was spawned beneath your house. Julia had complete control. The violent timbre of things worked both ways in her case: if any one boyfriend ever threatened her or tried to exchange help for sexual favors he would be dealt with by one of the others.

So for the next week, we watched as one gaucho after the next crossed the shallows upstream of Duck and Edith's and rode downriver toward Julia's. We would hear the dogs barking in the pasture and go to the window and call out the riders in a kind of protracted, slow-motion play-by-play. There were six in all throughout the course of the week, and when we saw them ride back—three hours or a day later—we would contemplate aloud the possibilities. "He got his hooves peeled," meaning that he got to take his boots off and get in bed; "He got salt in his *mate*," meaning he hadn't gotten the time of day; "He'll make for the trees," meaning he'd wait till the following day to try his luck again before riding all the way back to wherever he'd come from. There was a sort of magnificence to the way the aural excitement of Messages had been given the resonance of a visual image: the radio soap opera—and, through it, the world—had been, however fleetingly, slightly undressed.

*   *   *

The only horseman we didn't see ride downriver was John of the Cows. We didn't hear, even once, the barking of his dogs. I wondered at the end of the week if he was even around. Still, I woke at four-thirty on the morning he and I were going to the Inside. The fire was dying, and I added wood and watched my breath smoke in the glow. There were pieces of ewe meat caked with fat in the pot on the stove, and I waited for the fat to melt and took the pieces and wrapped them in a cloth and put them in a saddlebag. Someone stirred; the door to the bedroom opened, and Mariana stood there barefoot and giggling and wrapped in a blanket. She came over and plopped down on my lap.

I said, "Your daddy'll feed you to the bulls if he finds you awake so early."

"Then you shouldn't make so much noise," she whispered.

I said, "How old are you?" She held up five fingers, and then she hesitantly extended two more on the other hand. I closed those two and winked. I said, "Like that. And I've never met a five-year-old who talked like you."

She shrugged. She said, "Are you going to give me some *mate* or do I have to make it myself?" I poured the gourd full and passed it to her. She wrinkled her nose. "No thanks. You still don't know how to make it right, *che*," she said, pushing the hair from her eyes. "Where are you going?"

"Inside with Uncle of the Cows."

"How long?" she said.

"I don't know."

Mariana grabbed the *mate* from my hand as I was about to drink, drained it, and handed it back. She looked angry. She said, "I don't know what you want with that crazy Indian, *che*."

*   *   *

I put on chaps and a poncho, put a second poncho in the other saddlebag, and went outside. It was drizzling, and fog hung so thick that I had to find Broken Ear by the sound of his hobble. I bridled him and wiped the rain from his back, then put a blanket over him and then the pad and saddle and the first girthstrap. On top of the saddle I put two whole sheepskins (a "couch," as the gauchos called it, because the skins were comfortable to sit on and they could be unfolded at night to make a bed) and cinched the whole thing down with another girthstrap. I could see only twenty feet, and Broken Ear and I followed the fence, past the invisible outbuildings to the river. It took a long time to cross to the other side.

John was sitting his horse, which he called Gift, in the yard. He had another horse, this one nameless, fitted with two *chiguas,* one empty and the other with a side of ewe ribs stuffed into a sack; an *asador* was strapped over the top of the packsaddle. John wore a poncho and his Colorado Rockies baseball cap and bullhide puttees that closed with buckles at the ankles and behind the calves and again just below his knees. He smiled and turned his horse, and we rode side by side toward the northwest. Two of his dogs, recently untied from the fence wire that had bound them through the night, ran ahead in the fog.

When we cleared the first rise, we were above the thickest fog and we could not see the cabin nor the river nor the forests that surrounded them. We turned north and steered by way of a fence that started at John's cabin and ended two hours later at the farthest inward settled point in Cisnes. Broken Ear trotted ahead, and stamped when I reined him in. He was an old horse, fifteen or twenty years, and he'd been with John to the Inside many times; and, if he knew where we were going, the knowledge made him another animal altogether, eager and energetic, and he looked around with his bad eyes and shivered and rubbed his head up under Gift's chin.

We began climbing again, the horses frothing at the shoulders and where the skin rubbed between their haunches, and we came onto a wet plateau littered with the corpses of long-dead trees and ibis droppings. From it we could see a long way into the valley that ran through the Inside in other directions there was nothing but fog. John rode as though none of it were of any consequence, or as though the consequences had been accounted for and need not be again. Every few minutes he would lean far down out of the saddle and study the ground, though when I asked what was there, he would shrug and smile and slip his foot back into the stirrup and ride on.

The dogs ran in and out of the maze of gray trunks, hunting European hares. The first dog would dart around corners and put his muzzle under the trunks while the second stayed wide, on the constantly shifting flank, monitoring the escape routes. Twice the first dog harried the prey into a panhandle of trunks, and twice the second dog was three steps too late and the hares flew past him and were gone.

"You ever feed them?" I asked.

Another chase began. This time, the flank dog hopped onto the trunk of a dead tree that lay across the outlet of the greater labyrinth, and waited, tongue waggling and ears raised, for the chase dog to herd the hare into the trap. He did, and when the hare came bounding through without looking up, the flank dog hopped lightly down onto him. There was a squeal, and the horses started, and the flank dog made a slow-motion readjustment of his grip so that he had the hare farther back on the body, and when it made a croaking sound, the horses shook their heads. The chase dog slid to a stop and got the hare by the shoulders, and the two dogs set their legs like players in a tug-of-war and tore the hare, which weighed ten pounds and measured two feet in length, jaggedly in half, and ate the pieces in choking gulps.

"What for?" said John, finally answering my question.

We were an hour crossing the plateau, and at the far end a small herd of horses stood at the final fence. Behind the burned land the forest billowed and towered into the rainy sky, a green wall that seemed to be growing even as we rode toward it. The horses looked up and circled and fell in behind us. They were colts and mares and geldings, Appaloosas and blacks and a buckskin, all of them rippling and fresh, and their brands were a mélange of crescents and arrows and letters. John and I rode through the gate.

"Whose horses are those?" I said, as they lined themselves once again at the fence like inmates.

John of the Cows pulled back his poncho and drew a .38 revolver and opened the cylinder. He looked at the bronze feet of the casings and the silver rounds of primer at their centers. He closed the cylinder and reholstered the piece. "Whose horses are those," he said, as though it were a statement instead of a question. Then he rode into the shadows.

*   *   *

We followed game trails made by European boars whose forebears had been brought hundreds of years before, domesticated and tuskless, from Spain and Germany, only to go feral in the mountains. Their thin trails wound casually around *coigue* that existed before Europe even had, trees as big around as two Volkswagens set side by side, and they reached two hundred fifty feet above us. Rain fell from their green leaves in drops whose courses wavered in the wind and pelted and startled the horses. There were pines and cedars and austere mountain cypress growing in segregated pockets, and a dozen perennials whose names were Indian and Spanish, *ñire* and *lenga* and *mañiu* and *arrayán* and *huinque*. At the bases of the trees ordered phalanxes of ferns grew, some with leaves the size of the horses and some as tiny and delicate as the spiderwebs that stretched between them. Red and pink and yellow and white roses crept up their trunks. The forest floor was covered in lichen and peat, and the footfalls of the horses were dull and muffled against it. They trudged along, heads down, foreign entities in a retroscape made to mythic scale.

Only the dogs seemed comfortable in that place, nearly feral now themselves. They ran about and studied the world perched on outlandishly large rocks that jutted into the foreground like prehistoric dwellings. And after these brief respites, they would trot back off into the forest, tongues casually dangling, ears taut, and remain long out of sight, hunting for signs of anything they might chase and fight and kill.

The hog trail split and split again, and each time John and I would sit the horses and study the divergence, and John would superimpose over the actual trail a blueprint he had stored in his head, wherein existed every deadfall and impasse he had encountered in years of riding there, and which constantly had to be reorganized and updated, for the information was only good until it changed, and it changed each time he passed. Several times we split up to follow the forks separately and call the obstacles, and to argue, blind to one another's position, the merits and deficiencies of what we saw.

At one such place, John yelled, "This road isn't right." When I trotted Broken Ear over to him, he was sitting Gift in front of a dozen trees that had been burned by a lightning fire and had fallen onto one another to make a snarl the size of an apartment building. "We have to get into the swamp," he said. He whistled to the dogs, which loped toward us from the bush and disappeared to the south.

We crossed a stream and rode into the swamp that cushioned the stream from the forests, through grass that came to our knees. The horses' legs sucked into the mud. We put the horses forward into a spring creek where *calafate* and Devil's willow grew over us like a gauntlet. We turned west where the spring creek did, and it branched into two more and two more and two more.

We came to a corduroy road that John had built three years before. It looked more like a dilapidated raft afloat in the bog, thirty or forty logs that had been laid side to side before the spring floods destroyed it. Now they were sticking up and cracked and splitting, and some of them had been moved altogether out of the way. The horses looked at this mess and tried to turn themselves in the muck.

We worked for an hour and a half trying to coax them across, first by talking to them and then by whipping them and chasing them down when they turned and kicked at us in slow motion and tripped away into the undergrowth. Finally, we put lassos around the necks of the two saddle horses and picked our way across the corduroy road and leaned against them.

Broken Ear was the first to come, followed by Gift. I took my lasso from Broken Ear and put it around the packhorse's neck, and he backed down until John and I both were lying in the mud. John picked himself up. He said, "I'll meet you half a kilometer over that way," and pointed to the west. "I have another bridge back in there; maybe it's not broken," and he mounted Gift and rode him back across the corduroy road. Then he took the packhorse and went crashing through the bush toward the stream.

I followed the spring creek north for what seemed like a long time. I was about to turn back when finally it opened onto a beach of east-west running fist-sized rocks, a feature so out of place for its convenience that it was hard to believe it was there. Two hundred meters west, I could see John sitting his horse at the end of the beach, smiling. It had stopped raining and the sun was out. Clouds of no-see-ums yo-yoed on the still air. The rock beach had turned to sand where John sat his horse, and the stream cruised effortlessly through the sand. We dismounted and took off our wet ponchos and tied them across the backs of the saddles. The horses splayed their forelegs like foals testing their balance for the first time, and drank from the stream, looking up between long, loud drafts. John and I lay facedown on the sand upstream of them, and drank and washed the no-see-ums from our faces. Then we mounted and rode on.

An hour later, we were out of the swamp. There was a burned clearing ahead the size of two football fields. The trail here was a good one and riddled with dried cow patties and gnarled old horse droppings. In the middle of the pasture was a cabin. The door was open, as though someone had just left. The grass was so tall that it lapped against the kipskins flapping in the windows. The sight of this vague nod to civilization seemed to make the dogs nervous, and John looked down where they walked in the shadows of the horses. "More suspicious than a couple of one-eyed cats," he said. He looked at me. He said, "You, *che?*"

"You?" I said.

*   *   *

The floor of the cabin was dirt, and in the middle of it was a fire black. The ceilings were steep, to let the snow slide off, and crossed with beams from which hung an array of sheepskins, the fat yellowed and hard. John said, "At night the rats hang off of them by their teeth, like crabapples." Across from the sheepskins, as though watching from the great limb of a *coigue* tree, a puma hide had been elegantly draped.

The ceilings crested at ten feet, and in the crest was cut a square smoke hole. This main room was two hundred square feet. The furnishings were composed of a wooden chair and a stool made from the trunk of a young tree and a rough-hewn table. On the table was a Nido can and a blue *mate* cup filled with petrified *yerba,* and the *bombilla* sticking out as though someone had left in the middle of his draw and never come back. Next to this was an old plastic J&B mustard bottle, with a shrunken block of salt gone rock-hard with the moisture. The Nido can was sealed tight and was half-full of *yerba.* We could see where rats had tried to eat through the sides; the tracks of their teeth and nails ran garishly through the paper where it read "Nutrition Facts," and again where it read "Ingredients." In the corner by the table stood a seven-foot wrought-iron *asador* for tending the fire and roasting meat. Next to it was a single-shot .22 rifle with the receiver held together with a rubber band. I opened the breech and saw it was loaded.

I walked through a doorway off to one side of the main room into another of half the size. In it was a pile of skins for a bed, and a loft on one side in which nothing was being stored. Aside from these things, the cabin was empty.

John rolled the kipskin shades and tied them up with horsehide *pitas* chewed in half by rats.

I said, "How long did you live here, *che*?"

"It took me months to burn this fucking pasture, *che*," he said. "A lot of days I had to go one tree at a time. This valley gets more rain than the next valley back and the next valley over, *che*. That's why the grass grew like crazy once I got a little spot burned. I have another camp up in the forest," he said. "It rains there, too, but not half what it does here."

I said, "How come you have no herd here now, *che*?"

"Because, *che*," he smiled, "I'm in the fence-building business for the time being."

"What do you need another camp for?" I said.

"I like to have places to go to in case I get caught in a funny situation." He went outside.

"Like what?" I called.

"Like a vacation," he called back. He came back in with his saddlebags and the *asador* he'd packed. "Forgot I had one of these up here," he said. "I have to take this one to the other camp."

I said, "In case you get caught in a funny situation sometime soon?"

He laughed. "I guess," he said. He reached into one of the bags, and pulled the side of ribs out and tossed them on the dusty table. From the other bag he took a J&B bottle full of *chimichurri* and a plastic bag with fried bread in it. He fished a brand-new blue ski jacket out of the saddlebag and put it on. He held his arms before him and looked at the sleeves.

I said, "Is that for a skiing vacation?"

John said, "Sometimes I like to take a little vacation, that's what I said. Away from building fences or fooling with shit." He zipped the jacket. "Make a fire?" he said. "Wood's under the bed."

"You always vacation alone?" I said from the other room. The bed looked like a hanta virus incubator, dusty skins with holes eaten through and tracked-in rat droppings. I held my breath. Underneath was enough wood to burn the whole cabin down. Or to stay a long time in the cabin without having to worry about being warm.

"Mostly alone," said John. "Sometimes I vacation with Louse or Monkey or Filly."

"Where else do you have vacation spots?" I said, exhaling and wondering which "vacation spot" Louse and Monkey were hiding out at. "Any on the Argentine border near the *veranada*?"

"Maybe," he said.

I went to the rivulet outside and washed my hands and face. When I came back in, John had cut three slices through the meat of the ribs and had woven the *asador* through them. I took some matches and a corner of an old *mate* bag from my pocket and made a fire in the dirt, adding wood as it grew.

When I was done, John brought two skins from the other room and laid one across the chair and the other on the trunk stool. He offered me the chair. He said, "You know Soto, that dipshit paramedic in Amengual? He says the sun makes it so the virus can't walk. That's why I raised the shades on the windows."

He added more wood to the fire and set his feet apart and rocked the *asador* back and forth, pointed side against the ground, until it had set firmly. Then he pushed at it, leaning it toward the fire.

I said, "Where did you get that ski jacket?"

"Coihaique."

"How long ago?"

"A few months," he said.

"Looks new."

John said, "I've been saving it."

"What for?"

"Vacation."

I said, "How many cattle can you keep here?"

"Never more than a few."

"Horses?"

"Horses, too."

"And what about the other camp, up in the forest?" I asked.

"For building fences, like I told you."

"I thought you said there weren't any fences back here."

"I guess there aren't really," he said. He smiled and looked at me.

I said, "What is there, then?"

John stopped smiling and looked out the window. I'd lost my concentration. Since the first time we'd met the year before, John and I had spoken with one another in a kind of indirect language. It was in this way that we shared control of our relationship, and of the variables from which it had evolved. John had wanted to talk about things in his way, and I'd wanted to listen and to put the clues together. We'd become friends through this very particular understanding of the rules that governed our interactions. I marveled at the way his mind worked. The making of the bridle and the spinning of the murder story, for example, or building fences and taking vacations, which were John's metaphors for strengthening his herd of stolen horses and running from trouble. I'd never, until that moment, wanted to hear him say he was a murderer and a thief. I'd gone with him to the Inside without knowing how long we would be gone for the same reason he'd offered to take me: because we had an understanding. Now, it suddenly occurred to me, I'd ceded control completely to him, in the same way John had ceded control to the police by going, against his intuition, to see Brew Wheely.

We sat smoking cigarettes and watching the meat cook. When it was done on the front, John worked the *asador* out of the ground, turned it, and rocked the pointed end back into the dirt. The metal was hot, and he held it with a rag over his hand. The meat dripped onto the dirt, and each little rivulet caught fire itself and popped and sizzled. The flames ran back and forth between the *asador* and the fire, fed now and again by dripping fat, as though they would trace and retrace the same route until they found some new direction in which to travel. I looked again at the rifle in the corner. Then I said, "Do you like what you do?"

He said, "What?" There was no expression on his face.

I said, "Do you like your life?" It was too late to turn back. I said, "Do you like what you do, *che*?"

"That question supposes there's something else I could be doing?" I nodded. "Well," he said, "there isn't."

"You could go to Coihaique."

"What are you, crazy from *mate?*" he asked. "I can't even go to Amengual to play soccer. I can't run the rodeos in Tapera, *che.* I have horses—I have to give them to my old man to run."

He got up and, with effort, forced the meat closer to the flame. He watched it char under stress from the heat, and it seemed to give him an ironic sense of pleasure. John showed his long teeth in a smile. He said, "You know what would happen to me in Coihaique?"

"No."

"Me neither."

*   *   *

It was raining when we'd finished eating most of the meat. John went outside and urinated in the waist-high grass. He was slow coming back, and I couldn't see him, and then he was standing in the doorway. He said, "Are you still hungry?" I told him I was. His eyes didn't leave my face. He blushed and said: "What do you want to eat?" His voice was high, even sweet, and his mouth was taut, as though what might come next would have to do so of its own accord. He didn't blink.

I said, "I'll eat the rest of what's left." I cut another piece of meat and sat down and ate, though I didn't take my eyes from him except to look at the rain, which was coming in sheets, such that the contours of the horses were outfitted in a constant, translucent splatter of deflected water.

John leaned against the door frame. He said, "Nothing better than that?" He rested his hand on his pistol, and I looked at it. His fly was unbuttoned. I looked at his face and he looked away. There was something ashamed in the way he did this. Of the many things for which John of the Cows was wanted, Edith had told me, rape was one.

I said, "I don't see anything that's better." I was more afraid of John than I'd ever been of Duck, and, before John could sense my fear and regain his nerve, I stood up and got the rifle from the corner.

John took his hand from his pistol and smiled. He said, "The road will wash out."

"I know," I said. Then I walked outside and began saddling the horses.

*   *   *

John reined his horse sharply around toward the mountains. "I don't feel much like getting rained on in this fucking shit," he said. "We'll make for the forest. I might find a road up in there I used to know," and he put his horse forward at a trot.

The "road" was a game trail that weaved and climbed across a heavily grown saddle. We rode quickly, ducking under limbs, the horses stopping at deadfalls to calculate briefly before jumping over them. The forest was close, and then suddenly it was not there. Ahead was an outcropping of rock that hung over a cliff, hundreds of feet above the swamp and the valley. We put the horses forward to see about getting around, but there was no way, just a straight fall.

"Forgot about this little detail," smiled John. "If we cut back down, we might find another road. If we don't, we're here the night. Or we could lead the horses up over this thing."

We rode back down to where we'd come out of the trees.

I said, "What's on the other side? Another cliff?"

"I don't know."

"Well." I wasn't going to stay the night.

"I don't know if I have things mixed up here," said John dryly.

We dismounted. The rock sloped gently at first, and we got the horses halfway up the slick face. When it grew steeper, we went to our hands and knees. Near the top, the packhorse slid back down and tumbled over backward, and landed on its feet and trotted off into the trees.

John and Gift got to the top first. When I made it over the lip with Broken Ear, we stood looking at what lay ahead. A plateau opened out of the other side of the outcropping and petered into trees a hundred meters away. I stood with the horses, and John went back down for the packhorse. It took John half an hour to get him up and over.

"We're in a hurry now, *che*," said John, jumping on one leg, trying to get back on his horse. He had one rein in his hand, and he leaned over to grab the other and we galloped across the plateau into the trees.

An hour later, we came to his other camp. The *coigue* and *calafate* were so thick that I didn't see the camp until my horse was nearly standing on the remains of a long-dead fire.

"Jesus," I said, "how long did you live here?"

"Long as I had to," said John. The camp was a plastic tarp held aloft at an angle by two tree limbs in the front. It was held down in back by ropes tied from the corners to the bases of two *calafate* bushes. The tarp was a hundred square feet, and inside was a bed made of three six-foot one-by-twelves atop six tree trunks. A second and third trunk served as table and chair, and on top of the table was a *mate* and a tea kettle.

John dismounted and walked around looking at things, as though checking them off a list. He picked up the tea kettle and looked inside. "Give me the rifle," he said. I had it across the pommel. I didn't want to give it to him. John looked up from the tea kettle at me. "Give me the rifle," he said again.

I said, "How long till we're out of here, *che*?"

John said, "It depends how long you put off giving me the rifle." It was foolish to have taken it in the first place, and when I handed it down, John checked the chamber and smiled. He smiled at me for what seemed like a long time—long enough that I would know, in case I'd forgotten, exactly who was in control. Then he laid the rifle on top of the bed, and we rode on.

We passed muds where boars came to wallow and where I half expected to see the bones of dinosaurs. The horses were tired and moved clumsily, tripping and then trotting ahead and tripping again. Little gray-and-white birds called *chucaos* flitted in the trees, calling back and forth.

We angled for the lowlands and crossed the stream where we'd crossed it the first time that morning. When we passed through the gate, the little herd of stolen horses was not there, nor did they appear anywhere on the plateau. An hour later, we sat looking down onto the terraces of rock and burned land we'd ridden through in the fog fifteen hours before. Flocks of upland geese waddled and flapped into the dusking sky, calling. There was the fence and the piles of dead trees and the place where the hare had been torn in half, and, far below it, the Cisnes. Smoke rose from Pork Rind's cabin in the cottonwoods.

John said, "You look like shit." I'd gotten a sudden fever, and I was sweating despite the cold. He said, "Do *you* like my job?"

"Do you?" I said. I smiled at him, and we put the horses forward; each time Broken Ear took a step, I could feel it in the swollen glands of my throat. I wondered if these were not the flulike symptoms of the onset of hanta virus.

"You should have seen what it's like at night," said John.

"When?" I said.

I wanted, completely beyond reason, to go with him to Argentina. It was there, I suddenly felt sure, that he'd run, and I wanted to see what it would be like. He'd not ridden downriver all week because it was too much exposure: any of the other yellow jackets might have lessened the competition for The Grape by telling the *carabineros* where John was hiding. Anywhere in Cisnes, no matter how isolated, was too much exposure, because there was always something waiting to flush him out. If it wasn't Brew Wheely, it was The Grape. John had built for himself a beautiful fence, indeed.

"When," he said. Gift sidestepped like a dancer, and John brought him around in a tight circle. "I'll tell you when," he said.

Then we followed the fenceline back toward his father's *puesto*.

Dogs

M ariana was sitting in the long shadow cut by the corner of the barn, nearly hidden amidst the tall grass that grew there. In two days, she'd be, for the first time ever, accompanying Patricia to the little school in Amengual. What she did not know was that two weeks after that, she would find herself in a slum of Coihaique, vomiting from the chlorine in the tap water. Trucks would rumble down the dirt street, and long-haired valley gauchos would tether their horses to bamboo fences, and Pentecostal Christians from Brazil would come knocking on the doors at lunchtime. At night, packs of wild dogs would eat from garbage pails.

For now, though, Mariana was still in Cisnes, staring across the river as an equally novel event unfolded: Rosa, Pork Rind's daughter, was trying to figure out how to ride the first bike ever brought to the valley.

"Whore's milk," said Mariana, by which she meant to describe the bitterness of her envy.

I said, "Don't talk that way."

"Bastard, dingle-headed, shit-in-the-brain Rosa on a bike," said Mariana.

The day before, Pork Rind had ridden past Duck and Edith's cabin with a new pink Huffy across his saddle; now he watched from atop his horse as Rosa took the bicycle by one handle and leaned it from her, as though reading a sign. Pork Rind's horse pulled at his rein hand, and he crossed one arm over the short pommel and leaned forward. Mariana sighed and leaned one side of her head in her dirty hand as though listening to a boring lecture.

Rosa mounted the bike with the exaggerated motion of someone mounting a horse. The bike fell over between her legs. "Wednesday!" said Mariana.

Mariana got up and walked to the fence, climbed it, and sat on a rock at the bank of the river. Rosa's older sister came forward and inspected the bike. There was a discussion. Then the older sister got on the bike and turned the pedals, and cruised and turned the pedals again, bumping over the uneven ground. She built up a head of steam, and Pork Rind put his horse forward at a canter. He was alongside her, and the horse strained ahead, trying to gallop as the girl rode the bike past the corral and along the fence. Then she disappeared into the forest.

Mariana stood up.

A while later, the older sister came cruising out of the trees and put the brakes on well past Rosa. Pork Rind came fast at her side and reined the horse. That's when Rosa got on the bike. Mariana took two steps forward. She was standing on the uneven rocks at the water's edge. Rosa pedaled and steered unevenly around the ruined trees on the plain, and fought the handles of the bike, and disappeared, as had her sister, into the forest.

Mariana was wearing Duck's boots, and she was standing in the shallows of the river now. A long, expectant few minutes passed. Then Rosa came back into view, and Pork Rind spurred the horse and galloped past Rosa as she rode toward him; he reined the horse sharply and galloped back at her side. Then Rosa stopped and let the bike fall, and they looked at it there in the grass.

"That's how it's done," said Mariana, walking past me toward her parents' cabin.

*　　*　　*

Two days later, when the truck from Amengual came for Patricia and Mariana, Duck, Edith, and Oscar went with them because, they said, they couldn't stand the thought of Mariana going alone with her sister to school for the first time. It was a short week, three days, so that the newcomers would not be completely overwhelmed by their new surroundings. Still, Duck and Edith knew it would be hard for Mariana, so they rode with her, planning to turn around that same afternoon and hitch back to the ranch.

But when Edith and Oscar returned from Amengual, Duck wasn't with them. Edith said, "He found Soto. Who knows when he'll come home."

When Patricia and Mariana came back to Santa Elvira three days later, Duck still was not with them. I said to Edith, "Well?"

She said, "As long as he makes it back from that village before Alex arrives, I guess it doesn't matter. If not," she said, "I'll go alone with the children."

We both knew that whenever Duck showed up at Santa Elvira again, he'd be drunk, and, if he hadn't spent all his money, he'd bring with him all the alcohol he could carry. I looked at Patricia and Mariana playing with Oscar in the pasture and past them at Broken Ear moving clumsily in his hobble along the river, cropping grass. I didn't want to leave Edith alone to deal with whatever was going to happen when Duck arrived.

But there was something else. I wanted at the same time for Duck to get as drunk as he had the year before. I wanted to see what he would do, and the thought bothered me deeply for many reasons, not the least of which was my complete inability to understand why. I profoundly recognized that, were Duck to comply with my perverse desire, my life would not be the only one at risk. In 1998, Edith had done me a kind of favor by barricading herself in the bedroom: she'd lessened the variables available to Duck. But it might not happen that way again. What if, for instance, Duck had used Edith or me to heighten the stakes? What if he'd threatened Edith with the knife while I was in the room?

When I looked at Edith, I understood more clearly than ever that people in Cisnes did things not because they were evil, or even unkind, but to lash out violently against the unbearable weight of the boredom and the isolation and the fear of what the loneliness might drive them to do. The fact that everyone claimed to have seen their face reflected in that of the Devil moments, or even days, before something horrible occurred was a kind of admission of guilt—an admission that it was they, not him, who was at fault.

I didn't say anything about this to Edith. What I said was that I needed to see Tío and Uncle Ya Ya for a last time before we all left for Coihaique.

"Why, Nico?"

I shook my head. "I'm sorry." I didn't know what else to say.

* * *

I was about to walk out to the tack room and get my saddle when Patricia and Mariana came running into the cabin. Oscar wasn't with them.

"Where's your brother?" said Edith. She stood up.

"He tried to piss on me," said Patricia.

"You left him outside?" said Edith. Her voice was shaky. She walked quickly to the door. "Oscar!" she called. He was walking in little circles in the pasture. Edith jogged out and picked him up, and when she did so, he slugged her in the mouth. "Come on, sweetheart," she said. He didn't want to be taken back inside the cabin.

Edith said to Mariana and Patricia, "What were you two eggos thinking leaving him out there!" She kicked at Patricia, then fell off balance because Oscar was trying to slug her in the mouth again, and Edith was leaning her head as far away from him as she could.

Patricia looked at her in disbelief. "He tried to piss on me like a dog," she said. "I was wrestling around with Mariana, and he stood above me and started pissing. And now you're pissed at me?"

Edith leaned in to kiss Oscar, and he socked her on the lips so hard that it made Edith's eyes water. It was one of the many times that I looked at him and realized how much he looked like his father. Sometimes I looked at Oscar and hated him. "That's it, my little king," said Edith. She looked at Mariana and Patricia. "He's not to blame," she said. "He didn't know what he was doing." She bobbed her head like a boxer, and Oscar's fist glanced off her chin.

"Looks to me like he's got it all figured out," mumbled Patricia.

*   *   *

Tío had left the Big Island of Chiloé in northern Chilean Patagonia when he was thirty years old, which was probably around 1910. Then, for the next twenty years, he'd wandered through Argentine Patagonia. When the land there got "too crowded"—this was in the days when they were building the first roads in Chubut province—he'd come across to Cisnes, where, he said, you could still hope to be alone. It was around that time, 1950 or so, that many gauchos were making their way to Cisnes for the same reasons that Tío had: plenty of unfenced land, no roads, no law. No nothing. Among those Tío found upon his arrival in Tapera were Black Carl and the Eagles brothers and The Black, and a famous gaucho called Don Luis, who had since, like Black Carl, moved to Coihaique to die.

Uncle Ya Ya, too, was one of the men Tío had met in Cisnes five decades before, and for the last twenty years, the two of them had been living with one another, Ya Ya in a humble cabin with two bedrooms and Tío in a single-room hutch that attached to the cabin and where an open fire burned in the middle of the dirt floor. Like their separate but connected *puestos*, Tío and Ya Ya were a sort of case study of the recent history of change in Aisén, for while Tío often got on his horse and rode off to explore the valley where he'd lived for fifty years (sleeping "wherever the night found him"), Ya Ya had become more sedentary—and, as Tío also liked to say, more "civilized"—by running his illegal business selling whatever the truckers brought him.

The last time I had seen Tío was two weeks before. He was bringing up the rear of a huge cattle drive moving from La Junta, two hundred kilometers to the north, to Amengual. The riders had been driving the stock for two weeks. I rode next to Tío for three hours, until the drive crossed the Cisnes in the shallows above John of the Cows' cabin and continued toward Amengual. When I asked Tío what he thought about visitors in the valley, he said in his clear, perfect Spanish that he thought "civilization" was good for the people of Cisnes because outsiders could teach the gauchos things to make their lives easier. And he thought it was good for outsiders to learn from gauchos that people are the same everywhere, with the same desires and fears and the same aspirations.

Tío wore the pinkie and thumb nails of his right hand very long—the pinkie nail cleared his finger by an inch—and he was famous for using the nails to kill yellow jackets by separating them where their thoraxes met their abdomens. It had been a hundred years, he liked to say, since he'd been stung. When Tío thought about something, he would often scratch the back of his neck with two nails, which is what he did before asking me if I would accompany him to a gold mine he had discovered "a little while" before. I asked how long before, to which he replied, "Nineteen sixty-three." He said the mine was on the Inside, three weeks away by horse. His plan was simple: to take an Outsider to the mine and, for this, to charge a "finder's fee," with which he planned to quit working and to buy a small parcel of land on the Inside where he could build the first real cabin he had ever lived in, at the age of a hundred twenty.

I had yet to make this trip with Tío because he was so difficult to find—one had to more or less happen upon him—and on the day I rode from Santa Elvira to see him and Ya Ya, Tío was gone. So I hobbled Broken Ear in the yard and loosened the girthstraps on my saddle and followed Ya Ya inside, where he drank wine and listened to Messages.

I'd heard that Ya Ya had made a bad horse trade the week before with another gaucho called Fart-Fart. Fart-Fart lived in a shack hidden behind a grove of crabapple trees about an hour down the road. He was a famous ne'er-do-well. Ya Ya, I'd heard, had sold Fart-Fart a mare he hadn't realized was pregnant, so that Fart-Fart, in effect, got two horses for the price of one. Ya Ya said, "Did you hear about what Fart-Fart did to me?"

I said, "I heard you traded the mare and didn't know she was about to give the light, *che.*"

"What!" yelled Ya Ya, rising from his chair. "What! No no no no!" He sat back down. "Ya ya ya ya ya yaaaa," he said, calming down. Then, just as suddenly, he was worked up again. "That is not the truth! How stupid do you think I am? That is not the way it passed. I'll tell you the truth on that dirty shameless faggot son of a goat bastard!" We drank to punctuate the outburst and he filled the glasses again. He said, "You do want to know the truth, don't you, Mangi?"

I nodded.

"Okay, here's the first fucking fact, Mangicito: I gave Fart-Fart money. Last month, he hears on Messages his sister's dying in Coihaique. So. Who does he come to? Me. He knows I have a little put away. He stood right here and cried like a baby. I said, 'Gentle sir, whatever you need. Bus fare? Money to buy her flowers? Money to have a bit of the Mother Whore when you come back in case she might be dead and you want to have a bit of the Mother Whore? You got it.'" Ya Ya stood up and put his hand on his pocket and handed over invisible bill after invisible bill. The Mother Whore was what Ya Ya called *pisco*. "Fucking little witch," he said, and sat back down. He spit on the floor. Then he got up and cleaned the quid with a towel, and tossed the towel into the sink. "Fucking Anita'll have me clean it up sooner or later," he mumbled, referring to his niece, who lived in the second bedroom but was gone for the day. When he was seated again, Ya Ya said: "So fucking Fart-Fart comes back and says he wants my mare."

"The great big black one?" I said.

"The great big black one. Too big for me to ride anyway; the thing is like a dinosaur." Ya Ya was only five feet six and the horses he owned were not unlike the stout, short-shouldered Appaloosa war ponies used in the American South-west. "So we made a deal. And in making the deal, I say, 'She's for giving the light, Fart-Fart. Three weeks. When she foals out, I want the foal. That's the only way I sell that horse.' And Fart-Fart says, 'Well, of course that's how we do it, *che*. As soon as that foal gets her legs and is off the teat, she's yours.' Lying son of a whore. But so I sell him the mare. And the mare foals out."

We drank, and I filled the glasses. "Ah-ah-ah-ah-ah," he said, raising his hand. "Just the half-glass, now." Half the glass was like a shot of wine.

"So I go to get my damn foal when I know she's ready to be off the teat. Fart-Fart says, 'Why, what are you doing?' 'Getting my foal is what I'm doing,' I say. 'Let's see, now, just hold on,' says Fart-Fart. 'That foal's mine. What's her mama's is mine, because her mama is mine,' he says. Can you believe that pile?"

Ya Ya disappeared into the hallway; when he returned to the table, he placed a cookie tin on it. "Open it," he said, standing over me.

Inside were several cloth bags and handkerchiefs cinched with horsehide; inside the handkerchiefs were nuts, bolts, greasy pieces of a carburetor, puma claws, discarded pieces of wire, and an awl. Wrapped in newspaper was another greasy handkerchief. I unfolded the corners as Ya Ya snatched away the canister. Inside was a haphazard collection of cartridges, all of them Winchester, .44 and .38 and .22 long rifle and .44-.70, ancient and tarnished, bought in Argentina decades before. Ya Ya reached into the pile and picked out five shells and shook them in his hand. "These are for Fart-Fart," he said.

They were .38 hollow points, designed not to penetrate the target but to blow a tremendous hole in it. Ya Ya said he'd gotten them a year before from a truck driver. The truck driver, in turn, had picked them up in Argentina. In Chile, where buying relatively benign .22 cartridges requires a permit, hollow points are strictly and specifically outlawed.

"These are for that shameless faggot dirtbag Fart-Fart," said Ya Ya. He opened the cylinder of his pistol, emptied the shells onto the table, and put in the hollow points. Then he dumped them out, stared at them indecisively, reloaded the regular shells, and put the pistol back on the table. He put the hollow points in his pocket and puttered around the kitchen, looking for a new hiding spot for his canister of goodies. "My niece is nosy," he said three times, first at a small closet, then at a drawer, then at the closet again. When he came back in, red-faced, he said: "I make her think I'm deaf and senile. That's how I stay one step ahead."

Ya Ya sat back down and reloaded the hollow points into the cylinder and laid the pistol on the table. Then he said, "Would you like to come watch me blow holes in Fart-Fart?"

I wanted to go back to Santa Elvira. The guilt of having left Edith alone there with the children was too much. Hearing Ya Ya say he was going to kill Fart-Fart made the decision to return much easier. I didn't know what I could do for Ya Ya, but I did know what I could do for Edith: Duck might, under the scrutiny of an added person, lose his nerve.

Ya Ya and I went outside to saddle the horses. When we'd ridden a little way down the road, I sat my horse and said: "You can't just go shoot a man about a horse, Uncle."

Ya Ya said, "Are you out of your mind?" He threw back his poncho and reached for the pistol. "Goddamn it," he said, shaking his head. He'd left it on the table. "Wait for me?"

I said, "How will Tío find you when he comes back if you're in jail?" Ya Ya looked at me incredulously. Middle Cisnes was not a place anyone would go to jail for killing a man about a horse. I said, "Well, I guess I ought to go home."

Ya Ya turned his horse and rode up alongside to shake hands. "Come back when it pleases," he said.

*   *   *

When I walked into Duck and Edith's cabin, Duck was sitting at the table. He looked as though he'd slept in a barn. His short hair was matted on one side of his head, and sleep creases crisscrossed his face like scars. He'd gotten back late that morning, just after I'd left for Ya Ya's, and he'd drunk all of his money in Amengual. He'd been so drunk, he said, that he forgot to save enough money for more *pisco*, and, still drunk when Pork Rind came over two hours later to take *mate*, Duck had sold Pork Rind everything he owned that would link him to his life in the mountains. He had sold his chaps and poncho and saddle and all the riding crops and bullwhips and three sets of stirrups, all of which he'd made by hand over the last ten years. He sold Pork Rind the chickens, and the little black tea kettle he'd carried on cattle drives since he was thirteen or fourteen years old.

He sold him his guitar and his spurs and three lassos and the AM/FM radio on which we'd listened to Messages, and he sold him Sheep Shearings and Country Dog. The only thing Duck kept was the poncho his mother had made him when he was a boy.

As soon as Pork Rind left, said Duck, the dogs had started to appear. First one and then another and, before long, there were half a dozen of them milling near the barn and laid up under the oxcart in the pasture, and one was in the hole under the shed where Sheep Shearings and Country Dog had slept for years.

Duck and I watched through the open door of the cabin as the dogs circled one another and partitioned the outbuildings like a conquering army. Duck said, "They're smelling that bitch, eggo." He was talking about La Vieja, the mother of Sheep Shearings and the mate of Country Dog. For weeks, La Vieja had slept in front of the supply room door. La Vieja was in full heat. Duck said, "Tomorrow, will you take her to Julia's? You're the only one La Vieja will follow anymore, and I want Julia to have her. That way Julia gets several dogs if she can find her a mate." He looked at the pasture. "Which doesn't look like it'll be hard, *che*."

A cattle dog I recognized as one of John of the Cows' came slithering into view, sopping wet with river water. He'd chewed through the wire John used to keep his dogs from running off, and the tag end of the collar stuck out from the dog's neck like a dart. He came right up to the spot where La Vieja sat in front of the supply room and circled her. Then he looked at us, fanned his hackles, and plopped down to begin cleaning himself as though he had a date. Suddenly, ten dogs were crowding onto the little porch gate.

"I'll be goddamned," said Duck, and kicked at them. When the dogs bared their impressive teeth, Duck took my bullwhip from its nail in the supply room and beat them. Only then did the dogs run, though not far; they stopped in the middle of the pasture and sat down to wait like gargoyles, ears aloft and tongues waggling.

By dusk, one of the dogs had succeeded in luring La Vieja under the oxcart. He'd spent the latter part of the afternoon fighting, and now the other dogs left him alone, waiting for the night. He was built curiously, like a baboon, and had short hairs covering his abdomen and legs, and a tuft of salt-and-pepper fur along his neck that plumed and waved when the other dogs shifted around him. That night, La Vieja slept in front of my door as usual, accompanied by her strange mate. It was cold, and the rats were trying to eat their way into the cabin to build their winter nests; and I could hear them scratching and clawing at the floorboards and scurrying across the attic.

At three o'clock in the morning, the dog that had escaped from John of the Cows approached the porch. There was a tremendous fight. Their bodies tumbled across the porch and knocked into the door. The rats quit clawing to stop and listen. Two times the fight stopped and started and stopped again. After the third round, I heard Patricia crying in the bedroom; Edith spoke to her and muffled Patricia's cries in her shoulder.

The next morning, all the dogs had gone, except for John's. He was lying in the pasture, and I thought he was dead until I approached him and he tried to get up, but could not. His right eyeball was gone from its socket. A dollop of vitreous humor had drooled down his snout like a tear. He was shaking uncontrollably, and his chest was torn across one side.

Duck and Edith were packing things for the trip, and I went inside to get John's dog some scraps of mutton. Patricia was sitting on the throne holding Mariana; they were going to Amengual that afternoon for a final couple days of school, and Duck and Edith would pick them up on the way to Coihaique with Alex.

"Don't take that dog any food," scolded Patricia.

"He'll die," I said.

"Let him," said Patricia. "That dream was terrible, and fucking that dog caused it." She looked at the floor when I asked what had happened. "I don't know," she said. "I was sleeping, and a man came in the room from the outside and stood there till I woke. Then I saw *mamá* get up, and the man beat her. Only, *mamá* wasn't up, and there wasn't any man in the room except *papi*."

I said, "Who was the man?"

"*Papi* was the only one in the room," said Patricia.

*   *   *

A furniture truck showed up two mornings later at eight o'clock and a little mustachioed man with bowed legs got out of the cab. He looked at the ewe tied to the fence, and she bucked weakly against the rope at her neck. Duck and Edith were taking the ewe to Coihaique so they'd be sure to have a month's worth of meat. "Fatty, *che*," said the driver, and doffed his beret when he came inside the cabin.

It took twenty minutes to load everything that Duck and Edith owned in the whole world into the back of the truck: four chairs, the little cabinet where they stored the potatoes, the table and the throne, the bookshelf and the Spanish dictionary and grammar I'd given them, four plastic champagne flutes, the calendar, and the Gloria Trevi and Stihl posters. The ewe was the last to be loaded. Duck and the driver simply tied her ankles together, picked her up, laid her in the space that had been saved for her, and closed the rolling door of the truck. The only things yet to be packed were a *mate* cup and *bombilla,* and the book of Santiaguino slang I'd bought that year.

"Poor sheep," said Duck.

"Sucks to be a sheep," said the driver. Then he climbed back into the cab and drove away.

Alex was supposed to have arrived at eight A.M., as well. We sat around most of the day on the floor of the empty cabin drinking *mate* and eating bread with hot sauce.

"It wouldn't be too funny if Alex didn't show up now," said Duck. "We just about have no more food." He looked at his watch. It was one o'clock. "The girls will be out of school in an hour and wondering what the Devil is wrong. God forbid they think we abandoned them." Duck said this three times in the next twenty minutes. Neither he nor Edith knew, once they got to Coihaique, where or when or even if they would find a house to rent. Luisa, the cook at the lodge, had said they could stay at her cabin until they found a place, but neither Duck nor Edith had ever been to Luisa's, nor to the sprawling slum in which it was located. And Luisa would not be there to show them because she had to spend another week at the lodge. Duck and Edith had the address, and they were hoping someone, perhaps Luisa's boyfriend, Fried Bread, would be there to let them in. Two more hours passed before Alex drove his red Toyota pickup through the open gates of Santa Elvira.

I have a photo of Duck and Edith taken in front of the cabin just before they got into Alex's truck. Duck is caught taking a deep breath, his mouth open. He looks exactly like he did fifteen years before, in a photo taken of him leaving the army—caught off guard and confused—only now he has exchanged his ill-fitting fatigues for a new uniform, this one of scrubbed denim. Edith's face is taut, her eyebrows knit against the strong sun, and she holds Oscar in front of her, as though displaying him. Or as though she will defend herself with him. Perhaps she was looking at the scattered pack of dogs that had once again assembled in the pasture to fight among themselves for the next shot at La Vieja.

*   *   *

Duck had offered me a ride with him and Edith to Coihaique in the bed of Alex's truck, but I'd opted instead to stay a little longer at Santa Elvira. The lodge had one more week of operation, and Rex had said I could sleep on a cot in the military tent behind the main house that had been set up for the guides and, at night, take meals with Rex and his clients. I thought it would be nice to spend a few days in a place with hot running water and people who might be able to tell me, as ridiculous as it sounds, who had won the Super Bowl. Most importantly, though, I hoped staying at Santa Elvira would give me another chance to see John of the Cows, who had gone to the Inside the week before "to build fences."

I had never forgotten John's offer to ride with him to Argentina. And while I had no horse now with which to go find him—Pork Rind had taken Broken Ear to a rodeo in Tapera and Happy Fat and Happy Slim were now the property of the gaucho who would be moving any day into Duck and Edith's cabin—I at least had a better chance of John's coming to find me if I hung around as long as possible. It wasn't long before he showed up.

I was down at the river washing my face one morning when he rode across. He'd lost weight, and his eyes seemed to have sunk deeper in his head. He was wearing his chaps, and they were covered in mud and burrs. On his feet were a pair of black soccer cleats. I dried my face and John hopped off Gift, and the three of us walked toward the pasture. I said, "Where are you going?"

"The village, *che*," said John.

"The village?"

"We're having a soccer match," he said.

I assumed this was a metaphor for something else, although I also knew how much John liked to play soccer. And he was, after all, wearing cleats. I said, "Soccer match."

John smiled and nodded. He said, "Other thing is, I'm heading toward Argentina in a month, *che.* Wondering if you still want to go."

I said, "I'll need a horse."

"I have that taken care of," he said. We were nearing the gate. "Four weeks Sunday," said John. "The bus will drop you here at the road, and I'll be waiting with the horses."

I said, "How long will we be gone?"

John swung onto Gift. "It all depends on what we run into," he said.

I looked back to where his dog still lay dying in the pasture. I said, "Your dog is going to die, *che.*"

Gift was getting anxious at the gate, and I opened it. When John didn't let him through immediately, Gift turned in tight circles. "There are rules," smiled John, easily keeping the saddle. "Number one is, when you're ready to move out, you can't worry about a fucking dog, *che.*" Then he rode through.

We always carry it to foreign countries, all over the world, our pride and our powerlessness. We know its configuration, but there is no way to make it accessible to others. It will never be right. Something, the most important thing, the most significant thing, something remains unsaid.

—RYSZARD KAPUSCINSKI

The Soccer War

The Center of the World

*Slum*che

A gaucho on foot is fit for nothing but the manure pile.

—*Ricardo Guiraldes,*

Don Segundo Sombra: Shadows on the Pampas, *1926*

MacKay Hill lords over the entire southern limits of Coihaique, effectively shutting the town off from an expanse of *pampa* that runs first across the eastern edge of Aisén and then, largely unbroken, all the way across Argentina. MacKay is, even for country full of geological marvels, the most monolithic of the features on the landscape, and more than half of the hour-long bus trip from Balmaceda to Coihaique is spent trying to get around one of its many corners. At the top of MacKay is the radio antenna that broadcasts Messages to much of Aisén's forty-two thousand square miles.

It takes three hours to reach the antenna, first by walking through fields of chest-high grass, and then by scrambling up a dry riverbed for several hundred vertical feet, and then, finally, by crossing an ancient and rolling forest. With some effort, you can scale the crumbling walls of the antenna's cabin-sized concrete foundation, and once atop it, you can see the mountain ranges that bear down on Coihaique from all directions, quilted in purples and browns and deep grays and punctuated here and there with the blue of glaciers. The only relief in all of this rock- and snow-covered expanse is a narrow plateau blocked in the yellows of ripening wheat and maize and the verdant greens of irrigated grass. This is where Coihaique was built.

Two rivers come together at the north end of the plateau, and it's from them, the Río Coihaique and the Río Simpson, that Coihaique, which means "between rivers," derives its name. A hundred years ago, the gauchos cut trails and burned forests across the plateau, and calved and separated and castrated their stock in the natural corral formed by the convergence of the rivers. A few *puestos* became a village, and the village became a town, the center of which was located in the same area where the herding took place.

Holding on to one of the iron handles soldered into the concrete base of the antenna and looking down onto town from The Hill, as MacKay is called, with typical Patagonian understatement, you feel as though Coihaique, as the lone and expanding nod to civilization in an area so immense and so immensely unpopulated, is the absolute center of the world. You can see the town square and the shining, corrugated roofs of the downtown computer stores and restaurants and the arrow-straight, ostrich-gray pavement of the streets. You can see the slums built onto the stepladder formations of saddles and ridges that ascend into the mountains and surround downtown Coihaique on three sides like a fishhook.

As evening approaches, however, Coihaique shrinks. Even as lights flicker on downtown, the slums, which account for the large majority of Coihaique, begin to disappear in shadow, owing to the steep angle of the land onto which they're built. The Southern Highway, too, is overtaken with shadow, first where it enters Coihaique from the sheer mountains to the north, and then where the road leaves town to the south. By dark, Coihaique is glowing at its shrunken core like an oil refinery and all but vanished around the periphery. What two hours before had felt like the center of the world feels suddenly more like an anomalous outpost at the farthest reaches of the frontier.

In late March 1999, Duck and Edith and their three children arrived in Coihaique long after dark. Assuming they had found Luisa's house and that Fried Bread had been there to let them in, they would have started looking for a cabin to rent the very next day. And, assuming they had found a place, I knew I would have to go looking for them all over again and that, wherever they'd ended up, it would be somewhere in the vast and darkened world of the slum*che*, far removed from the glowing Center.

* * *

During the last week of the lodge's operation, Luisa and I had talked extensively about Duck and Edith and about what their lives would be like in Coihaique. Luisa and I had been friends since 1995, when I'd worked at the lodge, and I knew her to be well acquainted with the kind of journey that Duck and Edith had just begun, for Luisa had made it herself nearly fifteen years before.

Luisa had occupied into her teens much the same role that Julia occupied in Cisnes: *un gaucho más*. Luisa's father, Don Luis, had been, in his middle years, much like Tea Kettle Without a Spout—likely to be away in Argentina for months or even years at a time—and Luisa had in his absence ridden cattle drives with her mother and sisters. Their ranch was halfway between Coihaique and Mañihuales, and when the Southern Road made it that far in the early 1980s, Luisa decided to take her chances and move to Coihaique. Two years later, she was married and working as a domestic for a family that took Luisa with them when they left for Santiago.

Santiago's sheer magnitude, though, was too much for her to bear. It was nothing, however, compared to what awaited Luisa upon her return to Coihaique, when the *carabineros* came to her house in the slums at three o'clock in the morning and took her husband, Jimmy's father and a devout Allendeista, in for questioning. Luisa and Jimmy never saw him again.

Since then, she had been circulating between the mountains and town. Luisa had worked as a cook at a downtown restaurant called The Pot and as a cook at the lodge and, on occasion, returned to her mother's ranch. She had always saved her money and she'd been careful not to remarry. This meant she'd never had to cede control of her savings and the little house she'd managed to buy to a man. Marriage aside, Luisa had fallen in love twice since her husband's disappearance, first with a gaucho from Mañihuales and then with another, younger gaucho— Fried Bread—each of whom had fathered a child with her.

During much of the austral summer of 1999, Luisa had come to Duck and Edith's cabin during her breaks, but she never came when Duck was around because her intent had been to advise Edith on the finer points of moving to town—chiefly, how to avoid losing money to a man with a drinking problem. Luisa had told Edith that she must, first of all, never officially marry Duck; and second, that Edith should get a job of her own, which would allow Edith "to live in Coihaique same as Duck," by which she meant it would get Edith out of the house where, if Edith spent too much time, she would feel as isolated and powerless as she had felt in Cisnes. Any money that Edith made, said Luisa, should be kept hidden from Duck.

Whether Duck knew any of this was as unclear as whether Luisa and Duck liked one another. At any rate, during our conversations in the last days before we came to Coihaique, Luisa had not said anything more about it, and we moved from the subject of Duck and Edith to Luisa's father, the famous Don Luis, who had ridden with the Eagles brothers and Black Carl and The Black and Uncle Ya Ya in the 1940s and 1950s. I had been as anxious to see Don Luis when I got to Coihaique as I was to find Duck and Edith.

Gauchos, when they could no longer ride, did one of two things: they stayed in the mountains to die or they came to Coihaique to die. Three years before, Don Luis had chosen the latter. Like Luisa, he had meticulously saved his money throughout the years, and he bought a little house in a distant slum of Coihaique. Now he spent his time tottering about Luisa's place or his own house or making the rounds by bus of his old and dying acquaintances in the many villages where he'd spent some indeterminate part of his life.

I was well aware that I'd never again see the *viejos* of Cisnes. Don Tito, who already could barely lift a skinned ewe onto his packhorse and would no longer be able to pull the girthstraps of his saddle tight within a couple years, would die in his cabin in Cisnes; Alfredo, I guessed, would die at the *veranada;* Tío would die under a tree somewhere, and Uncle Ya Ya would, I assumed, die in his cabin. I was intent, therefore, with the six weeks remaining on my visa that year, on listening to Don Luis's stories and, in doing so, getting a last glimpse of the world as it had existed before the Southern Road.

There was only one problem: Luisa had come back to Coihaique from Santa Elvira a day before me, and I couldn't remember how to find her cabin. She lived high above Coihaique, at the foot of The Hill in a slum called José Miguel Carrera. In the weeks I'd spent in town during 1995 and 1998, I had been to the cabin many times, sleeping there occasionally when I'd been unable to find a room in a boardinghouse before dark, and the only two choices had been to sleep on a bench in the town square—which I'd also done—or to walk the hour or so to JMC, as it was called. But JMC was a humongous *población* with hundreds of dwellings—some of them wood cabins, and others nothing more than cardboard shacks—lining its steep, winding, narrow dirt streets.

So a few days after I got to town, I went to The Pot to see if Luisa had once again resumed working there or, if she had not, to see if someone might tell me where she was working. I was hoping that I could wait until she got off work and walk home with her. The Pot is where the lawyers and doctors and the rotating casts of government people and entrepreneurs from Santiago take their lunch. Here is where you'll find men in suits and ties and women in heels and with brooches on their lapels. It was owned by a Spaniard and his son, and the continental décor in the place is unmistakable: paintings of bulls and *toreros* that adorn the walls; wrought-iron wine racks; starched, regal flourishes of cloth napkins stuffed into water glasses; and three plates and two wineglasses—one for red and one for white—at each place setting.

Given the lofty clientele, The Pot is also the only restaurant in Coihaique where admittance is not guaranteed, and it took a long time for the son to answer the bell after I rang it. In a smoke-scarred voice, he said, "We're not open yet." When I told him I was looking for someone who might be working in the kitchen, he said to come inside and locked the door behind me. Then he disappeared behind the heavy kitchen door.

A while later, an old woman in a dirty apron came out of the kitchen. She had a shower cap on her head, and she wore slippers with tire-tread soles and cowhide footings that are ubiquitous among the world's poor. I begged pardon and asked if she knew Luisa.

"She doesn't work here." I asked if she knew where I might find her. "If she had a house," said the woman, "that might be the place to start. If she doesn't have one, then it wouldn't help to go there."

*　　*　　*

Satisfied that I would not find Duck nor Edith nor Luisa that day, I spent the next several hours wandering around downtown Coihaique, refamiliarizing myself with the place—and the century—I had been out of contact with for a month. I went to a newspaper kiosk and bought all three nationally circulated papers available. (The papers were from the day before, because they were flown in from Santiago each afternoon and today's had yet to arrive.) Then I went to

Coihaique's only seafood restaurant and ordered soup with *congrio* (a white-meat fish) and mussels and clams, and then two plates of grilled salmon. While I read the news, I drank a liter of beer.

When I was done, I walked up and down Calle Prat, Coihaique's main drag, past the cafés and the clothing and music stores and the bars. There is nothing in town that says as much about Coihaique's bipolar personality as the naming and gridding of its streets.

Coihaique's origins can be traced directly to a pentagonal "square" in what is now the extreme north end—the same area where the calving once took place—from which its first streets emanated. The pentagon was built in imitation of the *carabinero*'s badge, though, standing at the corner of Calle Arturo Prat and Calle Dussen, just off the square, the first settlers' preemptive efforts at organization seemed more like an exercise in disarray than an example of militaristic administration. The streets run willy-nilly; the blocks are an uneven collection of recessed cul-de-sacs with lopped-off ends and fused corners, and the houses and buildings are completely devoid of ninety-degree angles. One look at the threatening winter sky was enough to understand why: first-degree, premeditated construction was not as important as just getting things built.

But as the town grew farther and farther east, a grid system was initiated and maintained with the kind of precision that would impress a mathematician. It is taken for granted by many Latin Americans and many Chileans alike that the latter are the most orderly and disciplined people on the continent, which, it is said, is owed to the Chilean government's historical respect for and imitation of the English, the French, and, above all, the Germans. Reading the sketchy history of Aisén's colonization, one would think that the gauchos had nothing to do with it and the continental Europeans, often at the behest of the Chilean government, accomplished everything.

Whatever the reality of Chilean cultural predilections, the downtown, educated Coihaiquinos consider themselves to be Chilean first and Patagonian second, primarily because their town is the only place in Aisén that, like a telephone line or a circuit cable, is *eslabonado* (linked)—to Santiago, to the twenty-first century, and to Chile. And the streets of downtown Coihaique are named accordingly: Calle Arturo Prat, for the naval hero of the War of the Pacific; Calle Ramón Freire, after the Supreme Dictator who ruled from 1823 to 1826;

Calle Lord Cochrane, named for the man who captured Valdivia from the Spanish in 1818; and so on. In some cases, as with Calle Prat, the streets have been named and renamed several times, as though to imbue them with extra *chilenismo.*

Outside the city limits, though, Prat is unnamed. The fences and the homesteads give way to glacier-scarred hills. It is here that Calle Prat (formerly Calle Ibáñez and Calle Ogana) peters into what Coihaiquinos call simply *el campo*—the country—though it's unclear, exactly, to what nation the few people who live there belong. Farther east, the road crosses the Argentine border, leaving Chile altogether.

The slums that surround downtown Coihaique are also referred to by some as the *campo* or by others as the "settlements." They, like Calle Prat's easternmost reaches, do not seem to be a part of Coihaique or of Chile, and many of the streets are nameless. Those that do have names are no less part of the Center: they are named for trees or Indians or, in the case of one slum, other countries (Venezuela, Argentina, Brazil, and Uruguay). Sometimes, two or more will share the same name, as is the case with Myrtle Street and Myrtle Street.

Since 1998, I had not, aside from the two days I'd spent in Coihaique a month before, had much time to wander around, and the rapidity of change in that one year—not to mention the change since I'd first been there in 1995—was staggering, though at the same time understated: three stoplights and six ATMs instead of none; a new bank, bringing the total to four within the same sixteeen-square-block radius; travel agencies and phone centers on every corner; and, at just about the point where Calle Prat melded into Avenida Ogana, two new giant and opposing supermarkets: the Vhymeister and the MultiMás.

In each of the Vhymeister's thirty aisles, a teenage girl in a red miniskirt, tailored jacket, and black heels stood waiting, not to help with finding things but, rather, just to look good. Or as though, like the Stihl girls in Duck's posters, they'd found themselves in a conspicuously peculiar place to hitch a ride. All around them, men and women in white knee-length smocks stocked and restocked the shelves with cans and boxes and bottles and packets. There was a liquor section with hundreds of bottles of Chilean wine and beers from all over Latin America and the world. The deli case was long and clean and brightly lit and stacked with logs of salamis and bolognas and rounds of cheese. The meat case was piled with whole and halved pigs and lambs and ewes; buckets of ox-tails and knuckles in bloodied, salted water; mounds of hamburger meat; and the anemic steaks typical of beef fed on grass grown sparse and dry in what had once been forest. Everywhere in the aisles, people pushed carts with children seated in the wired child-boxes just aft of the push-handles. They spoke to one another with the bright-eyed, excited amiability of small-town folk who had just added to their limited world the unlimited convenience of not one but two supermarkets.

A friend of mine who had long since gone to Santiago when his father was forced to close the family fruit stand because he could not compete with the supermarkets asked the question: "What kind of sense does it make to bring two supermarkets to the Asshole of the World and drop them within fifteen meters of one another?"

It was not a rhetorical question, whether he'd meant it that way or not, and the answer was that it made a lot of sense. Coihaique is at once extremely insular and obsessively outward-looking. Like an awkward teenager, the more conscious of itself that Coihaique grows—by, among other things, aggressively courting adventure tourism—the more self-conscious it becomes. As the town builds, the natural instinct is to invest in the future, both literally and figuratively—to invest in the center. Where else would you put the Vhymeister and the MultiMás? At the dirt corner of Wild Horses and The Chieftain in The Stags settlement?

When I left the Vhymeister, I walked north on Prat toward the town square. The Hill, always visible in the near-distance, was outfitted in new white snow. Five or ten years before, the same would have been true of the streets and houses in downtown Coihaique. But the town's population, as it had done several times since the 1930s, had nearly doubled in the last fifteen years, and the concomitant increase in exhaust and woodsmoke (wood is still far and away the most common source of domestic fuel) had radically changed the climate. Locked beneath the wintertime haze that kept town in a three-hour dusk every afternoon was the combination of smells that has become Coihaique's trademark: sweet-burning *leña*, smoldering trash, a hint of diesel fuel and wet concrete, and, just before dark, the rich aroma of roasting meat.

I walked past the pharmacies, where men in pressed shirts and ties and white knee-length jackets stared at one of Coihaique's newest growing pains: the afternoon *taco,* or traffic jam, which backed up Prat all the way from Army Street to Admiral Simpson. I waited for the crossing light, then went into one of two brand-new phone company centers facing the pharmacy from separate corners.

Inside Chilesat, the walls were lined with curved, red plastic chairs and clear Plexiglas display trays of demo phones. Behind the central desk, a uniformed operator sat amidst a buzz of computers and fax machines, fielding requests with a hurried smile. I sat down next to a bowlegged old gaucho in riding boots and sloppy wool trousers. When it was his turn, he ambled up and handed the operator a piece of paper.

As I watched him, I couldn't help but wonder where in the world he was calling and, more specifically, how many people he knew who had a phone. I wondered if Duck and Edith would someday find Coihaique to be as small as they had found Cisnes—if they would adjust to their new surroundings enough to subsequently want to go in search of life in, say, Concepción.

The operator punched the gaucho's number into the switchboard, and the call rang on a speaker; someone answered, and before the operator transferred the call to a booth, she said, "Just a moment, Coihaique calling . . . please don't hang up."

*   *   *

I was walking on Calle Ibáñez to Mario's house (the doctor from the hospital) when I heard someone walking quickly behind me. When I turned to face him, I saw briefly as he passed that it was a man or a boy. I kept turning, only to realize that he'd expertly spun me around as if I had been a bull following a cape. He was behind me again, and he reached around with his arm and grasped my neck and wedged something sharp into the small of my back. "Fool," he said into my ear in a smoky, postpubescent voice, "thought you didn't have to worry about anything over here in the rich neighborhood."

I said, "I always did worry about you, *che.*" I thought I could hear him smile, and I leaned back into him to knock him off balance. When he loosened his grip on my neck and withdrew the knife, I turned around.

In the two years since I'd seen Luisa's son Jimmy, he'd grown several inches and gained fifteen or twenty pounds. He was dressed in jeans that needed to be washed and a canvas work shirt and worn black cowboy boots. His black hair was long and dirty, and his face had widened with age, tempering the protruding nose he hadn't quite grown into. When he reached around behind himself to put the knife back in its sheath, I asked him where he'd been the last couple of years.

"Coast." His accent was lisped, like that of John of the Cows, a country twang that was as high and singsongy as it was deeply indicative of the frontier where he'd picked it up. He straightened his shirt and snapped his arms to move the cuffs off his wrists.

He smiled. I said, "When did you leave the coast?"

"While ago."

"Fishing out there?" There were fish farms all along the coast of Aisén that the Japanese had once controlled and, when they no longer were profitable, abandoned. The Chileans took them over and began raising Atlantic salmon in the Pacific. Now Chile is the second-largest exporter of salmon in the world behind Norway.

"That," said Jimmy. "Then building road for a while. I was going to *mami's* when I saw you walking down this street, so I followed you." He looked at his watch. "It's getting time for dinner."

We walked back down Calle Prat and onto Avenida Ogana, past the park where they had horse races. Above that, a construction company was building summer homes, big two-story houses with west-facing windows and green roofs and blond-wood sides that shone in the fading light. Eight of them looked about ready to move into, and eight or ten more had foundations already laid; they were all built within a hundred feet of one another, as though herded together for protection. A half-mile farther toward Cerro MacKay, the southern *poblaciones* began in earnest.

Jimmy and I turned east at the Toyota showroom and walked up a paved, tree-lined street for a quarter-mile. There was a taxi stand at the corner. Standing there in front of it was like being at the confluence of two rivers. There was the tree-lined street which continued east and then north, circling back into Coihaique's middle-class neighborhoods and the little subdivision of vacation homes, and far beyond that, the quiet grandeur of Ibáñez, where we'd been half an hour before. Coming in from the south, a dirt and rock street cratered with potholes and littered with beer bottles brought with it certain muddied sensibilities. All the currents eddied at the confluence, right in front of the cabstand: a meat store, a cobbler, and a well-known whorehouse and bar in the guise of a "convenience" shop.

We were only a few hundred meters from the foot of The Hill. At the top was the antenna and the ancient forest, both set to disappear in the night. Jimmy and I each turned a circle, looking at all of this. Then we walked up the dirt street and entered the slums.

*   *   *

Inside Luisa's house there was a small kitchen with a peeling linoleum floor. The ceilings were low, and an open fire burned in the far corner of the main room. Next to that was a sofa and a wood table surrounded by chairs. Luisa and her lover, Fried Bread, were sitting at the table. Don Luis sat on a bench in the kitchen, alone, nodding to himself as though in conversation with someone who wasn't there.

Luisa stood up and gave Jimmy and me a kiss on the cheek. She was wearing tight jeans and a denim shirt and black motorcycle boots strapped and clasped across the uppers with bright silver buckles like on a belt. Luisa was bowlegged from all the years she'd spent running her mother's ranch with her six sisters, and her cheeks were flushed. She had black eyes and black hair and a wide, friendly face.

I looked around the room for any evidence that Duck and Edith had been there—furniture that had been moved to make way for extra sleeping space, a pair of Oscar's overalls—but there was nothing out of place in Luisa's house, save one of the few gas stoves I'd ever seen in Coihaique in any home, middle-class or poor or gaucho. The stove, which was much smaller than its wood-burning predecessor, was awkwardly situated in the kitchen, flanked by the bench where Don Luis sat.

When I asked after Duck and Edith, Luisa said that they had stayed at her place during the five days it had taken them to find a rental house in The Stags, one of the newest and farthest slums in Coihaique. Luisa said they'd come for their belongings a few days before and said they'd be sure to come back the following day with the exact address (Duck had written it down but had then lost the piece of paper), but they'd never come back and no one had seen them since. I wondered if this meant Duck had sensed Luisa's lack of confidence in him.

I sat down on the bench next to Don Luis, and we hugged and kissed one another on the cheek. Don Luis was in his eighties, and his one remaining tooth dangled from the middle of his upper gum, which, like his lower gum, was dark red and riddled with disease and coming apart in chunks. He had grown up around Coihaique and the *pampa* to the east, and he still dressed, like most of the old men in the slums, in a style that had been popularized one hundred and fifty years before by the gauchos of Argentina. He wore olive *bombachas,* felt or moleskin pants that were plain-fronted and slim at the waist and widened as they approached the floor, not unlike bell-bottoms, except that they buttoned tightly around the ankles so that they could be folded over and tucked into one's boots. The sleeves on his silk shirt had been cut too long and in a widening swath, and they were buttoned tight at the wrists. He wore a long, indigo silk scarf. He'd sealed himself tight around his waist, first with a cummerbund and then with a pinstriped wool vest and a fitted, double-vented suit jacket. His graying black hair was combed back with grease. A few wisps curved down in a rakish arc toward his eyes.

He'd arrived at Luisa's a few minutes before Jimmy and me and he smelled like the smoking remains of a fire; the cold was still on his jacket and his skin, and this, too, I could smell. Luisa said, "*Papi,* what in God's name are you walking over here after dark for?"

Don Luis puttered over to where Fried Bread sat looking at the uneven pruning job he'd done on his nails with a hunting knife. Don Luis said, "Would you choose to slaughter a ewe with a hand grenade, too? *Ojo!*" *Ojo,* or eye, is what Don Luis said when he wanted you to take note of something. He reached into the breast pocket of his jacket. In a cloth napkin, he had a dozen .22 long-rifle cartridges. He let them fall into my hand. "This," he said, making a crooked gun of his finger, "is how I can afford to walk wherever I want." But when he patted his side, he frowned.

"Forget the pistol again?" said Fried Bread. He took a handyman tool from a holster on his belt and opened the tool into pliers; the handles of the pliers were like two separate Swiss Army knives, jammed with blades and bottle openers and a corkscrew and a little saw. Fried Bread said to Don Luis, "Get one of these and you won't have to worry about forgetting things, *viejo.*"

"I've got half of what I need, anyway," said Don Luis. Then he said to Fried Bread, "You, on the other hand, your problem is different. Your horse has more tails than flies to smack."

Don Luis spoke beautifully and with great earnestness and humor, and he used a combination of high, formal diction and a great variety of words—Tehuelche and Italian and German—that with the generations that followed him had gone out of style or out of the lexicon altogether. In all of his monologues, there was one singular set of facts that he would return to over and over: that when he and his generation died, so too would gaucho culture.

Aside from this, Don Luis rarely came out and said anything directly. He preferred instead to make his points with stories, and when I asked him a question, his answer, if it could be called that, would wind its way slowly and thoroughly through the history not just of Argentina and Chile and Patagonia, but through the history of his own life and the lives of his many acquaintances. The answers took the form of parables, and they had neither end nor beginning, for Don Luis might leave off at any point to backtrack to a previous question and not return to the initial question at hand for several months, at which point I would realize he had been answering not only the (now) two questions at hand, but three or four others I'd asked a year before.

None of which anyone, aside from me, had any patience for. Fried Bread seemed simply not to care, in the way of a teenager who is neither living in the times being talked of nor is entirely sure of the direction being taken by the world around him, and therefore cannot be bothered to try and relate the one to the other. Luisa had likely heard many of the stories ten times, so while she obviously respected Don Luis, she, a terse realist, considered him a dotty philosopher. Then again, perhaps she preferred not to know more than was necessary about the years he'd spent away from her and her mother. Luisa had spent many years hating Don Luis for shirking his duties as a father and husband in order to compile the material for his unending litany of stories, though as soon as he could no longer ride, she had insisted on caring for him.

As Don Luis and I sat there on the bench in Luisa's kitchen, I remembered something that I'd always wanted to ask him: how it was that he'd learned to read. It was a skill that was virtually unknown among the gauchos, particularly gauchos of Don Luis's age. Not only that, learning to read was an event to which he had on several occasions referred, though he'd then either lost the thread of the tale or, more likely, decided it was not yet time that I knew. Whatever the case, it seemed to me that learning to read was an appropriate metaphor, given the varying novelty of the place in which all of us—Don Luis and Luisa and I and, wherever they were, Duck and Edith—found ourselves.

As soon as I asked Don Luis about this, Fried Bread and Jimmy excused themselves and went into the main room to watch *Heidi* on the TV. Luisa followed and sat on Fried Bread's lap. "It would please me," Don Luis smiled, "to tell you about all that. But it's better to start with something that displeases, like religion. Then, from there, we'll work toward the positive.

"A few years ago, I rode as far as Río Mayo, in the other country, and when I went to take a room there, I noticed lights in the schoolhouse. It was the time of the Second World War. Hugo Wast was the education minister of Argentina, and he had recently declared that the Bible should once again be taught in the schools.

"There is no better place for a fight than a schoolhouse, *che*! So I, naturally, was attracted to those lights. There were some thirty people sitting around and discussing things, and I walked in and sat in the back of the room. They were too busy talking to notice that I was there, and I listened to them for a long time. Then I said, 'Excuse me, but I'm very interested in all of this, and I would like to ask a question if I may.' I said, 'Who among you knows God?'

"The woman who was leading the meeting said, 'Who are you?'

"I said, 'That is just the right answer.' I waited until everyone had turned in their desks to look at me, and I said, 'Who are all of *you*? You are many people, and you are united by the fact that none of you knows God. Is He in this room? Can you see Him? Yes and no. But if you look for Him, he's not there.'

"The woman raised her Bible and said, 'This is God.'

" 'I beg your pardon,' I said, 'but although I am illiterate, I'm familiar enough with things to know that thing in your hand is a book. I don't see God in your hand.'

"She said that the word was God's word and that, if we read his word, we would come to know Him: the usual bullshit.

" 'Those are not the words of God,' I said, 'those are the words of men and women. They tell a story, and the story they tell is not God's story, but that of the men and women who wrote them. If I tell you I was in Coihaique and I rode to Río Mayo and that, during the trip, the sun did such and such a thing and the moon another, what I am telling you is more about me and my perceptions of myself than it is any kind of truth about the moon and the sun, *señorita*. What I choose to say and how I choose to say it sheds light not on the nature of the sun, *che*, but on my nature and how I interpret the nature of the sun. For the sun, in the end, is not here—I am.'

"There was another woman in the room and she stood up and said that this is only true in a world without God, and one in which man, not God, is the center. She said that God, knowing this, sent a son to show all others that men should focus not on themselves but on God.

"I asked her upon whom she focused her religious beliefs, such as they were.

" 'Jesus Christ,' she said.

" 'And was he a man or a god? He was a man, and he interpreted the idea of god as all of us do: in his own way. God is everywhere, for every man has his idea of god, and no two can be the same, just as no two men can be the same. For one man to say that there is only one god is for him to speak the truth, for each man has his god. But to say that there is only one god for all men is to say there is no god, and is that not blasphemy?'

"Oh! They didn't like that. It delights me sometimes to speak in riddles, and I could see that I had confused them. I could see it would take some time to discuss things fully if I was going to speak this way. So I found a job breaking horses for a *patrón* near Río Mayo, and I went back to the schoolhouse each time there was a meeting. I would walk in and they would say, 'Look, here comes the Devil's Lawyer!'

"I never convinced them, but why would I have wanted to do that? Their interpretations were just as important and unique as my own. Had I tried to convince them, *che*, I would have been a hypocrite. But I hoped that they might talk to their children about these things—even in anger, for if you tell a child angrily not to think a certain way, he is sure to try his hardest to do so—and that their children might understand that the only truth is that, by closing your mind, you will never see the truth. You will never, you see, learn to read. And besides all of that, the woman who ran the school was young and pretty. *Ojo!*

"Years later, *che,* I went on further south, to Comodoro Rivadavia. I found work there in a granary. I'd shown up and thought I would keep moving, but next thing I'd sold my horses because this town had me fascinated. All kinds of people, and things I'd never seen before. Industry, *che!*

"I've never attended one day of school in my life. But riding toward the horizon is what educates, for between it and you there lie many men, and each of them a lesson, like a tree on the *pampa,* and from it shade that keeps you from broiling in the sun and stewing in your own juices.

"Now the wheat that comes to a granary, *che,* is ripe. It can be fermented or it can be pounded into submission and made into bread for the men who are kept in submission by the bread made therein. A granary is full of ripe seeds, then, *che;* and there was fermenting in those days a revolution, and there were those for Perón and those for the right.

"The woman in Río Mayo had taught me that what gives one man power over others is the written word. If it is written, men believe it because the memory is weak, and written words are the crutch that aids the shortcomings of this weakness. So the Devil's Lawyer decided literally to learn to read.

"There was a man who stayed in the rooming house where I stayed. An educated man, a professor. I went to him one night, and we talked until the sun came up and it was time for us to go work. And when I came back the next night, there was a grammar book on my bed. He sat with me that night and every night for months until I could read the books he had brought with him to Comodoro. Lenin. Nietzsche. Trotsky. Simón Bolívar. I read all of them.

"And I came to understand something else. That the countryfolk have memories that far surpass those of the cityfolk. Many of us had been unable to count, for instance, and we would understand the numeric concept not in terms of the individual *quantity* of that number, but as an individuating *quality, che.* We saw differences in the hides of cattle such that each of them was differentiated as an individual entity far more profoundly than a mere number allowed for. I could recite entire stanzas of *El Gaucho Martín Fierro,* though I had never read them. I had committed them to memory by hearing. It was in this way that I understood something: that a man who could read and understand things and then relay them in a convincing speech had the greatest of all possible advantages.

"Let me tell you what happened for this. The police saw things the same way! Only they saw in each of us the individual expression of an evil concept: socialism. And I left Comodoro. I'm no martyr. What can a man accomplish as a corpse? Food for worms, Skinny. Change at the lowest level eventually filters up. But change that filters up from six feet below the earth sprouts flowers, and the flowers do nothing for the revolution. *Ojo!*

"I was now forty-two years old, and I went once again back into the country, armed with my knowledge, educated by the natural processes of curiosity, not because I'd been forced. And for this I was much more dangerous still. This was 1955. Perón was exiled, and the generals were in charge of the Argentine government. I was, in those days, with men like-minded to me. And we went back to what we knew: we went to the village of Buen Pasto.

"One day we were in the village resting around a bottle of red wine when a man approached and said there was a meeting of Peronistas in a barn in the country, and there they would discuss what was to be done now that the government was in the hands of the military. He invited us to join, and then he left. Nothing more.

"We drank for a time. I said, 'Brothers, did you see the pistol he carried?'

"'What of it?' they said. It was a government pistol.

"I said, 'Did you see how he stood at the table?'

"'What of it?' they said. He stood like a man trying to overcome a life in which he'd been trained to stand at attention.

"'Brothers,' I said, 'did you see his legs?'

"'What of them?' they said.

"'What gaucho is it has no bow to his legs, brothers?'

"But they did not believe me. Drink makes men willing to believe things they should not. Remember this, Skinny: If you drink with a man you don't trust, this is not the time to get drunk. In this case, drink vegetable oil first, which is heavy and keeps the alcohol from rising to your head. With men you trust, it is wise to get drunk, for you know them better afterward.

"I said, 'If the man was not who he appeared to be, it logically follows that the barn is not what he makes it out to be.'

" 'Nonsense,' they said. 'How could he have known we were Peronistas if we only got here a month ago, and we've never seen him before?'

" 'In that case, what harm is there in waiting to see what happens tonight? If a man can be trusted today, he can surely be trusted tomorrow, too. No loss in taking care, brothers.'

"But they would not listen, and they went to the barn that night. When they were inside, the police locked the doors and burned the barn to the ground. My friends had not, you see, learned how to read.

"The next day, I was riding back the way I'd come, looking to the horizon—the same horizon I'd left long before—for new clues."

Finding Chile

I spent much of the next week looking around Coihaique for Duck and Edith. The Stags, I knew, were the easternmost slums, though this was little help, for they had two "levels," owing to the fact that The Stags had been built onto two successive waves of striated ridgeline. Still, every morning I would walk the hour or so that it took to get to the slums from where I was staying to check the construction sites where I thought that Duck, given his experience as a carpenter, might be working. I went into the shops where they sold candy, liquor, cigarettes, soda, and firewood and asked if anyone had seen any newcomers. In the afternoons, I would go to the MultiMás and the Vhymeister in hopes of happening onto Duck as he was buying food or was simply wandering around what had to be, from his perspective, an unparalleled and mind-bending creation. Then, thwarted, I would go back to my room on Calle Magallanes.

Calle Magallanes is a short street at the extreme west end of Coihaique—it spans a mere four blocks before dead-ending at the hospital—and behind it are Calle 18 de Septiembre and Calle Gabriela Mistral, after which Coihaique comes to an end by falling abruptly into the Río Simpson. Calle Magallanes is lined with rowhouses. If you went through the gate in front of one of the rowhouses, into a small yard and past the woodshed, you would come to a tiny A-frame that stands hidden beneath apple trees. This is where I lived during April and May 1999.

The A-frame had two floors, though the second floor was so short that I couldn't stand up there. The ceiling on the first floor was just taller than my head. There were three beds crammed into that single room, and a table with a stool at which I could write. There was a tiny refrigerator and a sink with cold running water, and an FM radio. There was a bathroom, in which I had to stoop to shave or wash my hands, and a cold-water shower. Next to the bathroom was a space heater which ran on gas that, once ignited, flowed over a metal grate. You could not run it all night, or even for more than a couple of hours at a time, because a fair amount of gas invariably leaked and made you dizzy. Every year, a couple of people in Coihaique would die from leaving the heaters on too long, which filled their room with enough gas to blow the whole place up. More to the point, the amount of heat generated was so negligible as to be unworth the risk. It was better to wrap yourself in one of the dozen wool blankets piled onto the beds and leave it at that.

There was a little house on Calle Bilbao where you could take your laundry to be done, and I was heading from there back to my room one afternoon a week after I'd arrived in Coihaique when I saw Peeled on the corner, in front of the pharmacy. I'd met Peeled at the fly-fishing lodge that year, where he'd worked as Luisa's assistant in the kitchen.

I watched him for a few minutes. Peeled had close-shaved pitch-black hair (hence the nickname) and dark eyes and olive skin. He was wearing shiny black Adidas sweatpants with reflective white strips down the sides of the legs, and he didn't appear to be doing much, just leaning against the lightpost, watching the people go by and smoking. I wondered if he'd had a relapse and was waiting to make a deal.

Two years before, Peeled had been the second-biggest cocaine dealer in Coihaique. He'd gone straight shortly after his uncle—who was the biggest dealer in Coihaique and, by virtue of that fact, the biggest dealer in all of central Patagonia and the border areas of Argentina—had died of an overdose at the age of thirty-three. Peeled had gone back to high school and finished. He'd captained the basketball team, taking them to the national tournament, where they were crushed in the second round. He had a girlfriend whose name was Patchy, and he'd moved back in with his mother and father and grandmother on what was left of his grandmother's ranch, ten kilometers outside of town.

Aside from Don Luis, Peeled is the only person I've ever met with something like total recall. He either said nothing for long periods or talked incessantly. Often, he would narrate with astounding exactness the events of the many basketball games he had played in the year during which he finished high school. He could tell you every shot that had been taken, not just by him, but by all the players; the time on the clock; the position of the players on the court; and the score. He remembered the exhilaration of thinking that he might use his newfound, almost mystical interest in the game as a bootstrap by which to pull himself out of the centrifugal path of addiction. Then he would smile and talk at a remove about how in the end none of it meant shit because he was no good at basketball.

I came up behind Peeled and tapped him on the shoulder. He gave me one of these hugs where he would grab my hand like he was going to arm-wrestle me, and then we'd sort of bump chests, making sure not to touch cheeks. In heavily accented English, he said, "What up, motherfucker?" Then in Spanish, he said, "I've been looking for a job all morning. You?" I told him I was going back home to do some writing. All of a sudden, he seemed nervous, even sad. When I asked him what was on his mind, he said, "Nothing."

I said, "C'mon, man, what?"

He said, "It's just . . . catch it, 'go, you hear what happened the other day at the gas station, 'go?"

Abbreviating "eggo" to "'go" was, according to Peeled, the proper way to express "Chileanism." Only Argentines and outsiders, he said, pronounced the whole word. It was ironic, then, that the only word he employed almost as much was one he'd picked up from listening to hard-core Spanglish rap: "yo."

I said, "Station on General Parra?"

"Fucking, right there, 'go. You didn't hear this shit. Fucking brutal, man. Crime in this place is getting out of control, 'go."

He looked at me until I said, "What? What happened?"

"Fucking, seven o'clock at night, 'go. Motherfucker walks in the little shop where they sell the beer and cigarettes, catch, pulls out a gun and says, 'Give me the fucking money, yo. All of it.'

"And, catch it, the kid behind the register is like, 'No, yo.'

"'What?' 'go says to him. Puts the gun to his head and says, 'Gimme the fucking money out of the register.'

"Guy behind the register's like, 'No, man. I'm not giving you shit, catch it? I just got this fucking job and my boss'll kill me, man.'

"'Motherfucker,' says the robber, '*I'm* gonna fucking kill you.'"

I said, "Was this that kid, what's his name, the skinny one?"

"Yeah," said Peeled. "I don't recall his name. But it's that one. Tall, right?" I nodded. "Armando," said Peeled. "Armando's his name." I knew Armando—he'd given me a free pack of cigarettes the night before.

I said, "And where'd this 'go with the gun come from?"

"Fucking, the slums, yo. Where you think he came from? Fucking bad-ass motherfuckers that run around up in the slums. Either that or the kids that come down from Santiago or over from Argentina with the drugs to sell the dealers in the slums. Wanted to hit some shit up in Coihaique before they went back over the border or something. So, anyway, fucking Armando won't give him the money. And, catch it, kid with the gun isn't too patient. So he says, 'Give me that money or I'm gonna fucking take you to that pump over there and fill your ass with gas.' And Armando holds his ground, man. I can't believe it, man, but he says, 'Do it then, 'go.'

"So the kid drags Armando out there and puts the nozzle in his mouth and starts pumping, man. Fucking fills Armando up with petrol." Peeled looked down and shook his head. "All about not losing his precious job, man. Fucking heroic, you ask me."

I said, "So what happened?"

"Catch it, the robber couldn't get the cash box open, so he leaves Armandito there on the pavement. And, catch it, Armandito gets up and starts walking to the hospital. That's a long way to walk, 'go."

I shook my head. The gas station is eight or ten blocks from the hospital.

Peeled rubbed his lips against one another and lit a cigarette. He looked angry. "He never made it, man." He inhaled deeply and looked away.

"Died?" I said.

Peeled looked at me and blew smoke. "No, man. Fucker ran outta gas." Then he exploded with laughter. He laughed so hard his eyes teared up. We hugged one another we were laughing so hard. "Oh well," said Peeled. "I'm done looking for a job today, yo. Let's go have a beer and some pizza."

*　　*　　*

The pizza place was new. It was on Calle Bilbao, not far from the center of town. A Spanish woman owned it. She was in her fifties and she wore a black shawl and a gray ankle-length skirt and a white silk blouse with a red kerchief at her neck. She had gray hair and long features. She'd been divorced from the Spaniard who owned The Pot, and she was very elegant in a sort of tired way, though none of her sophistication was evident in the pizza place she owned. The tables and chairs were plastic, and the walls were covered in cheap drawings. Fake plants crowded one corner, as though waiting to be thrown out.

The Spanish woman was seated at one of the tables, smoking. She was watching *GI Jane* on the TV perched in the corner, and she rose wearily when we approached her and pulled the shawl tight around her chest and took her place behind the cash register to one side of the open kitchen. A stout young woman with strong indigenous features sat listening in the kitchen as we ordered, though she didn't make a move till the Spaniard entered the kitchen and handed her the ticket. Peeled and I sat down at a table.

"Oh, man," said Peeled, and lit a cigarette. "Wild times, yo. These are wild times around here. Three years ago, you'd have never believed me. Joke wouldn't have worked because there wasn't any crime."

Peeled was not a full generation removed from being a gaucho. His grandmother had owned a large parcel of land in the rich Valle Simpson and big herds of sheep and cattle. But with the land conglomeration brought on by twenty years of free-falling cattle prices and the competition from Argentina and Brazil, she'd sold off pieces of her family's land till all that remained was a mere pittance. Amidst the changes in Coihaique that had defined the trajectory of Peeled's life, he had lost his identity—he was not gaucho and he was not, because he lived in the *campo,* Chileno. But then, through his drug dealing, he had made a place for himself in the new order. His slang and his accent and his style of dress were studiously Santiaguino. He'd ridden his business right into downtown Coihaique—the Center had belonged to Peeled and his uncle alone.

But then Peeled had taken a gamble: he'd gone straight. He'd decided to go back to school. He'd not planned on having to stick around Coihaique afterward, nor on the 1998 Asian crisis, which had crushed the Chilean economy and was the event that made it impossible for him to go on to college and that made it hard to find a job in anything other than the tourist trade, which was largely being run by foreigners—North Americans and Argentines and Germans—an "invasion" that Peeled abhorred.

Worse was that, in just two years, the drug market had been taken over by the slum*che,* who enforced their law using the same handmade knives with which they'd slaughtered sheep while growing up in the mountains. Never were the lines that delineated the two worlds in Coihaique, that of *el* eggo and that of *el che,* as clear to me as when I hung around with Peeled. He hated the word *che* in a way he couldn't explain: it was *their* word, and if he wanted back into the world that he and his uncle had pioneered—if he wanted his identity back—Peeled knew to whom he would have to answer.

I told him I'd walked home from Luisa's a few nights before at midnight and had seen a bunch of boys standing on a corner. There were half a dozen of them, and they were dressed in black warm-up pants and black sweatshirts. Some of them had the hoods pulled over their heads, and the others wore black baseball caps so low you couldn't see under the visors. When they saw me, they moved to the middle of the street, like players in Red Rover.

Peeled interrupted me. " 'Go," he said, "first of all, you're the dumbest motherfucker in all Coihaique. Fuck is your problem walking around a slum at midnight? Especially JMC, yo. They see you and their eyes light up with dollar signs, dumbass. You think the *pacos* ever go up there at night? I bet you've never seen a *paco* in the slums at night, not once, right?

"I've never seen a *paco* in the daytime."

"You wanna know why?" said Peeled. "Because it's the same reason you don't see *pacos* at the whorehouses, unless they're there to get a trick or take kickbacks. Don't think they don't know all about it, 'go. And don't think it's a coincidence the paper doesn't report more than one out of every ten murders. If it happens in the slums, yo, no one gives a fuck. Not if it happens to you or to me or to Luisa or whoever.

"Second, let me tell you what happened when you saw those 'gos. You stopped and looked at them, and then you turned around, and guess what? There was another group behind you."

He was right. I'd turned around, thinking I'd swing onto a side street and avoid the gang at the bottom of the hill. But there was another half a dozen kids standing in the street behind me. They'd come out of the same dark street I'd planned to duck down, the one I'd just walked by seconds before without ever knowing they were there.

Peeled said, "So what did you do?"

"Walked down the hill."

"And one of them asked you for a cigarette or some shit, right?"

The Spaniard brought over two glasses of beer and put them down on napkins on the table. I waited until she was gone before I said, "Yeah. And I assumed that as soon as I had my hands in my pockets, he'd pull out a knife or something. But instead . . ."

"But instead he told you he didn't want the cigarette."

"So I lit it and walked away."

"Soon as he makes you get him a cigarette, the only way he can make it *more* clear who's in control is by not smoking the cigarette. Seriously though, 'go, I have to tell you something else about that, since you're not gonna see this on your own. It's a Chilean thing, maybe, or a Latin thing, I don't know. But when you smoked your cigarette and walked away, they were probably like, 'That's an icy motherfucker right there, man. That's a fucking *macho toro, ch*,'" he said, imitating a country accent. "They respected that. But if they catch you again in the trap, they're gonna think one of two things: one, that you're just plain stupid; or two, that you're *too* fucking *macho toro*. Either way, you'll be fucking fucked."

I got up and paid for the pizza. The Spaniard went and sat under the TV and continued watching the movie. When I sat back down, I said to Peeled, "So you know all this because either you and your uncle were like them or because you got run off by kids like that."

"Kind of," said Peeled. "We weren't really like that. First off, we were pretty much the only game in town. And second, we weren't any fucking slum monkeys. It was more of a gentleman's business. People deferred to us because there wasn't anyone else to defer to. Gangs and stuff, it probably existed, but it was like, out of sight, out of mind. I carried a gun, yo, but I never expected to *use* it. Half the time it wasn't even loaded. *I'd* be so loaded I'd forget where I'd put the bullets. I stole it from my dad, and then one day he was like, 'Where's the gun, you little bastard?' So I gave it back to him and moved out and started living with my uncle downtown.

"Now, it's like these motherfuckers watch movies from the U.S. and take their orders directly from fucking Robert De Niro or some shit. We didn't have to be like that. Like, one night I was walking home from some party where I'd provided all the coke. It wasn't even night. It was like six on a Tuesday morning. And me and my friend who used to deliver for me were going back to my uncle's, which was like ten kilometers from the house we were at."

I said, "Whose house?"

"Some rich kid who's a lawyer. Lawyers and government people and kids of landowners—that was our clientele. So we're walking home and we're like halfway, and we can't get a *colectivo* because they're not running yet, and all the sudden, we're like, 'Fuck, 'go, we *had* a truck at the party!' We'd fucking *driven* to the party and gotten so fucked up we forgot we'd driven there, yo. And it's cold and we don't wanna walk all the way back. There's this beautiful sunrise, catch it, and people are starting to make their fires for the morning, and it smells like smoke everywhere, and there's haze and the sun is like—pow!—massive in the haze, 'go. So what's the hurry? I mean, we could walk back to the house we were at and look for the truck—that'd be one way to spend some more time together walking around—but we don't want to *work* too hard, right?

"So, we're walking along and checking out the sunrise and we were just like, 'Let's steal a truck. We could use a new truck for the next few hours.' So we walked along checking out the trucks parked on the street and were like, '*This* one looks good. No, no, I don't like the color of the interior. *That* one looks good. No, no, tires are too bald.' Shit like that. We finally find this black Toyota four-door, and we're like, '*Mortal,*'" by which he meant "the best."

"So I hotwire it and off we go, doing a hundred and fifty kilometers an hour, flying all over the place, fucking blowing lines. We stopped in at the little illegal beer and sandwich shop—the one over there across the square, you know, where they sell twenty-four hours?—bought some beers and some ham and cheese sandwiches. Just, you know, having a good time.

"But here's my point, 'go: At nineteen, I'm a dinosaur. I've been naturally selected out of the dealer gene pool, 'go. Because it never would have occurred to me to sell the truck to buy more coke. I'm not mean, man. I mean, I stole the truck, but it was more like I was borrowing it, trying to have a good time in this fucking small town. I didn't want the guy who'd just bought it to wake up and, you know, his truck is gone, yo. When we were done, I just pulled it back in the same parking space we'd stole it from and rolled up the windows and locked it. I mean, after all that, we *walked* home."

We'd been talking in normal voices, though it seemed loud in the empty restaurant, and we both looked over at the Spanish woman. She was turned in her seat, staring at us, outraged. Peeled had a mouthful of pizza, and he smiled a bulging smile and wiped his lips with a napkin, then waved to her with the same hand. The woman in the kitchen was seated in the far corner, staring at the tubs of cheese.

"In those days," said Peeled, "there wasn't any crime. No monkeys, no crime. You and I went out and stole a truck right now, we'd be in jail by sundown. Then, 'go, it was a different world. Now, I wouldn't last till the commercial break."

*   *   *

When Peeled and I walked outside, I asked him, as an afterthought, if he knew anything about what had happened to Duck and Edith. He said he'd run into Duck the day before coming out of the Vhymeister. He'd written the address down, and I took it from him and walked across the street to a kiosk where *colectivos,* little black and yellow cabs that run on distinct lines and cost about a quarter, stopped to pick up passengers. The number of *colectivo* lines had doubled in the last five years, though they still ran mostly in circuitous routes around the slums, always somehow avoiding, except in the rarest of cases, the hearts of the places where the majority of the people in Coihaique lived.

I was waiting for the number six when a van pulled up and Señor Mansilla stuck his head out the window. He asked where I was going. When I told him, he looked at his watch and said, "Where's that?"

"Wherever the six line ends. I need to get to Wild Horses Street, number 397."

"I guess we'll find it," he said. We pulled onto Calle Bilbao, and I asked after his business. "Got three vans now, in addition to the buses," he said. "I've been running tourists to and from the airport and back. Then tours to the coast and down south."

I said, "Winter, too?"

"I'm the only game in town this time of year."

We'd been passing middle-class houses and small businesses—cobblers and tailors and liquor stores—but now, slowly, the scenery began to change. Row-houses painted garish colors leaned out of the ground; between the houses were high-grassed runs of *pampa* littered with tires and the rusted frames of cars and trucks. Herds of sheep and thick-necked Chilean mountain horses fed on the grass that grew through the windshields and the doors. Packs of half-wild dogs lapped at themselves in the sun. The signs refused even to designate the dirt pathways with the basic moniker *"calle."* Trampananda, the name of Patagonia before the word Patagonia even existed, was, according to the wooden cross that bore the name, something other than a byway, a theoretical entity unto itself. At Wild Horses, Señor Mansilla pulled off onto the dirt shoulder and I got out.

I walked down a steep hill. The rowhouses, like the country shacks after which they had been modeled, had steep roofs made of corrugated aluminum; tiny, stylized porches too small for someone actually to stand on were built into the fronts. The spaces between the rowhouses were so slim—four inches, a half a foot—that I could look over the tops of hundreds of other rowhouses as they fell, under the sky and the mountains, step by step toward the center of town, where evenly cleaved grids of streets shot up between the spaces like images seen through a pinhole camera.

Halfway down the block I came to the first house that had a number: 397. Duck was standing in the open doorway, smiling. Before I'd made it through the gate, he said, "Nico*che,* I dreamed you were coming."

*   *   *

The rowhouse Duck and Edith were renting was half again as big as the cabin in Cisnes. There were two bedrooms, one for the children and one for Duck and Edith, a small bathroom and a large main room in which the principal feature was a used television set Duck had purchased the day after they moved in. The dining room table was positioned at an angle so that everyone sitting there could see the screen. They'd also bought a little orange vinyl couch, and beside it sat the throne, covered now in pillows instead of sheepskins. Near the front door was the kitchen. A cabinet clung unconvincingly to the dry wall above a brushed steel sink that Edith had scavenged and somehow made shine; the pipes, which Duck had spent a day installing, were visible below the sink housing. Across from it was a used stove, much smaller than the one in Cisnes.

"That rip-off," said Edith, "doesn't burn right. The vent gives too much air when it's open and kills the fire when it's closed. I haven't had a decent haul of bread in a week."

"It's the water," said Duck, "not the stove."

"It's both," said Edith. "Chlorine in the water and the fact you can't keep a good fire going."

Patricia was sitting in a chair next to the front door, covered in Duck's poncho, the sole bearer, along with the throne, of the history of their lives in the mountains. Patricia got up out of the chair and tossed the poncho on the floor and walked slowly to the bathroom. A minute later, she was retching into the toilet.

"I thought that business was done," said Duck. "Chlorine in the water's had these poor kids sick since the word go. If they're not vomiting, they're shitting." When Patricia choked and began to cry, Edith disappeared into the bathroom and closed the door.

I said, "How's school?"

"Yesterday was the first day they could go," said Duck, "they've been so sick. It's nice because it's right down the hill there. Patricia's teacher is a nice lady. We went and talked to her, and explained where we come from and said we were worried about, you know, the girls adjusting. She said she'd keep an eye on them both. She said she herself was from the south and knew what it could be like for kids.

"Mariana's teacher, though, acted like she didn't know what we were saying, like we weren't even speaking the same language or something."

I asked how the girls had liked it so far.

"Oh, kids, you know, they don't give you much slack. They're like mares with an old gelding, and they'll nip right at where the nuts used to be. Mariana's having a hard time. She's so shy, and she doesn't fight back. Patricia learned how not to take shit in Amengual. But Mariana, she'll have to learn."

I looked to where she was sitting at the table, in the uniform Duck and Edith had bought her. The navy pants were too long, and the navy sweater was too big, and her white shirt was untucked; her belt was buckled to the last hole and still it hung loose. She was putting pencils and paper in her knapsack with the kind of rehearsed concentration I'd seen many times, the kind that meant she was faking interest in some task to mask the fact she was listening to what we were saying.

I walked over and lifted her up by the arms and sat down and plopped her on my lap. She looked at me as though she'd never seen me before and hopped down and went across the room to the couch, which was as far as she could get from everything else.

"I guess she's toughening already," Duck said. "Know what there is around here more than anything? Dogs, *che*. There's more goddamn dogs than work on ten ranches. I mean, just whatever number. And they don't stay away from one another, either. Like in the mountains a lot of times, you know, dogs from different owners won't run together, unless there's a bitch in heat. And then not so much together as they are, you know, staying close to get at the bitch, not because they share the same views, so to speak.

"Here, they pack up, *che*. I mean, thirty at a time. I guess they have no owners. A pack came here the other night to steal the garbage, and I'll be damned if they didn't knock the whole container over. That's how I knew you were coming: I woke up to the sound of the dogs and remembered my dream."

"Dogs," said Edith, "and dogs—bad people." She'd just come from the bathroom, and she was cleaning her hands with a damp towel. "Music, too. More fucking music than you could dance to in about ten years. Our neighbor—that woman, I swear to God—every morning eight o'clock sharp, *che,* the music starts. Fucking *ranchera* all day and no end to it till late at night. These walls are thin. And on the other side, nothing all day but damn *cumbia*. All this music and I haven't heard a ballad since we arrived. It isn't quiet like the country."

Edith tossed the towel onto the table and sat down on the kitchen chair in a heap. Patricia was still in the bathroom. There was the sound of running water, and Edith listened till it stopped. She said, "We can't let Oscar out of the house. He thinks the trucks are like horses, thinks they'll stop and let him on. He wanders out there with his little string and he wants to ride. Makes me nuts. And he's big enough he can undo the latch on the gate, *che*."

Mariana went over and turned on the TV. It was time for Messages, but when I looked around the house, there was no radio anywhere. "Is it time already?" said Edith.

"*Sí,*" said Mariana. She didn't turn around. She seemed to be refusing to acknowledge my presence, the same way she had the very first time I'd ever entered Duck and Edith's house in Cisnes.

I Love You, Paquita Gallego was just starting. It was a Colombian soap opera about a young, beautiful woman who had married a rich old man who'd died shortly after the wedding. Now Paquita lived all alone in an old, gigantic house, and there were all kinds of young men trying to get her to settle on them. She had this old woman—her mother, maybe, or her grandmother—who was also dead, and the old woman came to her in dreams and gave her all kinds of advice that didn't make any sense. The old woman spoke in riddles, and she didn't come only at night, she'd come in the middle of the day while Paquita was sitting in her house having tea. There was a maid who served Paquita the tea, and some gardeners, and no one seemed to take any notice when Paquita, like Don Luis, began having a conversation with a person no one else could see. Then, every once in a while there was a scene with two old alcoholic witches who sat around plotting in a studio apartment somewhere in Bogotá or Cali or Medellín. They dressed like gypsies, and you could tell they were actually young, attractive women who, through gobs of makeup, had been made to look old and ugly. Duck and Edith loved this.

But not so much as they loved the Brazilian soap opera that aired in the evenings. It was called *Chica da Silva,* and it was about the Portuguese colonists who ruled the country in the eighteenth century. There were men with white wigs and makeup and who wore knickers and kneesocks and ornate frock coats, and they were by turns brutal with and charmed by the army of *mulata* slave women and black witches who populated their great estates, and the creamy-skinned, big-breasted Portuguesas whose passions were inflamed by everything from the searing tropical heat to the sight of fields of laboring men.

"Oh man," said Duck, "do I ever love that show."

"They do the best shit to one another," said Edith. "Those Brazilians, they don't stop for anything. Sex, murder, all kinds of bad stuff. I can't get enough."

"And the history," said Duck, "that's the best part. It's informative. I bet that's what this country was like a long time ago. Not here, though—too fucking cold all the time. But in the north, that must have been something, up near Santiago, near the beaches, where they grow the wine. I bet that's really something."

I couldn't help but think that part of the attraction of *Chica da Silva* stemmed from the fact that it was about a time that didn't exist anymore, and about the people—however sordidly they were depicted—who had brought the place into being. It occurred to me that Duck and Edith, as refugees from another time and another place—the indeterminate *campo*—saw in *Chica da Silva* many things they could relate to.

I said, "What about the Chilean shows? There have to be some Chilean shows on the TV, too, *che*."

"They suck," said Edith. "Nothing happens. Nothing I can connect with, anyway."

"Yeah," said Duck dismissively, "I don't see anything in those shows that seems real to me, *che*. It's all a bunch of jerks in school, and doing business, and they don't really ever *do* anything but sit around."

"It's like here with me now," said Edith. "Like, I can't go out because I have Oscar, and I can't have him in the street because he's likely to run out in front of a truck he wants to pet. No one can go out at night around here, *che*. There's too many gangs, and these Indians that want to rob you. All I ever do is sit around in this cabin. It's like Cisnes that way. And all the neighbors, they do the same thing, *che*. Who wants to watch a bunch of losers on the Chilean shows doing that in Santiago? I mean, I can relate to the Brazilian show, even the Colombian, more than the Chilean, because in the other ones, people act like people."

"Or with the Brazilian one," said Duck, "what makes it the best is that they do that, *and* it's real. It's *history*. They should do a show about Santiago like they do about Brazil. But Santiago in the old days, at the beginning. That would be *Wendy*."

I said, "It's real because it's history?"

"Well, Nico, I can see you're trying to put words in my mouth. No, I mean, it's obviously made up. It's a show. But, it's . . . it's history. I don't know, I can just relate to it better. It's more real to me."

"It *is* real," said Edith. "Of course it's real, *che*. Maybe, like, these people didn't actually exist, like their names are made up and so forth. But you don't think people really did that kind of shit to one another? I mean, they did it to one another in Cisnes all right."

"Then how about a Patagonian soap opera?" I said.

"We just came out of that," said Duck. "We don't need to go looking at that again."

Edith was getting frustrated. She snapped her lips. "The Chilean soap operas," she said, "I don't know about the Chileans. I'm just not there with them yet."

❀

CHAPTER SIXTEEN

God on a Wednesday

Do you wish to curb our nomadic gaucho in his vaga-

bond instincts? Root him . . . with the only bond that is

lasting: property.

—*Nicolás Avallaneda,* Estudio sobre las leyes de tierras públicas, *1865*

O nce I'd found Duck and Edith, I began developing a bad case of dysentery, though I quickly learned to deal with it by eating nothing except avocados and salami. For some reason, these were the only foods that didn't make my stomach hurt so badly that I would have to lie down for a few minutes until the pain passed. Aside from *pisco,* the only liquid I could keep in was *mate* with loads of sugar.

I spent the weekends, when Luisa wasn't working and when Don Luis was most likely to show up, at Luisa's cabin in José Miguel Carrera. I divided the days of the week between sitting with Edith and Duck in their cabin in The Stags and just wandering the slums, talking to people I met there. In the evenings, I often went to pass the time with Mario, whose fourteen-year-old son was a brilliant pianist; he could play Chopin's Études without ever looking at the music. When Mario and his wife went to bed, I met Peeled at a pool hall or at the Red Skin.

Then, at the end of my first two weeks in Coihaique, something happened that would change everything: Duck got a job. A construction company was building low-rent housing in one of the dwindling number of pastures that pocked The Stags, and Duck, when he talked to the foreman, was hired on the spot. From that point on, Duck and Edith's lives began leading them in opposite directions.

The houses Duck helped to build, though small, were being made to twentieth-century specifications, and they were a dramatic departure from anything else around, with their shiny aluminum roofs and walls made of a synthetic material that looked like wood. As soon as a road crew surveyed the pasture, they would cut a dirt street in front of the houses and, by the following summer, pour the street over with new concrete, thereby creating a clear delineation between two classes of slums: those with pavement and those without. Duck was already talking about putting his wages into an advanced payment program that would enable him and Edith to buy one of the houses he was building.

Duck was suddenly, just as Luisa had predicted, living in Coihaique in a way that Edith wasn't, and there was a shift in power in their marriage. In Cisnes, Duck and Edith had been more or less on the same footing—more or less, at any rate, stuck in the same place. Now Edith could only watch, at home in an outdated cabin, as Duck went about literally building the future for them.

Because Duck was gone so much, I spent most of my time with Edith as the weeks passed. She was not, by any means, unaware of the two distinct places in the world that she and Duck occupied, nor of the cruel irony of the situation. Edith, who had for so long prepared for the trip to the Center of the World by imitating the townie slang she heard on the radio, was now, in a way, farther from the Center than she'd ever been. She was stuck in limbo between two *puestos:* the *campo* which she had not quite left and the town in which she had not quite arrived.

Whenever I did see Duck, he wanted to know what stories Don Luis had told me, and he listened intently and delightedly as I repeated them. Now that Duck was in the place where Messages was broadcast, he replaced his old addiction to the radio with a nostalgic need to know about the world he no longer lived in. Don Luis became, albeit in absentia, Duck's preferred New Messenger.

Edith, meanwhile, became addicted to her own New Messengers: the Evangelical church and the television—both of which, in very different ways, offered glimpses of what might lie ahead.

*　　*　　*

Mariana wouldn't eat. She and Patricia were no longer physically ill, but the fact remained that Mariana would not—or could not—eat. And she was having problems at school. Her teacher assured Duck and Edith it was nothing out of the ordinary. Children who came in from the mountains, she said, experienced a kind of vertigo when suddenly surrounded by so many people. It was to be expected. Still, the teacher admitted, Mariana was having quite an extreme reaction. And the word she'd chosen to describe Mariana troubled Duck and Edith deeply.

"Unresponsive," said Duck. He wiped his mouth on his napkin, reached across the table and picked up Mariana's fork, and tried to feed her. He spoke with her as you would with a horse—coaxingly and sweetly. But Mariana wouldn't even look up. Then she started to cry. "Oh, sweetheart," said Duck, "c'mon, now. Please, c'mon."

"It isn't that," said Edith, "it's *huasa*. It's what any of us would be if we were Mariana. In the country, you worry about the Devil. Here, it's people. People are a hundred times scarier than the Devil. Fucking townies."

"It's just kids," said Duck. "Kids everywhere are the same with the new arrivals. Amengual, Coihaique, Santiago—it's all the same."

"Never in a thousand-thousand years in Amengual, *che*," snapped Edith. "Not like this it wouldn't happen."

Mariana had come home with new bruises each day she'd been at school. She and Patricia had separate recess, and Mariana, alone and scared in the school-yard, had no one to help her when the boys pushed her around.

Edith pushed her own plate away despite the fact it was covered with mutton stew.

Duck said, "Don't tell me you're going to quit eating, too, Daughter."

"I'm on a diet."

Duck looked at his watch. "Time to go, daughters. Get your things."

Hearing this only made Mariana cry harder. She was sobbing and hiccuping and trying with difficulty to catch her breath. Duck rubbed his face with both hands. He pushed his palms against his eyes. When he uncovered them, Edith was looking at him, waiting. He shook his head, and she moved her eyes back and forth, as though she were making his head move. "Come on, now, girls," he said, "they're waiting for us down there."

Patricia put on her jacket and stood by the door. When Duck tried to get Mariana out of the chair, she went limp and slid to the floor. Duck picked her up and brushed the hair from where it stuck to the wet skin around her eyes and on her cheeks. Her face was swollen, and she'd lost weight in the past two weeks, and it made her head look too big for her body.

Edith put Mariana's boots on her feet while Duck held her against him. Edith tied the boots and took a napkin and licked it and wiped the scuffs off the leather. When Duck put Mariana down, Patricia came over and tucked Mariana's uniform shirt into her pants and fastened the belt and zipped the zipper. Then Edith slid Mariana's arms through the backpack straps.

Duck watched for a moment and then he went to the window and looked past the herd of sheep in the pasture and down onto the skeletal beginnings of the new houses. He took a match from his pocket and whittled a toothpick. When he was done, he inspected the work and put it in his mouth. His shoulders were sloped. He could not have known, given the variables that the move had introduced into all of their lives, where in the world his children's lives would end up. At least in Cisnes he had known this one thing.

When Duck turned around, Edith was crying. It was the only time I ever saw her do this. Duck didn't move from the window. His children and his wife watched him, and no one spoke. He shook his head and turned around and zipped his jacket. When he tried to kiss Edith goodbye, she turned away.

"God," said Duck.

*   *   *

The four of us walked out the door and turned left onto Wild Horses Street. We walked down the hill in a staggered line. Patricia was holding my hand, and Duck was moving slowly between us and Mariana, who would not let anyone touch her. We got to the series of stairs that descended into the first level of the slum like scaffolding at an archaeological site. At the bottom was a dirt street that wound east, toward the next slum and, beyond that, the naked *pampa*. There was no wind, but the clouds moved in the sky like ships on water. Mothers walked along the street holding their children by the hands, and they stopped to stare at Mariana and Duck and Patricia and me. Duck looked at his feet each time one of the women looked at him. Then he tossed the toothpick aside and scooped Mariana up into his arms and hid her face against the shoulder of his jacket.

The school was a three-storied rectangular building of concrete, and each floor was lined with green-tinted windows. Bright chimneys stuck out from the roof. Two dozen children, most of them boys, played tag in front of the school while five or six dozen other children stood around watching the melee. When a bell rang, the games moved inside the school, and Duck and I followed with the girls. There was an atrium formed by concrete walls. It was light inside, and the floor was waxed and shone in the light. The children, who ranged from six years old to twelve or thirteen, tucked in their uniforms as a dozen or so young women watched them from the walls. They were the *profesoras,* and they wore carefully applied makeup and knee-length skirts and long white coats, like doctors. The oldest among them was forty; most were in their mid-twenties, and they had been educated in Temuco and Valdivia and Santiago. They could not have looked more out of place.

Patricia pointed to a group of second-graders. "There's the brute who fucks with Mariana the most: Fucking Julio."

Duck smiled, I think, for the same reason that I did. Julio looked nothing if not unintimidating. His teeth were blocky and much too big for his mouth. He had dried marmalade stuck to his lips, and the blue tie he wore was clipped haphazardly to a lapel. Perhaps sensing that the four of us were herded too protectively in benign-enough environs, Duck said to Patricia, "Go on, *che.* When we leave, though, come find your sister and don't leave her side till you're made to go to class. Me or your uncle will be here to walk you home this evening."

When Patricia kissed all three of us on the cheek and walked away, Mariana once again broke down in tears. One of the teachers left the wall and walked over to us. She wore braces, and her face was powdered slightly, and there was a subtle line along her neck where the makeup melded into her skin.

"*Señorita,*" said Duck.

The teacher reached down to take Mariana's hand, and Duck let her. When she tried to run her fingers along Mariana's head, Mariana backed away like a dog that didn't want to be hit. The teacher knelt down and held her there, at arm's length, until Mariana relented. She bent her elbow slightly as the woman stood up again.

Duck watched with no visible reaction. There was a confidence, a sort of aloof resignation, about him. "There it is, *che*," he said.

Then he thanked the teacher, and we turned around and walked back the way we'd come.

*　　*　　*

I went back up to the cabin to spend the rest of the afternoon in the kitchen with Edith taking *mate*. After I sat down, I lit a cigarette and shook the pack so that the filters of two or three others cleared the lip; I held the pack out to her.

"Quit yesterday," she said. "This whole thing—moving to Coihaique, living near my mother, all of it—is a new start. So I quit. Duck hasn't had a drink since we got here, so I figured I could go without something as a kind of, you know, support to him. And," she said, "we've been at church every Sunday evening, *che*. I go on Wednesdays, too."

She looked over at the TV in the corner, under the window. *I Love You, Paquita Gallego* was on. Then she looked at Oscar, who was asleep on her lap. It was a Wednesday, and I asked if she was going that night. She nodded. I said, "What do you do at the church?"

"It's a Pentecostal," said Edith. "A Brazilian outfit on Baquedano, not far from the jail."

I said again, "What do you do there? Listen to sermons?"

"Some. Mostly it's Devil exorcisms." I was about to ask if she participated, but I hadn't even begun the sentence when she said, "Yes. Yes, I do have it done." She might have been talking about a pedicure.

"And Duck?"

"Not yet," she said. "When he's ready, he'll have one. The other night he had one of his dreams again. He hasn't had one since we moved into town. He wouldn't tell me what it was about, but I sensed him having it in the night. When I woke up, he was talking to himself, trying to let the cassette fall," by which she meant spill the beans. "But I didn't catch any of what he said, though it was same the script he used to follow in the mountains: mumbling, tossing, getting up and walking around. Next morning I asked what he'd dreamt about the night before. He shook his head. I know it scared the hell out of him, though. I could just tell by the way he looked. He thought he was through that. But I'll tell you," she said, "if he keeps on, he'll be right up there in line at the church to have the Devil drawn. No question in my mind, *che.*"

"Do you know anyone else who goes to that church?"

"We don't know anyone, Skinny, except Duck's damn mother. She goes. Drives me fucking nuts, too," she said, then added with a self-conscious smile: "But I'm working on that."

Edith still hadn't looked away from the TV. I leaned back and watched, too. Paquita was at an airfield with this guy she was in love with, watching a skydiver. The skydiver, too, she'd been in love with, but he'd broken up with her, and then, to spite Paquita, he'd brought his new lover to the field to watch him jump. Paquita was watching the plane as it circled, gaining altitude, and she was saying to her soon-to-be new lover that she was afraid the skydiver was going to die. The woman who appeared to Paquita in dreams had told her as much—or, rather, she'd said, as was her habit, some things that could have been interpreted about fifty different ways, though Paquita had decided it was a prediction of impending doom. Edith had read it the same way. "He'll die," she said. "Parachute won't open, and splat! He's gonna hit the ground like a bag of shit."

I said, "Really? Duck hasn't had a drink since you arrived?"

There was a commercial. Edith suddenly relaxed and looked at me. "Sorry," she said, "I get a little carried away with that crap. Nico," she said, "it's God's truth the man hasn't had a sip since we got here. I just, I mean, we've never been happier. It's like we're a team, like we were a long time ago. We talk about things. Don't get me wrong. We have a long way to go. But we're on the road.

"This church has changed us so much. Like, for example, the other Sunday we got word the wood trucks are in town to sell for the winter, catch it? Duck comes home from the Vhymeister, and he's in a great hurry. That right there made me nervous, *che.* I said, 'What's making you so rambunctious?' He said, 'Well, I need to get downtown again—the wood truck's here selling cheap, and I don't want to miss our chance.'

"He asked for the money I'd hidden. I'd told him I was in charge of the money till he proved himself capable of not drinking it away, catch it? I wasn't about to let him know where it was hidden, either. I said, 'Well, let's go.' 'Edith,' he says, 'you know damn well we can't all go trudging downtown with three sick kids to haul wood. Now just give me the money. There'll be a line to get that wood cheap.'

"So I gave him the money. What else could I do but trust him, *che*? How else can we build this life if we can't trust, just like God tells us to?

"The whole time he was gone, I cursed God about my luck. I thought, 'That son of a whore, this'll be the first of many times he runs off.' I was ready to pack the girls and head to my mother's, Nico. And God said to me after I finished cursing Him: 'Woman, what's wrong with you? He might well be going to get the things this house needs. You know you can't be out in the streets with sick children, *che,* and here he goes out there alone, and you're cursing him and Me both!' God said, 'You know, it'll serve you right if he comes back drunk, catch it?'

"That calmed me, hearing God's voice plain as dogs barking.

"But it takes a long time to get wood and hire a trucker to come bring it up to a slum. By the time it was nightfall, I was at it again, cursing him and God, and about to dress the girls and Oscar and leave the bastard. And I'll be damned, Nico, if Duck didn't come back an hour later with the wood. Not a smell of booze on him, *che*."

She looked at Oscar, who was beginning to open his eyes. He looked up at her and at me and then he looked over at the TV. In the commercial, a man was riding a horse across a river. Great explosions of water erupted all around the horse's legs. Oscar let himself down from Edith's lap and ran over to the TV. He hitched his pants on the way, skipping steps. "Ooohhhhh!" he called. *"Andale!"* He bent over to pick up the string that he'd left next to the TV and that, like the string he'd had in Cisnes, he used as his riding crop and reins. When he stood back up, a woman was talking about skin cream.

Oscar looked around, confused. He walked over to Edith and climbed onto her knees and stood up, looking out the window. "Horse," he said. Then he climbed down and walked over to the sofa and looked out the back window. "Horse!" he yelled running the string through his hands like a gaucho checking a whip for weak braids.

"It's gone," said Edith.

"Horse!"

"The horse is gone. There's no more horse, child."

There were plastic toy cars on the floor next to the couch that Oscar had rounded up and surrounded with strings, as though keeping them in a corral. He seemed to be counting them, and then he stood up and kicked them across the room.

"Don't be a wild man!" yelled Edith. "And pick up those cars and put them back where they belong!"

"In the corral?" I said.

"Don't be a smartass, Skinny," she said. "Oscar! Do as I say!" He was howling, and he held his hands over his groin like he had to pee and stuck his chin out.

I'd brought my sleeping bag over that day. I wouldn't need it anymore, and I thought the family might be able to use it sometime. It was stuffed inside a blue bag the size of a saddle made to Oscar's proportions. I walked over and put it at his feet. "There's your horse," I said. He looked around the room again and grabbed the sleeping bag and heaved it onto the couch. Then he climbed up and mounted the bag.

Oscar rode at a walk, with his string casually in one hand and his hips moving rhythmically. The whole time he was watching the TV as the plane kept climbing and Paquita nervously looked on.

"Nico," said Edith, "those exorcisms are the most real thing I have ever seen, *che*. No mirrors and smoke. Really. It's like . . . I can't explain it. It's like, you can see things that look real—like what Oscar thinks of the horse in the commercial—but you can't *feel* them if they're not there. You just can't. And it's all there in that church, *che*. The Devil's there and God, too. And then you feel them fighting in *you*. Like they're exploding out of you."

"So you've had the Devil exorcised."

"I've had him pulled twice. Or called out, I guess. I mean, the preacher, he puts his hand to your head and, like, sucks the Devil out of you, *che*. Or hooks up to your head like a cable, and God goes inside and finds the Devil in you, and they knock the shit out of one another for a while. I don't know, really. I had the TV turned off on me," she said, meaning she'd passed out.

"Does everyone have the TV turned off?"

"Everyone, yes. Some convulse and shake and writhe on the floor with their tongues out. A lot of them are old, old women, and you worry they'll bite their tongues off. But they keep the preacher's wife there to hold you and with a wood piece to make sure the tongue question doesn't happen."

"And what happens afterward?"

"You go home."

* * *

Another commercial interrupted the soap opera, and Oscar stopped riding long enough to watch. McKay, according to the man on the TV, was the best chocolate in Chile—or, for that matter, in the world. Oscar put the bag forward.

Edith said, "That's the problem with these soap operas, *che*. Just when they get to the punch, they either take forever to happen or they get right to the edge and end the program." She looked at her watch. "Five minutes till the hour. They can't really watch that stupid plane circle for another five minutes, can they?"

"When did you get a watch?" Edith had never had a watch since I'd known her.

"The other day."

"In town?"

She looked at me and didn't say anything. Her face flushed. She said, "Yes."

Edith is a horrible liar. "Out with it," I said.

"Soto's in town. I thought it might be nice to, you know, look nice."

"Has he been here yet, *che*?"

"No. Duck doesn't want to be tempted to drink."

"And is he coming here?"

"Yes," said Edith. "In an hour."

Paquita's ex-lover hopped lightly onto the jump steps under the wing of the plane. He held on to the railings in the door, and looked back at his friend inside and smiled. Then he let himself fall. On the ground, everyone stood looking up. Paquita, her lover-to-be, the skydiver's new lover—a whole crowd of people stood looking up. TV crews trained their cameras to the sky.

The falling man pulled the ripcord. Only, the chute didn't open. The man pulled the ripcord again and again, and then he pulled the backup ripcord.

But that one didn't open, either. In the final scene of the soap opera, there were paramedics racing over to where the man had hit the ground. Then there was a commercial.

"I knew that would happen," said Edith bitterly.

Oscar watched the commercials—one for a bank and the other for a grocery store—and kissed the air, though he didn't put the bag forward. It was more like he was putting the commercials forward. When another soap opera began, Oscar dismounted from the sleeping bag and fell to the floor in a heap. He screamed hysterically.

"God!" yelled Edith. "What do you have?"

CHAPTER SEVENTEEN

Coffee and Rice

Peeled had been staying at my place off and on for a week. His girlfriend
Patchy was a schoolteacher, and she lived with another teacher in town in a
small apartment. Sometimes the other girl didn't want Peeled around. We'd go
out and then Peeled would call Patchy to see if the coast was clear. If it wasn't,
he'd spend the night at my place instead of hitching a ride to what was left of his
family's ranch.

Mostly we'd go to the Red Skin or just sit around my place at night and drink
pisco. No matter where we were, Peeled would pass the time telling jokes. Once he
got started, he couldn't stop; it was a compulsion. He would change his voice and
his body language to play nuns and gangsters and oversexed burros and Cubans
and Gallegos and priests and parrots. Any given monologue might last two hours,
and as Peeled shifted his focus, side characters from three jokes or three days ago
would become the main characters in a new joke. If you listened closely and long
enough, every joke could be fitted into something like an ongoing novel or a collection of serialized short stories. And all of his stories took place in Peeled's own
private Santiago or Buenos Aires or La Habana, none of which Peeled had ever
been to, but to all of which he was always, somehow convincingly, going.

Peeled came down the steep stairs that went up to the second-floor room,
where he slept. He sat down on one of the beds and lit a cigarette. He was hopelessly hung over, and in a sour mood. Peeled didn't tell jokes when he was in a
sour mood; in fact, if you asked him to tell you a joke then, he'd tell you to
go fuck yourself. So we drank *mate* and listened to the disco show on Radio

Rainbow. Finally, I said, "How do you remember all your jokes? Where do you get this stuff?"

"What are you talking about, yo? I make this shit up as I go. I've heard about five jokes in my life. I wouldn't know Santiago if it fell on my head."

"How come you almost never tell any jokes that take place here? The only one about Coihaique was about the gas station."

"Living here is why: I know you don't have to leave nowhere to know that everywhere else, people are the same. It's like, you ever read that essay Borges wrote, about the time he was in Rio Grande do Sul?"

"And the river was too high to cross and he had to spend, like, ten days in that gaucho village there?"

"Yeah. He said getting stuck there was, at the time, about the worst thing that ever happened to him. All he could think about was getting the hell out, right? And then it becomes the one thing he always came back to in his stories. Those ten days in the middle of nowhere directed his writing for the rest of his *life,* 'go. I'm the same way. Only Borges had ten days, catch it—I've had fucking nineteen years in this shithole."

I thought Peeled was as talented and smart a comedian as I'd ever heard. It was the one thing he wanted to build his life around, and I wanted badly for him to succeed. He lit another cigarette and sharpened the ash to a fine point. He said, "So there's a large Latin population in the main place of New York, right? What do you call the main place?"

"Manhattan."

"Manhattan. So what about my chances as a comic there?" said Peeled.

"I think it would be a shame if you didn't do something with it. Get to Santiago, get anywhere."

"That's what I think. Only, fuck Santiago. Santiago's beat."

Peeled changed the station, and we listened to the traffic report in Puerto Montt, in northern Patagonia, an hour and a half from Coihaique by plane. Peeled said, "Can I ask you a weird favor?" I nodded. "My name is really Jorge, right? How's that in English?" I told him it was George. "Call me George from now on, will you?" said Peeled.

I said I would, and then I got up to start packing my things. I was supposed to go out to Cisnes the next day to meet John of the Cows. The last time I had seen him, a month before, he'd said to meet him in the road, where he'd be waiting with the horses.

Peeled said, "Where are you going?"

"Argentina."

"What for?"

"I'm not sure." I wanted to get out of Coihaique, where for a month I'd been waiting for something to happen without knowing what it might be—or if, in the end, it would be something I really wanted to see.

"With the cattle thief?" said Peeled. When I nodded, he said, "You're the dumbest motherfucker, yo. Haven't you learned anything yet? Can't you just leave before one of these people kills you, or before you end up in jail?"

When I didn't say anything, Peeled laughed and tried to take another drag of his cigarette, but he'd smoked it to the filter, and the heat made him wince. He put the cigarette out. Then he went to look for Patchy.

*   *   *

That afternoon I went to Luisa's house. I was surprised to see Julia sitting in the kitchen. Julia almost never left Cisnes; and when she did, it was to go to Mañihuales to see The Grape. I went to the new stove and filled the *mate* and waited for the water to heat.

Luisa said to Julia, "Jimmy didn't pass through Cisnes, did he?"

"No."

Jimmy had left town again, and no one knew where he'd gone. Luisa and I had talked many times about what to do with him. She didn't want Jimmy behaving badly, and she wouldn't put up with him doing as he pleased in her house. As she'd said, she had two other children to raise, and she didn't want them to be influenced by Jimmy's inability to get his life together. It was better, she'd said, if he wasn't around. But now he'd left again, and it was painfully obvious that things were not this simple.

I said, "What does Luis think?"

"His stories don't help in times like this. He just sort of talks, you know, about this, that, and the other. None of which does anyone any good, *che.*"

Julia shifted in her seat. She was wearing jeans and a homemade sweater of brown, raw wool, and the barrettes in her hair were red. Luisa took the *mate* and looked at it. Then she looked at the floor. After a while, I said, "What's the news in Cisnes, Miss Julia? How's John of the Cows?"

"He's in jail," she said. "You didn't know?"

"How could anyone know?" said Luisa.

"I thought Nico would know."

"No one knows," said Luisa.

"For what?"

Julia rolled her lips as if evening her lipstick, though she wasn't wearing any. "He killed someone in Amengual."

I wondered if John, the last time I'd seen him, had encoded his plans to commit a murder by referring to it as a "soccer match." And, if so, whether Argentina had been planned ahead as his escape. I said, "What would he kill someone about?"

"Who knows, *che,*" said Julia. "Maybe he did or maybe he didn't. He was wanted for many things."

"Does his mother know he's here?"

"I don't know."

"Will the police tell her he's in jail?"

"No."

"Will you?" I said. I poured the *mate* full and handed it toward Luisa.

"No thanks," said Luisa, "I've had all I can take." Her eyebrows were knit with annoyance. She said, "If I told you where his mother was at, would *you* go see her, *che?*"

"Where does she live?"

"I don't even know her name."

I said to Julia, "Who'd you hear it from, *che?*"

"I just heard it."

"Are you going to see him?"

"No."

I poured water onto the *yerba;* it stayed dry at the top while the water seeped into the leaves at the bottom of the gourd. The water bubbled up and ran over, and still the *yerba* at the top was dry. Luisa said, "You spilled the water, *che.* His mother must be crying." She had a pained look on her face, and then her eyebrows unfurled and her face was totally expressionless.

I said to Julia, "So you're not going to go see him nor find out what happened?"

"You, Nico?"

Luisa said, "Why would she do that? To make trouble for herself?" Luisa knew what it was like to have the *carabineros* come for someone. She knew better than to associate with a known criminal. Julia had come all the way from Cisnes to see John. Luisa said to her, "When are you leaving?"

"Tomorrow, I guess."

"You have a bed here for the night, then," said Luisa.

I watched Luisa, and then I looked down. The *yerba* had soaked up the water like a sponge—soaked it up as though no one had ever poured the water in the first place.

*   *   *

The jail was made of an off-white concrete, such that it might have grown out of the ground like a massive lime deposit. Its designers, it seemed, were worried more about attack from outside than escape from within. The cells were cut high into the walls. Of all the men I knew who had been incarcerated there for a night or a month or a year, the most common complaint I heard was not of the treatment by the guards nor of the food or the crowded confines but, rather, of the cold. Looking up on the day I went to see John of the Cows, I imagined him sitting there on his bed, wrapped in a poncho.

I skipped the front office and went right to the cellhouse gate, where a sergeant stood guard in a uniform of olive wool. The cut and insignias had been borrowed from the Prussian army, whose military code and prowess had been greatly admired by Chile's generals at the turn of the nineteenth century. The sergeant opened the gate and waved me onto the front steps of the cellhouse, and closed the gate again. He said to knock on the heavy door, which I did. When I did so a second time, the sergeant came over and said, "What are you looking for?"

He looked me up and down. Although I'd been in Coihaique for a month, I'd continued to wear the clothes of the gauchos. Jeans and riding boots and a wool sweater and a scarf and a leather jacket. I wore a long mustache with a triangulated patch under my lower lip and a week's worth of stubble, none of which had ever made me feel out of place till now. The sergeant, who was much shorter than I, stood up two steps. "Yes?" he said, raising his eyebrows.

"I'd like to see someone here at the jail."

I thought the sergeant was going to smile. Instead, he said, "Where in the world did you come in from, eggo? Argentina?"

"Cisnes."

"You mean Puerto Cisnes."

"Middle Cisnes."

If he knew where that was, he didn't give any indication. He said, "What are you looking for?"

"John of the Cows." I didn't know his last name.

"John of the *Cows*?" he said. "What kind of name is that?"

"I don't know. It's just his name, sir."

"We have fifty criminals in here."

"There can't be more than one gaucho in here from Cisnes. There's a hundred twenty people out there, *che*. How many of them can there be in jail?"

"Fifty," said the sergeant. "What's your business?"

"He's a friend a mine."

"A friend of John of the Cows," said the sergeant, more to himself than me. Then he lifted the skirt of his jacket and took a thick pad from his back pants pocket. He opened it with an exaggerated flip of the heavy leather cover, and took a pen from beneath a lapel of his jacket. "Your name."

"Why is that important?"

"Your name." He smiled.

"I don't see what that has to do with anything, *che*." It was hard for me to imagine in that moment why I'd not just given him the first name that came to mind. Nick of the Sheep, I thought, had a nice ring to it.

The sergeant stepped down a step so that we were at the same height. "I think I just asked you a question, eggo."

"And I think I just answered it."

He readjusted his saddle-leather gunbelt and waited for a response, and I waited for him to grow tired of waiting. "Nationality?"

There had been a general reaction against foreigners in Coihaique in the last four years, and a more specific reaction against North Americans, who were not only visiting more often, but were starting lucrative tourist businesses the Chileans couldn't easily finance. It was growing more common when you went to the Red Skin, for instance, for a group of Chilean men to ask what the fuck you were doing in their country, and then to wonder aloud what they could do to convince you to leave. This resentment extended to the *carabineros,* though in a different way: the government had told the police not to screw around with the tourists, which the police took as the unwanted meddling of a newly elected and nonmilitary governing body. I said, "German."

"Where are you staying?"

"Cisnes."

"Puerto Cisnes," he said, and I let him write that down. "May I see your identification?"

"It's not on me."

"Are you aware that's a serious crime in Chile?" said the sergeant. He put the cap back on his pen and slid it smoothly under the lapel of his jacket into his shirt pocket. He closed the book and stood at ease with it in his hands. He said, "What are you doing in this country?"

"Leaving," I said. Then I smiled at him and lifted the latch on the gate and hurried onto the avenue.

* * *

I went to Duck and Edith's house. They were taking *mate* before Duck had to go back to work. When I told them about going to the jail, Duck said, "Well, that was dumb." Then he got up and walked to the window and looked out onto the street. He said, "Did you come here directly from there?"

I said, "Do you want me to leave?" He shook his head. "I'm sorry. I hadn't even thought of that."

"Well, it's just different in this country than what you're used to, I guess. Did you tell him where you live?"

"I don't even know my address."

"If I were you, two things, Nico. First off, don't go near that fucking jail again, you hear me, *che*? Second, I'd walk home different routes some days than others." He tried to stifle a giggle, but couldn't.

We laughed. Edith laughed the hardest. Something about the way she was laughing seemed out of proportion. But it was infectious, and Duck looked at her and he seemed suddenly very happy.

I said, "Had you heard about John?" Duck nodded. "Don't you wonder what's come of him?"

"He's in jail, Skinny. That's what's come of him." Duck looked at his watch. It was one o'clock, time to go back to work. "I wish you'd not get here after lunch all the time. Why don't you come early and be with us to eat instead of rolling in afterward when I don't have time to talk and the girls have to go back to school? Why don't you come tomorrow at noon so we can all be together and eat, *che*?"

"I can't eat. Any kind of food makes me sick. The only thing I can stomach is *mate*. I didn't want you to be offended if I sat down and then couldn't eat."

Duck looked at Edith. She said, "I'll give him some when I give Oscar the next dose."

"What're you talking about?"

"Coffee and rice," said Duck. "Oscar's sick as the Devil himself. Coffee and rice fixes you. And who cares if you can't eat. Just come and be with us. I don't hardly see you anymore."

Mariana and Patricia marched over to where I was sitting and gave me a goodbye kiss on the cheek. Duck stood up and we shook hands, and he took his jacket down off the nail in the wall like I'd seen him do so many times in Cisnes before going to water the horses. He gave Edith a kiss on the cheek. He put his beat-up hat on and took each of the girls by the hand so they were on either side of him. Edith and I stood in the door and watched them walk downhill toward the school.

When Edith closed the door and we sat down, I said, "What do you think happened to John of the Cows?"

"You mind running the *mates,* today?" she said. "I need a vacation from that job." Oscar was asleep on the couch; he'd thrown his blanket, and Edith went over to re-cover him. She picked up the dishes from the table and brought them to the sink.

I said, "C'mon, *che,* you can't just pretend this whole thing doesn't exist. I mean, don't you wonder what he did?"

"Look alive if you're running the *mates* show," she said. Then she went ahead and filled the gourd herself. We drank quietly for some time. "You bastard," she said. "You're really worried about him, aren't you, *che?*"

"Aren't you? Besides, I'm convinced you know something more than what you let on, *che*. You have the rat's tail hanging out of your trap." Edith shook her head. "Open up, now," I said. "Let's see what color of rat you have."

"Soto moved to town."

*   *   *

I'd assumed that Edith had seen Soto when he'd come to Coihaique a couple weeks before. I had also suspected ever since the night he and Fat Will had come over to the cabin in Cisnes that she and Soto were in love with one another. But I'd never imagined he'd move to town for her. I said, "Did he come for you?"

"I don't think he means to be renting for long, if that's what you mean."

"And you're going with him when he leaves?"

Edith shook her head. "What do I have here I didn't have out there?"

"Doesn't it make you nervous Duck will do something violent?" Edith looked at me as though she'd never in her life seen me. "What?" I said. "Is it so outlandish to suggest that Duck won't be fit to be tied when he finds out you're about to leave him for his best friend?"

"I didn't say I was leaving anything," snapped Edith. She looked at Oscar, who was just beginning to wake up.

"That's hardly the point, is it?"

Edith took the tea kettle from the stove and poured the gourd full and drank. It was supposed to have been my turn and, according to *mate* etiquette, not passing the gourd to me was as good as asking me to leave. She poured it full again and drank a second time.

"You're right," I said. "It's none of my business. None of it has ever been my business unless you wanted it to be. I apologize." We sat there for some time without looking at one another. Then I said, "Do you remember the night before Duck and I went on the cattle drive with Tito last year, the one to bring the whole herd down?"

"You went on a lot of cattle drives," she said dismissively.

"Only one began with Duck breaking everything in the cabin two nights before."

"What happened?" She sounded completely disinterested.

"You tell me."

"I heard some things." Edith looked at me steadily, even condescendingly, as though challenging me to say something more. Then she dumped the *yerba* into the stove fire and set the empty *mate* in front of me.

I said, "What the fuck are you talking about, you 'heard some things'? If he'd killed me, guess who was next? You think he won't kill you for fucking Soto, eggo?" Calling her eggo was, in this instance, like calling her a bitch.

Edith giggled. She said, "I'm proud of you," then added: "*che.*"

"What?" I could feel the throbbing of blood along my hairline. "What're you talking about?"

"I've never ever in all this time seen you betray a single emotion. I've never," said Edith, "seen you scared, I've never seen you angry—I don't know if I've ever even heard you raise your voice. Duck and I used to talk about it. It drove him nuts you never gave any indication of what you were thinking, *che.*"

"What was that, his elaborate plan to get a reaction out of me?"

Edith looked at Oscar, who was grouchy in his newly awakened state, and wandered around the room, mumbling and on the verge of tears. "How come you didn't kill Duck that night?"

"Is that what you wish had happened?"

"There's never been a better chance," she said.

"So you did hear the things he said that night."

"And the things he said every night he put a knife to my throat and said it all to me. And the things Black Carl used to say to my mother when I was a child and hiding under the table when he came home drunk. Black Carl used to say the man from Campo Grande was the Devil. Black Carl was the Devil, Skinny."

"And Duck?"

"I don't know," said Edith, shaking her head. "Sometimes yes and sometimes no."

"Why don't you leave?"

"Leaving Duck leaves him alive." Oscar walked over to Edith, and when she took him in her lap, he hit her in the face. "Sometimes I look at my own child and think about the blood in his veins, and I hate him. Leaving it all leaves everyone alive."

I said, "So what are the other options?"

"There's no way to kill the cycle unless . . ."

"No."

"I could never in a thousand-thousand years kill my own children," said Edith, "even if they do have the Devil's blood. No sooner than I could actually kill my husband. I'd sooner kill myself. I've got the blood, too, Skinny."

Edith held Oscar's arms till he stopped flailing. There was a pan of burned rice and a pot of boiling coffee on the stove, and Edith asked me to put some of each in a cup. The rice was hard and black, and I chiseled a chunk and did as she said. I said, "What does this stuff do, anyway?"

"I don't know. Something about it takes the diarrhea. But it has to be black or else it doesn't work. Can you get me a spoon, too, please?" I handed the cup and a spoon to her, and she stirred it all together and spooned it up and dropped it back in the cup to cool. Oscar had cried himself out for the time being. Edith said, "*Che,* could you put some cold water in here?"

She turned Oscar so he was facing to the side, and I gave her the cup and she fed him. It smelled like charcoal. Edith said, "You know, there's one other solution to all this."

I asked her what that was. Oscar grabbed the spoon midway down the stem and all but fed himself. He seemed to like it.

"To exorcise the Devil from us all, *che.* The church says that God is the center of all things if we make Him the center. If we allow God into our bodies to do battle with the Devil, *che,* then God will clean the blood. Catch it?"

Edith turned to Oscar, who didn't want any more. "Come on," she said, "just one more bite. Get all that bad oopa out of you."

❋

The Estancia of Gómez

In truth, the creole spirit is filled with broken promises

and radically suffers a sublime discontent.

—*José Ortega y Gasset, "Intimidades," from* Obras completas, *1966*

Four days before I left Patagonia, Luisa had a party. It was a Sunday, and I'd not fallen asleep until five o'clock that morning. There was a man in my room, and I didn't know who, and I couldn't see him. It was dark, though it was past sunup and I'd left the shades open. Whoever it was in the room with me was taking his time looking around, checking beneath the sink, inspecting the bathroom. It was only a matter of time before he'd be standing over me.

I was having trouble breathing. It was as if someone had placed a wet paper towel over my face. I could, if I tried hard enough, get oxygen. Then the man dipped a second towel into the water and put that on my face. I could feel it with my tongue, but I couldn't bite through it. By the time he'd applied the fourth paper towel, I could no longer breathe. Then he sat down on the chair where I wrote, and he watched. I could hear him there shifting. That's when I bolted upright and slammed the left side of my face against the low-angled wall above the bed.

A little while later, I stood up. My left eye was swelling, and my stomach hurt so badly that I had to sit back down. I was accustomed to the fevers from the dysentery at that point—they were constant and, therefore, seemed to me benign. I normally didn't wake until after they had broken. But that morning, my chest was wet and my hair was sopped, and sweat ran in streams from under my arms and down my ribs. Since I'd been in Coihaique, I'd lost twenty-five pounds, nearly fifteen percent of my body weight.

When I tried to stand once again, the pain loosened my bowels, and I barely made it to the bathroom in time. I took a shower, but as soon as I dried off, I immediately became dripping wet again. It was comical, in a way; there was something pleasing about the choreography: drying off and sweating and then drying off. I finally gave up and sat down on the bed and began dressing myself. I'd just buttoned my jeans when I blacked out.

When I woke again, it was eight in the morning. I'd only been unconscious for ten or fifteen minutes. I could feel my eye still swelling, and this, too, was pleasing insofar as it gave me something specific—the thump of the blood—on which to concentrate. The muscles in my neck and at the base of my skull tingled, and my knees and calves were weak. I've had several concussions of varying severity in my life, and I knew that, in hitting my head on the wall, I'd more than likely given myself another. I've also had two vertebrae fused in my neck; in wrenching myself awake, I'd aggravated that injury. I tried turning my head, but couldn't.

The idea of a concussion didn't bother me as much as the fear that I'd had a seizure and that, should I have another, I might crack open my head on the headboard or on the cement floor, and that, in the days it would take for someone to find me there, I would bleed to death.

The hospital was six blocks from my room. I got to the door and opened it. It was cold outside, and there was frost on the grass, and new snow had fallen yet again in the mountains. Thousands of people had built their morning fires, and a sweet haze hung in the air, moving slowly on the wind like a fine dust. Through the haze, the sun was red and perfectly round, and I could look right at it without blinking my eyes. I could see all of this from the little backyard, see all of it through the chilled, static drape of the apple trees and above the roof of the teachers' house and above the woodshed, all of it perfectly and clearly.

I remembered a gaucho I'd seen in the hospital months before. He was standing with his retarded son, both of them dressed exactly the same. I remembered the smell of the hospital—the reek of urine and mucus, and the stained walls of the place, and the lighting. Above all, I remembered the lighting: the exposed bulbs, and the harsh and septic feel that they engendered, like an operating room. There was something medieval about it, the gutters that lined the hallways and the wandering mongoloids and the men who knelt along the walls.

I went back into my room and closed the door. When I tried to get my boots off, my feet were too swollen. So I kept them on and lay down and fell asleep.

*   *   *

The party that Luisa was giving in honor of my departure was to have begun at noon. I woke at one o'clock. The fever had subsided considerably, and I was ravenously hungry. I took a sweated shirt from where I'd hung it to dry on a hanger above the useless heater. The day before, in anticipation of the stores being closed on Sunday, I'd bought the things Luisa had requested: three bottles of dark malt liquor and several packages of *chorizo.* I'd bought flowers, as well, and I got all of it from the knee-high refrigerator and walked outside.

The day had turned warm and sunny, and the sky was pressed to its limit by a late-season high-pressure front—a fall sky dyed a dark, rich blue, and broken here and there with immense white clouds. Everything on Calle Prat was closed. There was no one anywhere. A truck would occasionally rumble up from behind and shift gears and rumble past and shift again and disappear. Whenever it got to be too warm, a cool wind would blow in from the *pampa* to the east.

When I got to her house, Luisa was in the kitchen making flan. Don Luis was watching her. Luisa said, "You're late." Her hands were dripping with egg yolk, and she wiped them on a towel and came over to give me a kiss. She looked at my eye and shook her head. She said, "I don't want to know, *che.*"

I put the bottles of malt on the counter and filled a pitcher with water, then put the flowers in it. Don Luis shuffled over and we kissed one another on the cheek, and he opened the bottles with his knife. He was wearing a loose white shirt tucked into a red cummerbund and olive *bombachas* and a red-and-yellow silk scarf. He said, "Your state, *che,* requires emergency procedures."

He took a plastic bowl from the rack and poured a handful of sugar into it. He separated the whites from a dozen eggs and dropped them into the bowl. Each time he did this, he would say, "Like that, then, my little friend." Then he poured a bottle of the dark malted beer into the mixture and beat it with a whisk until it frothed. "Smell it," he said, putting his nose so close to the bowl that he came away with a dollop of froth on the end of his nose. "Smell the protein."

It had a moldy quality—a damp, dank air like the smell of the cork from a bottle of wine. While watching Don Luis make the stuff I had not been in any hurry to drink it. But when I smelled it, my stomach gargled and I salivated. The taste was earthy and strong and dull at once; it coated my mouth and stomach like blood.

We drank the glasses at one go, and then he filled them again and we drank and poured another. When I began pouring a fourth glass for each of us Don Luis stopped me and put the glasses aside. *"Ojo!"* he said. "Too many emergency procedures yield a separate emergency."

Luisa had filled another bowl with malt and vegetable oil and vinegar and garlic. She dumped the *chorizo* into it. Don Luis untied a burlap sack that hung from the wall, and reached in and pulled out a quarter of a ewe and part of the shoulder of a calf-bull and several plucked chickens with the heads and innards intact. We stood there, the three of us, carving steaks and gutting and cutting the chickens into pieces and adding them to the bowl for a traditional Argentine barbecue called *parrillada*. Last of all, Don Luis pulled two handfuls of calf testicles and three ewe tongues from the sack and dropped them in.

Don Luis and I went out to the little backyard, and he took a hoe and began raking a fire pit out of the ground. He did this meticulously, stopping every time he scraped away a patch and stepped back as if looking at a painting. He dug the pit a foot deep on one side and half that on the other. Then he made a fire in the shallow side and let it simmer and pushed it with the hoe toward the deep end. He did this several times, until the coals had piled up a foot deep and were glowing hot. Then we went inside the cabin to wait for Duck and Edith and the children.

* * *

They arrived an hour later. They'd run across Fried Bread coming back from the store, bringing cucumbers for salad, and he walked in with them. Duck and Edith were dressed as twins in new denim shirts and jeans and hiking boots. The children were dressed in matching denim overalls and hiking boots and green or red T-shirts. They'd been scrubbed and brushed, and the hair on all of their heads was still wet. It was the first time any of them had seen Luisa since they'd stayed with her upon their arrival in Coihaique, six weeks before. After the initial round of hugs and kisses, the two families stood back from one another and looked at the floor or looked around the room uncomfortably.

Fried Bread, who'd exchanged his motorcycle boots for flip-flops, came back into the room. He said, "You heathens look as surprised as two Indians who bumped into one another coming around opposite sides of a tree."

Everyone laughed, and Fried Bread offered seats to Duck and Edith, and then he poured himself a glass of malt and egg whites and offered one to Duck.

"Thank you, no," said Duck. Fried Bread offered the glass to Patricia. "She's sick again," said Duck. "She and Mariana both. Flu."

Fried Bread said, "Sick and shy. This'll take care of them on both accounts."

Don Luis stepped in to snatch the glass. He drank it down. "I could use some help with the meat," he said to us, and Duck and Fried Bread and I followed him outside. Don Luis placed an iron tray on the grate and poured vegetable oil onto it. He rubbed the oil around with his handkerchief to season the tray, and when he spit onto it and the spittle bubbled and evaporated, he began spreading pieces of meat evenly around.

As he spread the meat with his *facón,* Don Luis told a story about the time he'd worked breaking horses on the ranch near Río Mayo, Argentina. "There were several houses for the gauchos," he said, "but we were more often on the plain, riding among the cattle, and we slept under cattleskins. When we were hungry, we killed a beef and ate until we moved on again with the herd, and left the carcass for the dogs and the little things that needed to eat, just like we did. 'At the *estancia* of Gómez,'" said Don Luis, and Duck joined him to finish the cliché: "'It's he who has a knife that eats.'"

Duck looked at the wine warming over the fire; he handed the glasses out among us. Duck drank his down and watched us do the same, then he filled them again and set them to warm.

"*Ojo!*" said Don Luis, delighted. "It's he who has a knife that eats, no matter where he came from. That's just it, Don Duck, a beautiful thing—beautiful. Natural. Sharing. And the *patrón,* he rode with us and took his meals at our fire. Now look: someday, the little things will eat me, and I'll be happy for them. They have their knives affixed to their mouths, the little things. Ants and dogs and so forth. They, too, reside at the *estancia* of Gómez, like all things in the world. I try to maintain a little fat just for that reason. Remember the little things near the end of your life, Skinny, and try to fatten up some, for Heaven's sake."

We all drank, and Don Luis filled the glasses anew. Duck said, "What kind of stock did the man keep?"

"Herefords," said Don Luis. "And his *cabalde* was piebalds and bays. Fast, lean horses that could run down an ostrich. We hunted ostrich on the plain with *bolos* when we were taking the cattle to market. There were shallow ravines in places on the *pampa,* and three of us would ride in a great arc around the ostriches and dismount and lead the horses through the ravines. The rest would ride slowly toward the birds, with their heads laid along the flanks of the horses. Then, when we got close, we'd herd three or four of the birds toward the ravine where the others waited. And when the birds approached the ravine, we put the spurs to the horses and trapped the birds between us, and at that point it was only a matter of throwing well. But we only killed what was needed, and never more."

Duck said, "It's been fifteen years since I threw a *bolo.* I used to carry one as a child. We all did. I bet I could still do it, though."

"Just like us," said Don Luis, "the *patrón* understood all of these things. He was a hunter and a rider. When we rode back to the compound, he slept as often as not in the quarters we kept, which were nothing more than little *puestos* of cattle skins and dirt on the floor. As you can imagine, there was a reason for this."

Don Luis looked up. The smell of the *parrillada* had awakened the neighborhood. The woman in the house next door opened her windows; she put in a *ranchera* tape and played it loud. A child from across the street wandered in through the open gate and sat down on the ground next to Don Luis and eyed the meat.

"Ha!" said Don Luis, "a little thing has arrived! Go get a knife from the kitchen, little thing," and the boy disappeared into the house. "So," said Don Luis, "there was a reason for the *patrón* to act this way: *política*! The wife of the *patrón,* you see, would ride out sometimes to watch the work, and afterward she would come to the fire and take her meat and stand apart. She wore a long dress, and she would chastise us for throwing the bones to the ground. She said it was unsanitary, *che*!

"One day, we saw her riding out, and we made camp under a tree. There was nothing for miles and then there was this tree. And like all living things, men are attracted to the lone part of the whole that is different. Birds come to the tree, and foxes make their dens close by. Horses go there for shade, and cattle the same. Ants, too. *Ojo!*

" 'Dismount,' I called to her, 'and take to the shade of the tree.' She did, and she didn't ask that we join her. She sat down under that beautiful tree growing there in the middle of the plain like nothing in the world, the leaves green and bursting with water in their veins and shining in the hot sun."

Duck laughed and reached for the wine. He said, "I love this shit, man."

Fried Bread said, "The stories?"

"Todo," said Duck.

The boy from across the street came out with plates and a knife for himself, and put the plates on the grate to warm. His name was Victor and he was eight years old. He sat down on my lap. He looked at Don Luis and said, "Is this that one about the ants?"

"Quiet," said Don Luis.

"I love the one about the ants," said Victor.

Don Luis smiled and poured malt onto the hot tray. The malt sizzled, and when it had cooked off, he knifed a steak for Victor and laid it on his plate. Duck and Fried Bread each speared a steak. When Don Luis saw that I didn't have a knife, he fished a second, smaller *facón* out from the front of his cummerbund and handed it to me. "Listen," said Don Luis. "And pretty soon, well, the *patrón*'s wife jumped up. What could be the problem? She danced around and swatted at herself. 'What's wrong, *señora*?' we called out to her.

" 'Ants!' she called back, aghast.

" 'Ants?' I said. I walked over and I could see them on her hands and scrambling in the pleats of that skirt. 'We don't have any over where we are,' I said, 'and that just outside the reach of the roots of the tree. Isn't that something!' Like that." He giggled.

Duck and Fried Bread laughed out loud. They held the steaks in their hands, close to their faces, and shaved strips of meat off and into their mouths in one motion. The party was in full swing. Danikza, Luisa and Fried Bread's two-year-old daughter, had come to the fire and Oscar sat on Duck's lap; even Victor's three younger brothers were now seated among us and eating from the tray. Patricia and Mariana had woken up and come outside, and they stood at Duck's side; he shaved bits of meat for them. Dogs came in and out of the yard, snatched the bones piled at the fire and left again.

Don Luis said, "Oh! She jumped around, that lady, hitting herself with the bone. I said, 'Throw the bone to the ground.' She called to her husband and he said, 'Throw the bone to the ground!' He was giggling, for he knew the joke I'd played on her.

"But she wouldn't drop the bone. Instead, she got back on the horse and rode out of there fast. I'd tried to impress on her the fact that, if you give the little things what they want, they'll be happy and stay away. How can you expect to take shade from the lone tree and not share with the tree's rightful owners? They won't come looking in the pleats of your skirt if you give them what they want, *che.* But she was a fascist."

Duck picked around the tray with the point of his knife. When he'd found what he wanted, he stuck it and held the knife to Victor, who took the meat in his hands. Duck leaned over and carved Victor a piece from the bone so that the piece was hanging off the end. "Now just put your mouth to it and pull it away," he said. Victor did as he was told. His mouth was smeared with grease. "Like that, then." Duck smiled.

*　　*　　*

Edith and Luisa were the only ones who didn't eat. They stood in the entrance of the woodshed, watching the party. They were fifteen feet from the fire, and they stood side-by-side, with their hands in their pockets. When the food ran low, they would go into the house and emerge with a pot of boiled potatoes or with more *chimichurri* for the meat, but they did not themselves eat from the tray.

After one trip, Edith stood behind Duck with her hands on his shoulders. She said, "Are we going to church?"

"We're in church," said Duck. "Don't you want something to eat?"

"Not hungry, *che,*" she said.

"C'mon, sweetheart, you have to eat. Let me fix you a plate," and he bent forward toward the stack that was warming on the grate and that no one had used.

"Really," said Edith. "I'm not hungry. Luisa and I have been snacking in the house."

Don Luis watched them. He was only on his second piece of meat, because it took him a long time to gum each sliver before he could swallow it. It was a process that, to watch him, required a lot of warm wine, and his cheeks were flushed. He offered Edith a glass.

"Thank you, no," said Edith.

"One glass wouldn't hurt anyone," said Duck.

She said, "Church is in two hours. It'll take an hour to walk there. I think we ought to go soon."

Duck nodded. "What about the children?"

"Them, too," said Edith. "They're feeling better, it looks like." Mariana and Patricia were sitting in the grass with Victor and his brothers. They picked at the grass and smiled while Victor gesticulated and played out the characters in a story which, from what I could tell, included a man on a horse, because Victor moved up and down from his knees and looked around whatever country it was in which he rode. "So, another forty-five minutes and we need to leave," said Edith. Then she went inside the house.

Fried Bread said, "Fuck church, *che.*"

Duck said, "I promised I wouldn't go to church drunk."

Fried Bread smiled and filled Duck's glass. He said, "Let me help you make good on the truth, *che.*"

Duck giggled. He looked at Don Luis, who was nodding and mumbling to himself. He'd not stopped talking, either to himself or to whoever would listen, since the time he'd begun cooking. "Don Lucho," said Duck, "tell us another story, *che.*"

*   *   *

The sun was setting, and the exorcisms were due to start in forty-five minutes. I went inside Luisa's house to get my jacket while Edith rounded up Duck and the children. I was alone, looking at the photos on Luisa's walls: Don Luis as a young man just back from Argentina; Luisa and one of her sisters at the age of twelve or thirteen, double-mounted on a horse at their mother's farm; Jimmy at six or seven, galloping in a race. On the wall opposite the photos was the new stove and a hot-water heater Fried Bread had installed above the sink. It was funny, I thought, how much harder the burners on an electric stove made it to get the water just the right temperature for *mate:* Luisa, when she first got the stove, had put a cookie sheet over it, to better approximate the cooking surface of a wood-burner.

Don Luis came inside. He didn't know I was there, and he stood in the dark-ening hallway with his hands clasped behind his back. I knew it was the last time I'd ever see him, and I'd been saving a question.

"Hey, *che,*" I said. He came over and put his hands on my shoulders for bal-ance. I said, "Where are you from, *che?*"

"The North."

"Where?"

"I don't know," said Don Luis.

"How long ago did you leave?"

"Too long to remember the name of the village, or even to know exactly where it is, *che.*"

"And your brothers and sisters?"

"Dead," he said.

"And your wife?"

"I never had a wife, *che.*"

"Then who's the mother of your seven daughters?"

"She's the mother of my seven daughters," he said, and took his hands from my shoulders.

"And when is the last time you saw her?"

"Right before she left me."

"She left you? But she still lives on the same ranch where she's always lived, *che.* Where you lived once."

"I never lived there. I stayed there, *che,* but I never lived there. I always lived wherever I wasn't."

"So you left."

Don Luis rubbed his face with his hands. He was very thin, and he wore his pants and his cummerbund high on his waist—nearly to his chest—and his hands were disproportionately big. "What could she say to a man that looked out the window all day and wondered what lay on the horizon?" he said. "In this way, she left, *che*. I went back from time to time, but you can never go back."

"And what did Coihaique look like when you got here?"

"It hardly existed. Now, *che,* there's a million people here."

"A million?"

"At least, *che*."

"Why don't you go back to the ranch at Mañihuales?" I said. "She's there. I know because I've been there." I'd gone with Luisa.

"I don't even know where that is anymore."

"You know where that is, *che*."

"You've misread me," he said. "When one stops moving, *che*, everything looks the same. The tracks blow over and the whole world stays in place. You can't, *che*, without the benefit of forward progress, know what direction lies where, which is forward and which is back. Nor can you start moving again, unless something pushes you. It's a question of physics, if I understand correctly."

"Where are you living now?" I said.

"I'm not, *che*. I'm dying."

*   *   *

Duck and Edith and I walked toward the center of town. Duck carried Mariana on his shoulders; his hands covered her feet like boot-shaped stirrups, and her arms and head rested atop his head. Edith carried Oscar the same way. Patricia and I walked behind them, hand in hand. When we'd gotten a few hundred meters from Luisa's, Patricia whispered: "Wait till you see the weird shit in this church, *tío*."

"Like what?"

"Just wait," she said, then added: "Maybe I'll tell you if you give me a horseback ride."

I got her up on my back. "Like what?"

"Not telling," she said. "And I'm not getting on my tired hooves again, either, so don't get any ideas about letting me down, *che*."

Duck and Edith stopped on a corner to rest, and Patricia and I caught up with them. Duck looked like he was about to fall asleep. "God I'm tired," he said.

Edith said, "Let's not cut for the center of town, after all." The shortest way to get to the church would have been to walk through the town square and up Avenida Baquedano, thereby arriving at the church from below. Another, longer route would have us go back uphill and skirt the slums so that we came out well above the church. It was also the way to avoid the brightly lit streets of downtown, where Soto was living.

Whether or not Duck knew that Soto was in town was unclear. He said, "That doesn't make any sense if you're late already."

Edith said, "What do you mean 'you're late'? *We're* late, *che.*"

"I wonder if I might go home with the girls and Oscar," said Duck. "They've had a long day. In fact, we've all had a long day. What do you say we just go home and wait for Wednesday?"

"Wednesday will be a long day, too," said Edith. "And Sunday next and Wednesday after that. There's no God any day unless you go looking for Him."

We walked on for twenty minutes in silence. We passed streets of rowhouses where the fences were spray-painted with *Los MegaRapers* and *El Tribe*. There was no one in the streets yet, and the rowhouses were dark. Dogs ran with us as we passed, and stood barking when they'd run out of room in their yards; each time this happened Patricia tightened her grip on my neck.

When we got to Avenida Baquedano, we were high above the church. The pavement was starting to give way to the earth beneath. We stopped again. In the distance was the prison, and there were no lights where we stood.

Duck swung Mariana down off his shoulders and shook his head. "I shouldn't do anything when I'm drunk like this," he said.

Edith slid Oscar from her shoulders to the ground and took him by the hand. Duck looked down on the church and, below that, on the oil refinery lights of the Center.

"What's waiting there," said Duck aloofly, "won't have any effect on me," and he started up the hill.

Edith looked at her watch. "We're late," she said.

Chapter Nineteen

Exorcising the Country

The congregation was standing when Edith, the children, and I walked into the God Is Love Pentecostal Church. Five dozen little chairs stood neatly in rows under two strips of naked fluorescent lights. Buckets set on the floor caught the rain that leaked through the ceiling, though we couldn't hear the dripping for the ravings of the preacher.

His face was red and his lips were wet, and his voice blared from two speakers set on tall tripods. The speakers, which were three feet high, framed a long table draped in a white sheet that nearly reached to the floor. The sheet was held in place by a small podium, behind which the preacher stood yelling into a microphone: "Gloria gloria gloria gloria gloria gloria gloria gloria gloria gloria gloria." Just like the name of the woman in the poster that had been on the wall in Duck and Edith's cabin in Cisnes and was now nailed to their wall in The Stags.

Midway through the next barrage, and without stopping, the preacher looked up at the receiver hidden beneath the table and adjusted the reverb so that each "gloria" hit the one before it and was hit by the next one, and they all ricocheted off the concrete walls like bullets.

Edith and the children and I were still standing in the doorway. The volume and chaotic repetition of the reverberation was disorienting. Edith yelled to me: "That preacher isn't the good one. The good one is from Brazil. This is the assistant, who's from Santiago. Still," she said, "he'll do."

Aside from Edith, I had never met a gaucho or a gaucho woman who believed in God. They had been, though they didn't apply these words to themselves,

Taoists and Buddhists and atheists—Tito and Alfredo, after all, had used the word "Christian" as an insult. The only thing that had united the gauchos' fiercely individual beliefs was a universal fear of the Devil, and agreement on what he looked like: the black-clad rider of a gilded black stallion, in whose face a man saw only his own reflection.

And it was impossible, listening to the preacher's heavily accented Santi-aguino Spanish and looking at the strong Indian features of some of the gauchos of his congregation, not to think of the seventeenth-century missionaries from Santiago who had come to Aisén looking for "heathens" to convert, and who had not, with few exceptions, come back. Or, for that matter, not to think of *Chica da Silva,* the Brazilian soap opera in which conversion was predicated not on the premise that God is love, but that a man without God, like the Devil, is unsalvageable.

"Come on," yelled Edith, "let's take our place," and she walked up to the empty row of chairs three back from the stage and stood in front of her seat, holding Oscar in her arms. Mariana and Patricia stood next to her, each of them separated by a chair-space. I stood in the row behind.

Of the twenty-one people in the church, only four were men, and they stood at the back, in front of the last row of chairs. They were short and mustached, and they wore pinstriped wool trousers and cummerbunds and leather jackets, and they yelled "glory glory glory glory glory glory," each of them in a different cadence, and they seemed to be trying to outdo one another. One man said, "Glo glo glo glo glo glo glo glo glo." Like everyone else in the church, the men stood with their left hands raised in the air and bent at the elbow, as though sig-naling a right turn.

The rows of chairs were divided into two sections, separated by an aisle. In one row there stood five generations of the same family, a great-grandmother, a grand-mother, a mother of thirty, and her daughter, fifteen. The daughter, like Edith, held a three-year-old boy in her arms. They were all dressed in black dresses, and the two oldest women wore black shawls around their shoulders, and one had the shawl covering the back of her head. Behind them was another group of old women in their sixties and behind them, alone, stood Duck's mother. I could tell by the way Edith didn't look over that she knew her mother-in-law was there, looking at her.

The preacher had not stopped his raving in the five minutes since we'd arrived, but now, as he began to tire, he put his hand on the table for support and leaned his head against the podium. His white shirt and black tie were soaked, and his black suit was blacker still around his shoulders, where the sweat had soaked through the fabric. The reflection of fluorescent lights traced the even plane of his crew cut. He went to his knees and was hidden from the congregation; and then, suddenly, he stopped. Nothing happened for several moments, and the people in the aisles shifted uneasily.

"Remain standing," panted the hidden preacher, "for the Beast is still among us."

When he stood up, he looked at the congregation and closed his eyes to receive his instructions. He said, "The Lord tells me that four women in this room are unhappy. That domestic problems are ruining their lives. That the Beast has entered their homes and made a nuisance of himself, fouling their relationships, taking money for his own and wasting it on drink."

One of the gauchos at the back said, "Blood in the blood oh the blood of the body in the blood is running in the blood of GOD*che* and the Devil and the HOME*che*!"

"Four!" yelled the preacher.

He had seven-year-old twin sons who sat next to their mother, an Argentine *mulata* with a thin mustache and Buddy Holly glasses and a dour black skirt-suit, in the third row. The twins, whose names were Ramiro and Ramón, looked at one another and smiled, though there was nothing mocking about it: the church was simply the place in which they found themselves every Sunday and Wednesday night, and they had grown used to carrying on there in the same way that they would have carried on at home. They wore matching blue corduroy jeans and cowboy boots and white oxfords with starched lapels and the collars buttoned to the neck. They got up and walked over to the far right corner of the stage.

No one seemed to notice them, save Mariana, who turned to smile at me. Ramón launched a little yellow rubber ball so that it ricocheted three times and careened toward the back of the room; Ramiro went running after it. But when he saw Mariana looking at him, Ramiro came over to her. He stopped a foot away and stared. Then he smiled.

The preacher closed his eyes and shook his head, disappointed in the unwillingness of the crowd to divulge the identities of the four women that God had assured the preacher were there in the room. The preacher did not use the word "eggo," because it was a word that, given its euphemistic origin, was clearly inappropriate for a preacher. Instead, the preacher salted his pleas and admonitions with *mi gente*, my people, which, from the perspective of the convert*che* in his congregation—orphaned, in a way, from their irreligious gaucho past—must have been an altogether welcoming new moniker.

"The Lord Jesus—can I get an amen?—tells me the great pain that four women in this church feel: a weight, a catastrophic weight that they cannot budge from their shoulders, *mi gente*. Women who are married yet alone, strong yet walking into the Devil's trap, the same that has consumed their husbands and is consuming their children and will consume their children's children. Evil like the stink of fetid water, and that stink is in the infected blood, and it is running in the bodies of four women, and they KNOW EXACTLY WHO THEY ARE!

"And only the Lord has the answer, *mi gente*! But that answer will not show itself through words. It will show itself through the hand of the one true God." And with this proclamation, he raised his own hand into the air, slowly and with outstretched fingers.

The great-grandmother across from us looked at her companions and rose and stood before the preacher. He put a hand on her shoulder.

"One!" yelled the preacher.

"One one one one one one!" screamed one of the gauchos at the back of the room.

"Ramiro!" yelled Ramón.

But Ramiro was still busy looking at Mariana. He looked her up and down. Mariana lowered her raised hand and squirmed and chewed on her fingers. Ramiro bent his neck to the side and pretended that the weight of his head was making him fall, and just before he did, he followed his head with his body and walked down the aisle, past Edith and Patricia and Oscar, to join Ramón at the back of the room.

The great-grandmother at the front of the room turned to look at the grandmother, who looked at the mother and walked to the front of the room.

"Two!" yelled the preacher. "Can I get an amen, *mi gente*!"

"Amen!" came the response.

Mariana took her hand from her mouth and raised it. I looked at Edith's as she whispered "amen," and I remembered how, a year before, she had been so shy that the day I showed up in Cisnes she had refused even to look at me. And then I remembered, for some reason, what Soto had said to Duck the night he and Fat Will came over for the party: "Not nearly so docile as she looks, eggo." Edith watched the preacher, and she raised her hand to cover her diseased mouth, the whole time whispering "amen amen amen."

"I tell you that Jesus has informed me of great evil in two more of my sisters!" said the preacher. "He tells me of households where desperation has replaced unity. Where drink has replaced love, *mi gente*. Where fear of neighbors has replaced tranquillity. Where confusion has replaced peace of mind. Where a woman has been left by her husband, and another has been beaten. The solution is not to flee to the hands of Don Satanás, *mi gente,* but to the welcoming hands of God. The solution is not to hate, because to hate is to concede victory to the Devil"—and here the crowd joined him—"WHO IS HATRED. We—God and I and every witness in this room—have two. There are two more," he said. "Who are they?"

This time the mother went to the front, and something about this prompted Edith, who set Oscar on his seat and put his hand in Mariana's. The three gauchos at the back of the room clapped. The *mulata* came forward, stopped behind Edith, and crossed her arms. Then the *mulata* spread her feet for balance.

"Who is it that believes in the power of God to heal this woman?" called the preacher.

"We do," came the muted response.

"And who is it that saw a lame woman walk away from here last week?" he said, louder and more insistently.

"We did," said the congregation, still unsure. "We*che*!" screamed one of the gauchos.

"And who is it that believes the Demon will be vanquished in this battle?"

"We do!"

"What's your name, *señora*?" he asked, calmly holding the microphone to Edith's mouth and smiling, and she told him. "And how old are you?" A long pause and a shake of Edith's head. "And how long have you felt the presence of the Demon?"

"Forever," she whispered.

*   *   *

Ramón marched up the aisle, trailed by Ramiro, and launched his rubber ball into the corner of the ceiling so that it bounced wildly about before disappearing behind the table. "Good shot," said Ramiro. They stood next to Edith and looked up at their father.

"God will perform this miracle if you have faith," said the preacher. He put his hand to her head, and Edith bowed uncertainly as he began. "God! God! Take the Demon from the body of our sister. I command you, Don Lucifer, leave the body of my sister, in the name of the blood of Jesus Christ. LEAVE this vessel that stands in testimony to the goodness of the Lord. LEAVE the body of this woman who stands against you in the name of Jesus Christ." Each time he said the word "leave"—*salga*—he hissed the "s" and prolonged the rest of the word—*ssss-ALga*—like a piece of coal that whines under the stress of a fire before popping. "*SSSSalga* from the body of this woman who has come to God that you may *SSSSalga* from her life and her home forever. *SSSSalga!*"

The preacher took his hand away from Edith's head as if he had touched a hot stove. He looked at his hand, then showed the palm to the congregation. When he put his hand once again to Edith's head, it was the only thing that kept her from crumpling.

His hands were large, and his fingers were long, and he locked them on Edith's temples. He raised the microphone and said, very loud and very slow: "I feel you inside this body, Don Satanás—I feel inside this body the destruction that you have wrought. This room stands in witness to your evil. I feel in the blood of this blood the power of Christ and the blood of my blood and the blood of God and in the name of the blood *leave* her in peace, *leave* her and be vanquished." He pulled his hand from her head as though he were starting a lawn mower; she fell forward, and before she dropped too far, he propped her up once again. Her body was rigid. The preacher turned to put the microphone down on the table behind him. Then he gave Edith a slight push, and caught her with his other hand, to show that the TV had been turned off.

Some in the congregation stood dazed, and others spoke in tongues and writhed and yelled to her to yield to the Lord; some swore at the Devil, and one of the gauchos fell to his knees and beat the floor with a Bible. The preacher hissed into the microphone. "*SSSSalga!*" he yelled. "*SSSSalga* from there! *SSSSalga!*" Each time he said this, Oscar howled and stamped and tried to break from Mariana's grasp, but she held him fast.

Edith let out a sigh and her knees buckled, and the preacher pushed her backward from the head so that the *mulata* could catch her and let her down to the floor, where Edith began convulsing. Her face was white and drawn, her lips were blue, and her mouth remained wide open.

The *mulata* held Edith's head and looked at the preacher, who also knelt. "Get up," he said plainly. He was exhausted, and he still had three more women to get through before the end of the night.

"She's dead," said Ramiro.

The preacher and the *mulata* hauled Edith up by the shoulders into a sitting position, and she opened her eyes and looked around.

"How do you feel, *señora*?" said the preacher.

"My heart," said Edith, and clutched her chest.

"No, she's still alive," said Ramón.

Oscar had stopped flailing, and I stepped over the chairs and stood between Patricia and Mariana and him. All three watched their mother there on the floor.

"Stand up, sister," said the preacher, and he and the *mulata* lifted Edith to her feet. The preacher put his hand over her heart and asked her to breathe steadily and not to be afraid. Then he told her that the Demon was in her heart, and he screamed at the Demon to be gone from this last foothold; then he pulled his hand away, pirouetted, and opened his eyes and approached her. "You feel fine," he said. Edith shook her head. "You feel fine," insisted the preacher.

"Yes."

"Say thank you."

"Thank you, *che*," said Edith.

Oscar ran over and grabbed onto his mother's legs as though he would bring her down. He was livid. Edith looked at him dreamily.

She seemed, for a moment at least, not to recognize him.

*   *   *

The last time I saw Duck was on a Wednesday, my last day in Patagonia. Following the exorcism, I had walked Edith and the children part of the way home. She was still so weak that I had insisted on walking her all the way to The Stags, though she had asked that I not, and I relented. I said I would come to see her and Duck for lunch two days later, on Tuesday, though I had known when I said it that it was a lie.

I have always had an aversion to saying goodbye to people, particularly when I know I'll never see them again. It makes me very uncomfortable, because, as at a funeral, there is nothing in the world that you can say that sounds right. Instead, I had planned to spend that Wednesday walking, one more time and haphazardly, around as much of Coihaique as I could cover in a day.

But as I headed up Baquedano past the church and the prison, I knew where I was headed: the construction site below Duck and Edith's cabin. The afternoon shift was just about to begin when I got there, and it was snowing. We were high enough above town, and the heaviest concentration of woodsmoke, that the snow didn't turn to rain. A few men stood around barrels with fires built in them, warming their hands. They were just beginning to cut the street, and snow filled in the graded filings of land. When Duck saw me, he walked over, but he did not stop, and I followed him. We just walked, without saying anything, right off the site and down the stairs into the lower level of The Stags.

We turned onto a street where the houses were separated by driveways twelve or fifteen feet wide. There were no cars in any of them—they were hardly big enough for cars—but in one driveway two gauchos were changing the shoe on a horse. They were young, and they wore chaps and scarves and ponchos. The horse was saddled, and two others stood in the driveway with their heads resting on one another's flanks. Of the other two horses, one was saddled and the other was fitted with a packsaddle and two *chiguas* covered by sheepskins. The horse on which the boys worked had its foreleg tied up in a sling, to expose the bottom of the hoof. The boys kneeled on the ground like they were changing a tire, or looking at the axles of a truck.

Duck leaned on the fence in front of the house and said, "How's it coming?"

"Pretty good," said one of the boys. He stood up and walked over to lean on the other side of the fence. The second boy looked up at us, then bent back to his work. "The mare threw a shoe, *che.*"

Duck nodded. A while passed, and the first boy and Duck looked around. They watched the sky and commented on the wind and the weather they thought it would bring. The boy had a friendly, warm face. He said he was fourteen. "Where are you headed?" said Duck.

"North*che*," said the boy, pointing with his chin.

Duck fished a battery of wine out of his jacket pocket, and took his knife from its sheath behind his back and sliced the nipple. He drank and passed the wine to the boy. "What for?" said Duck.

The boy shrugged and looked around and squinted. "Oh," he said, "you know."

Duck nodded. The second boy stood up, undid the sling from where it was tied to the lasso ring on the saddle, and gently lowered the mare's foot. He pushed her to the side and made her walk to set the shoe. Then he grabbed her fetlock and looked again at his work. "Come on," he said to the first boy. He let the mare's leg down.

They mounted the horses, and the second boy took the packhorse by its lead. Duck opened the gate, and the saddle horses squeezed through onto the street. The *chiguas* of the packhorse caught on the fence and would not pass. The second boy dropped the lead. He put his horse forward and swung around and charged the packhorse from the side. When he did this, the packhorse broke through the narrow gate opening. There was the sharp sound of cracking wood, and the fence tottered, and one side of it fell to the ground. The other half of the fence remained standing.

The boys sat the horses, and Duck and I stood near them in the falling snow and shared the wine till it was gone. Then the second boy, who was last to drink, dropped the empty box on the street. He reined his horse around, and the first boy did the same, and they passed each of us in turn and shook our hands. Duck handed the second boy the lead to the packhorse.

"Very lovely," said the first boy, smiling, and touched his beret.

"*Vamo', che,*" said the second boy.

They started down the street at a trot. The packhorse nodded and stuck her neck out, and they turned onto the street at the bottom of the hill and disappeared from sight, though it was a few more seconds before the sound of clopping hoofs was gone altogether.

Duck picked up the wine box and held it in both hands. He said, "When are you coming back, Nico*che*?" I shook my head. "Well," he said. Then we shook hands and hugged one another.

Duck dropped the box and turned to walk back up the steep grade of the street. He had his hands in his pockets, and his shoulders were slumped, and he was kicking the box ahead of him like a soccer ball. When he got to the street where he would turn to go to work, he spun around on the empty battery of wine and kicked it back down the hill.

Then he jogged off to where they were building the new houses.

Epilogue

❋

After I got back to New York in June 1999, I sent several letters to Duck and Edith. When there was no reply a month later, I sent a letter to Luisa asking if she had seen them. Luisa and I had been in touch off and on since 1995, so I knew that the mail was reliable in José Miguel Carrera. I was less sure about The Stags—a newer slum and, in Coihaiquino terms, a lesser-known entity—and wondered if my letters had ever arrived there. Luisa responded with a short note saying only that she had neither heard nor seen anything, a response that, due to its "I don't want to get involved" brevity, prompted me to write her back asking again after Duck and Edith. Luisa didn't respond, and still has not.

None of which did anything to put to rest the thing that I had obsessed about for three years: What would become of Duck and Edith? The difference now, in New York in 1999, was that I could no longer see whatever was happening, and I knew I was never going back to Patagonia. I could only imagine, and my ideas ranged ungoverned from one extreme to another. Were Mariana and Patricia and Oscar adjusting to the chlorine in the water and the townies at school? Was Edith now living in Amengual with Soto? Had Duck ever found out about their affair? Had he left her? Had he finally killed her in a drunken rage?

Rex had continued to live in Coihaique for much of the off-season, and through our irregular e-mail correspondence, I found out little bits of information about many of the people I'd known in Patagonia. He did not, though, ever go to see Duck and Edith, nor even know where they were living. He was busy, he said, and his business was doing well. So well that he and a small group of investors had bought a ranch of several thousand acres above the Río Moro, where they are planning to build a new lodge.

Then, on April 28, 2000, Tío died. Rex didn't know any of the details of his death, only that Tío had been been buried in Amengual under a large concrete tombstone which said Tío had been born in 1901, though there is no way to know if this date is accurate, because Tío, in strictly bureaucratic terms, had never existed. A week later, Rex said that he'd seen Louse, one of John of the Cows' brothers, riding on the road in Cisnes. Louse said that John had not been jailed for murder, but for the rape of one of his half-sisters. Then, just before Louse rode away (he was headed toward Coihaique), he added a cryptic addendum to the news: that John, he felt sure, would be out of jail very soon.

Rex confirmed some of the changes that I'd heard predicted in Cisnes over Easter weekend in Coihaique in 1998. The pavement on the Southern Road had, indeed, been advanced past Mañihuales, and, as soon as the summer weather allowed work to continue, would advance to Amengual and Tapera. By the winter of 2001, said Rex, the engineers were confident the road would be paved all the way to Argentina. The number of lodges and adventure tourism businesses had doubled again in Aisén by that winter, mostly south of Coihaique around Río Baker and Chile Chico, two other sectors very similar to—and even more beautiful than—Cisnes.

Then, in November 2000, Rex sent the first word about either Duck or Edith since I left Patagonia in May 1999: Duck left.

The fly-fishing guide who had taken my place at Rex's lodge in 1996 is named Curt, and he has continued, every year since, to work at Santa Elvira. It was in this way that he was familiar with Duck and Edith. Curt is from Alaska, where the PanAmerican Highway, which begins south of Coihaique and passes through two continents, ends. At the village of Puyuhuapi, two hundred kilometers north of Coihaique, the Southern Road turns up the Pacific Coast after a long westward swing around Middle Cisnes, where it circumvents, among other things, the valleys that run through the Inside.

Puyuhuapi is also the village where the two youngest gauchos who had accompanied Duck on his first cattle drive had gone with half the herd, while Duck and the others had continued on to Coihaique. Curt, at any rate, was driving outside the village when he saw a group of men standing alongside the road. As Curt drove past, he looked more closely at them, though he didn't stop or get out of the truck—it was raining and windy and cold.

The men were building a road, said Curt, and Duck was among them.

BAKER & TAYLOR